"Probing the depths of human experience, Ingrid _____, _____, how it works, and how God in his goodness overcomes it. Breathtaking in her honesty and relentless in her biblical scholarship, Faro broaches the subject we all must eventually face. *Demystifying Evil* is a masterful treatment of a fundamental issue from a voice uniquely gifted to write this book. A truly overwhelmingly powerful book."

David Fitch, B. R. Lindner Chair of Evangelical Theology at Northern Seminary

"Jesus taught us to pray, 'Deliver us from evil.' Jesus believed in the destructive power of evil, and he warned us to avoid and combat it. Ingrid Faro equips us to do just that by explaining what Scripture says about evil. She masterfully moves between simple explanation, rich theological analysis, and poignant personal stories. This is not a dull treatise on evil; it is a call to embrace and participate in the grace of God to bring goodness to the world."

Nijay K. Gupta, professor of New Testament at Northern Seminary

"Ingrid Faro offers readers a gift—of her scholarship as well as her life. Her study of the Bible, along with personal stories and practical insights, can educate as well as encourage those who try to make sense of the vicissitudes of life. Faro says evil is not the absence of good but the corruption of good; she invites us to be agents of God's goodness in our world and to let God make beauty from ashes."

Dennis Edwards, dean of North Park Theological Seminary and author of *Humility Illuminated: The Biblical Path Back to Christian Character*

"Philosophers and theologians frequently distinguish between the 'emotional' and 'intellectual' problems of evil, and they make the point that these matters need to be approached differently. Ingrid Faro's *Demystifying Evil* beautifully brings together both the emotional and intellectual, the personal and the intellectual—and biblical and theological. In a wonderful and truly powerful way, Faro draws out the richness of the biblical text as it speaks to evil in the world and attests to God's confrontation of and victory over it in the gospel of Christ. While doing so, Faro weaves in her own honest and penetrating story of traumas and abuse, of encounters with deep evil and the demonic realm, of inner struggles with perfectionism and pride and failure, of anger at God, and of brokenness before him. But she also came to realize the power of Christ to transform lives bludgeoned and ruined by sin, evil, and demonic powers. The book also includes rich and practical lessons of gratitude, contentment, trusting in God, and allowing his grace to transform us. It is a compelling book, and I highly recommend it."

Paul Copan, Pledger Family Chair of Philosophy and Ethics at Palm Beach Atlantic University and author of *Loving Wisdom: A Guide to Philosophy and Christian Faith*

"Ingrid Faro weaves her stunning story throughout this richly researched and deep, biblically based study. A journey for both the mind and soul, *Demystifying Evil* draws from Old and New Testament scholarship and the author's own experience and expertise; it guides readers through a depth of understanding of the evil within, the evil without, where evil comes from, and most vitally, how to be truly and faithfully strong in the Lord. I am so grateful to Ingrid for her transparency and generosity as she shares her own journey so readers may be changed by the powerful and transforming love of God and gain an understanding essential for every Christian."

Tommy Lee, president and founder of Resource Global

"'Life is hard. The world is filled with evil.' These are the first words in chapter one of Dr. Ingrid Faro's wonderful book, *Demystifying Evil*. The reality of evil is everywhere, and we must have tools and strategies to navigate our approach to evil. Dr. Faro does a fantastic job of weaving both the theological and practical, which enables us to face the evil in our world and not be stifled. Dr. Faro is an outstanding biblical scholar and a tremendous communicator. I highly recommend this book without hesitation, and hopefully you, too, will gain insights as I have from Dr. Faro."

Wayne "Coach" Gordon, pastor emeritus of Lawndale Christian Community Church and professor at Northern Seminary

"Blending personal testimony, biblical study, and theological reflection, Ingrid Faro probes evil—our world's greatest menace. She is readable, intelligent, chilling, and, at last, reassuring."

Cornelius Plantinga, author of *Not the Way It's Supposed to Be: A Breviary of Sin*

"Ingrid Faro's *Demystifying Evil* is profoundly philosophical and theological, passionate, and practical. As long as evil remains mysterious, it cannot be directly opposed and overcome. Evil defined can be defeated. Alas, we are not helpless against evil. This book offers each of us a stark challenge to live our lives fully embracing God's flourishing goodness, or we will find ourselves acquiescing and participating in wickedness. We cannot remain neutral. We are either a force for evil or good. Faro urges, let's choose the good!"

Marshall E. Hatch, senior pastor of New Mount Pilgrim Church and associate professor of ministry at Northern Seminary

Ingrid Faro

Foreword by
Heather Davediuk Gingrich

Demystifying EVIL

*A Biblical
and Personal
Exploration*

IVP
Academic

An imprint of InterVarsity Press
Downers Grove, Illinois

InterVarsity Press
P.O. Box 1400 | Downers Grove, IL 60515-1426
ivpress.com | email@ivpress.com

InterVarsity Press® is the publishing division of InterVarsity Christian Fellowship/USA®. For more information, visit intervarsity.org.

All Scripture quotations, unless otherwise indicated, are taken from The Holy Bible, New International Version®, NIV®. Copyright © 1973, 1978, 1984, 2011 by Biblica, Inc.™ Used by permission of Zondervan. All rights reserved worldwide. www.zondervan.com. The "NIV" and "New International Version" are trademarks registered in the United States Patent and Trademark Office by Biblica, Inc.™

While any stories in this book are true, some names and identifying information may have been changed to protect the privacy of individuals.

The publisher cannot verify the accuracy or functionality of website URLs used in this book beyond the date of publication.

Cover design: Kate Lillard
Interior design: Daniel van Loon
Images: Getty / 1256177926–snake head shape

ISBN 978-1-5140-0493-7 (print) | ISBN 978-1-5140-0494-4 (digital)

Printed in the United States of America ∞

Library of Congress Cataloging-in-Publication Data
Names: Faro, Ingrid, author.
Title: Demystifying evil : a biblical and personal exploration / Ingrid
    Faro.
Description: Downers Grove, IL : InterVarsity Press, [2023] | Includes
    bibliographical references and index.
Identifiers: LCCN 2023023805 (print) | LCCN 2023023806 (ebook) | ISBN
    9781514004937 (print) | ISBN 9781514004944 (digital)
Subjects: LCSH: Good and evil–Religious aspects–Christianity. |
    Devil–Christianity.
Classification: LCC BJ1401 .F368 2023 (print) | LCC BJ1401 (ebook) | DDC
    241–dc23/eng/20230725
LC record available at https://lccn.loc.gov/2023023805
LC ebook record available at https://lccn.loc.gov/2023023806

30 29 28 27 26 25 24 23 | 13 12 11 10 9 8 7 6 5 4 3 2 1

To those who mourn

Isaiah 61:3

CONTENTS

PART 5: GOD AT WORK

TRIGGER WARNING

THE MATERIAL PRESENTED and the personal stories told in this book include accounts of violence, abuse, and trauma. A cautionary warning is advised to the reader that these may reactivate memories and trigger subsequent reactionary responses.

FOREWORD
HEATHER DAVEDIUK GINGRICH

I REMEMBER BEING FASCINATED by M. Scott Peck's book, *People of the Lie: The Hope for Healing Human Evil*,[1] when it first came out in 1983. In it, Peck recounted the story of Bobby and his parents as an illustration of human evil.[2] As a Christmas present, Bobby's parents gave him the gun that his brother had used to kill himself. Bobby's psychiatric symptoms indicated that he clearly had received the message that his parents were inviting him to follow in his brother's footsteps. That example haunted me for years.

When I read *People of the Lie*, I was young, I had grown up in the sheltered environments of a relatively healthy Christian family and supportive church environment, and I was a fledging therapist. So, while as a devoted Christ-follower I believed in the concept of evil as the antithesis of God's goodness, personified by Satan, evil was not something I had encountered up-close either personally or in my counseling work. According to Peck, human evil, in contrast to Satan, is present when individuals make choices that are so destructive to others that they cannot be explained simply by mental illness. As a psychiatrist, Peck well understood that mentally ill people can do evil things, but in his book, he explains and describes the depths to which people absorbed by the lie of evil can go in perpetrating evil against others.

Within a few years of beginning to practice, I came into more direct contact with evil as my counselees began sharing memories of child sexual abuse. While all child abuse is horrific, the stories that stood out to me were

---

[1]M. Scott Peck, *People of the Lie: The Hope for Healing Human Evil* (New York: Simon & Schuster, 1983).
[2]Peck, *People of the Lie*, 47-69.

narratives of torture, such as young children being beaten almost to death, starved, violently raped, and left in cellars for hours or days only to be brought back into the world to have the cycle perpetuated multiple times over many years. Evil started to take on some new meaning in the midst of listening to those stories.

Several years later, counselees began to ask me specifically about possible demonic involvement within their life situations. These discussions forced me to think beyond human evil and come to grips with the reality of evil spiritual entities. One counselee, whom I'll call Nancy, made an appointment to see me two years after her weekly counseling sessions had ceased. Nancy told me that she had experienced some strange things during the time period in which she had been receiving regular counseling services. Being afraid that I would think she was crazy, she had decided not to risk sharing them with me earlier on. But as the months passed, Nancy had continued to wonder how I would interpret these events and so had made this particular appointment specifically to hear my response. Nancy told me that objects in her house changed location overnight, and that she saw objects levitate and then settle back down to their original position. "Could this possibly be spiritual, like maybe caused by demons?" she asked, "Or do you just think I'm imagining it all?" I knew that I did not have enough information, nor did I have adequate understanding of such things, to ascertain whether this was a spiritual matter, a psychological one, or, perhaps both, and I told her so. That was all she needed to hear. She expressed immense relief that I did not automatically conclude that she was experiencing psychotic episodes, and that I at least allowed for the possibility that some malevolent force could be behind these experiences.

Within the same several-month period, another client, Sarah, came to her regular counseling session distraught. A fairly new but dedicated Christian, Sarah reported that she had been unable to attend Easter services despite her valiant attempts to do so. She described mounting the church stairs only to find herself turning around and going back down them despite her willful efforts to enter the church. Extremely distressed after multiple attempts, Sarah gave up on the idea of attending the service and went home. Was her inability to participate in the celebration of Christ's resurrection due to the actions of evil entities that did not want Sarah pursuing her newfound faith?

Or were there deep-seated levels of ambivalence about her faith within Sarah of which she was unaware that led to her strange behavior? I did not know, but her situation certainly got my attention. I began to study what Christian scholars had written about the demonic, evil, and how to help individuals who were struggling psychologically and spiritually from the impact of evil forces.

In prompting me to research this area, I believe that the Holy Spirit was gently leading me into a better theological and psychological understanding of evil before I would be plunged headlong into facing the horrific effects of evil as I began working with individuals who met diagnostic criteria for what we now call dissociative identity disorder (DID). DID is strongly associated with a history of chronic, relational trauma in early childhood. In addition to horrendous familial neglect and abuse, and familial sex trafficking (where parents pimped out their children for financial gain), some of these counselees had also been subjected to Satanic Ritual Abuse.

When I entered the counseling profession, I knew that I was making a choice to enter into others' suffering and pain to an extent that not every person is called to do. What I did not know is that I would also encounter evil in ways I could not have previously fathomed. If I had recognized the extent of the cost, I do not know if I would have begun this journey. I think that God, in his mercy, shields us from knowing aspects of our futures that would be too scary to contemplate before we have no choice but to face them. But despite the price, I am exceedingly grateful that I have glimpsed the depths of the darkness of evil, because I have also borne witness to the immensity of God's love, power, and victory over the forces of darkness! I have stories . . . many of them. I will just give you one example to illustrate how God has triumphed over evil.

Several days before a regularly scheduled counseling session, I was filled with fear. I had no idea what I was afraid of and in several years of working with this client I had never before felt this way. But the feeling persisted to the extent that I asked my husband and some godly friends to pray for me specifically during the upcoming session. Ten minutes into the therapy hour I faced an evil spirit that attempted to strangle me. I do not know how many minutes the counselee's hands were inches from my throat, but I do know that I experienced the presence of the Holy Spirit so strongly that despite my previous fear, I felt no fear in the moment. Only after the demon was forced to flee did my client tell me that she saw my guardian angel spreading her wings across my neck and chest, effectively preventing the demon from harming me! I do not visually see demons, nor have I seen angels, but I have witnessed God dramatically vanquish evil!

I suspect that most of us do not want to address evil because we hope that by ignoring it, we will not be impacted by it. In fact, the opposite is true. It is analogous to an individual that refuses to go to the doctor to get some physical symptoms checked out because they do not want to believe that anything could be wrong. But if they actually have cancer, the sooner the diagnosis is made and treatment is started, the greater the chances of survival.

Demystifying Evil, therefore, is an important book. If it had been available to me several decades ago, it would have saved me much confusion and struggle in my attempts to understand what I was seeing. Ingrid Faro explores evil from every angle, allowing the reader to understand better what it is, how we are impacted by it, and even how we may, often unwittingly, be participants in it. It also looks at the role of demons and Satan in the perpetuation of evil, but then finishes on a victorious note, with how God works and restores in the midst of the evil. Once we better recognize evil and understand it, we are in a much better position to choose what we do about it. My own journey with encountering evil has strongly reinforced what Scripture says: God is more powerful than Satan (Acts 10:38)! Light penetrates darkness (1 Jn 1:5)! Goodness wins out over evil (Prov 11:27)! Remember these truths as you read.

Heather Davediuk Gingrich, PhD
Coordinator, Graduate Certificate in Trauma Therapy
Toccoa Falls College School of Graduate Studies

Author of *Restoring the Shattered Self:*
A Christian Counselors Guide to Complex Trauma
and co-editor of *Treating Trauma in Christian Counseling*

ACKNOWLEDGMENTS

THIS BOOK IS THE CULMINATION of fifteen years of wrestling to understand evil through my studies and my story, and of rising up from its impact. The people to thank for walking with me are far more than I can list, including the many with whom I have spoken, cried, prayed, hugged, and exchanged knowing looks into each other's eyes.

I'm grateful to InterVarsity Press for publishing this book, first to Anna Gissing for inviting me to write it, and especially to Rachel Hastings for your insightful edits and comments all the way through, along with the anonymous external readers who challenged me to make it better.

Thank you to Kevin K. Peters for your work editing my manuscript. Special thanks to Dr. Mark E. Hattendorf (psychologist and trauma specialist) for your valuable feedback and conversations chapter by chapter. I'm also grateful for the helpful edits of selected chapters by Heather Macon, Sally Seekins, and Walter Faro Jr.

I'd like to thank my colleagues for their support and encouragement. First to Drs. Willem VanGemeren, John M. Monson, and Dick (Richard E.) Averbeck, my mentors and friends since my early years of theological study. I'm grateful for my colleagues at the Scandinavian School of Theology (Skandinavisk Teologisk Högskola) for reviewing drafts of some of my chapters as part of our faculty meetings: Drs. Anders Gerdmar, Torbjörn Aronson, Göran Lennartsson, and Hans Sundberg. Thank you to my colleagues at Northern Seminary for feedback on the concepts of this book: Drs. Dave Fitch, Marshall Hatch, "Coach" Wayne Gordon, and Scot McKnight. I'm grateful for Drs. Michael Heiser, Catherine McDowell, John Peckham, Paul Copan, and Craig Keener for your writings that have been inspirational in my work. Thank you also to Trinity Evangelical Divinity School and

Dr. Dennis Magary for the opportunity to teach two PhD seminars on "Genesis and the Theological Foundations of Evil," and to Northern Seminary and Tommy Lee for the opportunity to teach a class through The Grow Center using an early draft of my manuscript. Thank you to all the students who have participated in interacting with the material and shaping this work.

I'm grateful to my pastors, Chip and Cyndi Block and Pastor Isaac J. Ampil, and to Pastor Daniel Ho for asking me to preach a series in their churches based on this book. Thank you to Mark Lanier and David Capes for inviting me to lecture at the Lanier Theological Library.

I'm forever thankful for my friends, and for their support and encouragement in innumerable ways: Maria Plummer, Gail Vida Hamburg, Dr. Katherine Jeffery, Caysie Cannon, Reviah (Eunmi) Kim, Dr. May Young, Dr. Willem and Evona VanGemeren, Bethany Wheeler, Kim Karpeles, Mette Schultz, Sharay Thomas Rochelle, Jennifer Flannigan, Sophia Gerdmar, Julie Ann Rose, Pam Ernest, Diana St. Leger Lindbergh, Tiffany McChesney, B. J. Hilbilink, Amy Allen, my cousin Else-Marie Gerdmar, and so many more.

Special thanks to my family for their ongoing love and support throughout my story, my studies, and my writing: Walter and Laura Faro, Michelle and Forest Banks, Paul Maxwell, and Dr. Solveig Spjeldnes and John Molinaro.

Foremost, I give thanks to the LORD who loved me first, walked with me before I even knew it, opens my heart and my understanding, and is my greatest joy.

Part One

WRESTLING
WITH EVIL

*Underlying all trauma, violence, and abuse lies evil, and
the result of evil is always some kind of suffering.*

DIANE LANGBERG

FACING EVIL and doing something about it take courage. Most people
seem to be afraid of evil. We tend to ignore it, hide from it, and cover it up.
Sometimes we would rather overlook evil than face what we don't want to
believe or don't understand. Through many hardships, I have found that
ignoring evil is unproductive. Fear ruled much of my life and kept me silent.
The process of reconstructing my life began when I started to face evil and
take it apart. Hiding keeps us a perpetual victim, confined and imprisoned
in our emotions.

Evil is often perceived as shrouded in mystery, ready to pounce without
warning or cause. We fear evil because we're afraid of what we can't control
or don't understand. The purpose of this book is to demystify evil by taking
it out of its dark corners, finding out where it comes from, asking why, and

exploring how it operates to disrupt and disable our lives. You can approach this book as a type of mystery-novel solver, asking the question *Whodunnit?* We're breaking down evil to examine who or what are the agents that bring harm to your life or those around you. If you or someone you love is paralyzed by evil or trauma into silence, fear, anger, bitterness, or resentment, this book is written for you to pull evil out of the shadows. As Nelson Mandela said, "I learned that courage was not the absence of fear, but the triumph over it. The brave man is not he who does not feel afraid, but he who conquers that fear."[1]

It's tough to face your deepest fears, greatest shame, or inner rage resulting from the wrongs you have experienced or done. The goal of demystifying evil is to expose its sources, strip it of its power, and thereby empower us to take action to prevent or reverse its blows—and turn entrapment into freedom, and mourning into joy.

TRIGGER WARNING

The material presented and the personal stories told in this book include accounts of violence, abuse, and trauma. A cautionary warning is advised to the reader that these may reactivate memories and trigger subsequent reactionary responses. Pay attention to your own emotional health. Take a break if you notice past memories or present circumstances arise with strong emotions. Connecting with a qualified counselor and/or trusted friend may be advised. As you reengage with the material, continue to process the memories in the light of truth, which will allow you to navigate the evil you have seen and experienced.

In addition, you may have questions that I will not answer. There may be pain or loss you have experienced that I will not address. At times my writing may not be sufficiently sensitive to your suffering or your experiences. While everyone's story and journey are unique, most of us who have not resigned to despair want to know why evil happens and if healing is possible. If you're on this journey, join me. My hope is that you will find answers to some of your questions, healing for some of your woundedness, and that hope will rise.

---

[1]Nelson Mandela, *Long Walk to Freedom: The Autobiography of Nelson Mandela* (repr., London: Abacus, 2004).

Chapter One

ENTERING THE CONFLICT

To everything there is a season, and a time for every purpose
under heaven . . . a time to tear down and a time to build up.

Ecclesiastes 3:1, 3

Life is hard. The world is filled with evil. Pain and suffering, anguish and anxiety often drive people to despair. Many of us hold God responsible for the evil in our lives. Others have abandoned the idea of God because of the suffering they've experienced. People are often blindsided by tragedy and trapped in their trauma, anger, or fear. Most never find the exit. Bad things, and sometimes horrendous evils, happen to good people who are trying to live moral lives. We struggle to understand. Life is supposed to be fair. People are not supposed to be brutalized. Parents are not supposed to molest children. Accidents are not supposed to happen to loved ones. We are supposed to be valued, not treated like scraps or objects used for the benefit of others.

The contradictions may overwhelm us, and we are unable to rise from the despair. "The world feels worse than random, it feels cruel."[1] Most of us are at a loss to handle the blows that come against us, much less to define evil or figure out what to do next. Confusion ensnares us, entraps us in triggers that we don't recognize or understand. As moral philosopher Carol Neiman writes, "The problem of evil can be expressed in theological or secular terms, but it is fundamentally a problem about the intelligibility of the world as a

---

[1] Rachel Hastings, in a comment to the manuscript, August 3, 2022.

whole."[2] When we have a sense that things *are not the way they're supposed to be*, we're entering the problem of evil.[3]

Most literature on the problem of evil in the last few centuries has focused on the philosophical arguments of theodicy, which seek to condemn, vindicate, or eliminate God based on a three-point structure claiming that if God is good and all-powerful, and God created this world, then God is responsible for evil.[4] However, the intrusion of evil is not simply a philosophical, intellectual, or theological issue; it is an extremely personal one. Evil, like a phantom, waits to strike undetected. It lurks in dark corners, in shadows, and in unknown and unexplored regions. We never seem to be prepared for its attacks. Biblical scholar N. T. Wright observes the human reaction to evil, "First, we ignore evil when it doesn't hit us in the face. Second, we are surprised by evil when it does. Third, we react in immature and dangerous ways as a result."[5] Universally, I've found that it's grueling for people to understand what's happened to them when they encounter evil and the question of why God, gods, people, or the universe allow these serious breaches of goodness. How we navigate evil not only impacts our personal lives in the short and long terms, but potentially has lasting consequences—rippling through our world and affecting whole generations. In this book, I seek to pull evil out of the shadows, define evil, examine sources of evil, and identify things we can do to either prevent evil or greatly alter the wake of its destruction.

In this book, I do not specifically address how to deal with the societal evils that surround us. At times, we may be powerless to do so. However, our

---

[2]Susan Neiman, *Evil in Modern Thought: An Alternative History of Philosophy*, Princeton Classics (Princeton, NJ: Princeton University Press, 2015), 21.

[3]"Every time we make the judgment *this ought not to have happened*, we are stepping onto a path that leads straight to the problem of evil." Neiman, *Evil*, 18. See also Cornelius Plantinga, *Not the Way It's Supposed to Be: A Breviary of Sin* (Grand Rapids, MI: Eerdmans, 1999), 5.

[4]For more on philosophical approaches to theodicy or the problem of evil, see, for example, Walther Eichrodt, "Faith in Providence and Theodicy in the Old Testament," in *Theodicy in the Old Testament*, IRT 4 (Philadelphia: Fortress, 1973), 17; Gottfried Wilhem Leibniz, *Theodicy: Essays on the Goodness of God* (LaSalle, IL: Open Court, 1985); James L. Crenshaw, "Introduction: The Shift from Theodicy to Anthropodicy," in *Theodicy in the Old Testament*, IRT 4 (Philadelphia: Fortress, 1973), 2-3; Antti Laato and Johannes C. de Moore, "Introduction," in *Theodicy in the World of the Bible*, ed. Antti Laato and Johannes C. de Moore (Leiden: Brill, 2003), vii; Brian Davies, *The Reality of God and the Problem of Evil* (New York: Continuum, 2006); Ulf Görman, *A Good God? A Logical and Semantical Analysis of the Problem of Evil*, Studia Philosophiae Religionis 5 (Stockholm: H. Ohlsson, 1977).

[5]N. T. Wright, *Evil and the Justice of God* (Downers Grove, IL: InterVarsity Press, 2014), 24.

personal response to evil along with our proactive engagement against it does impact whether systemic injustices will be prevented or perpetuated. As Abraham Heschel pointedly observes, "Few are guilty, but all are responsible" for the corruptions in society. "In a community not indifferent to suffering, uncompromisingly impatient with cruelty and falsehood, continually concerned for God and every man, crime would be infrequent rather than common."[6] Every movement to stop systemic evil begins with one or two individuals deciding they will not tolerate the wrongs any longer and persevering in the risks to stop them. As we heal from our hurts and traumas and grow to be no longer afraid of evil or those who perpetrate it, we become powerful agents for healing, restoration, and the establishment of goodness.

THE STORY THAT STARTED MY QUEST

My search to understand evil began in spring 2001, after working myself into a disability while managing two startup companies and consulting for a third in the insurance field. Not a likely occupation to begin such an inquiry. The cause of my disability was more than just fatigue from working eighty plus hours a week. My symptoms manifested as severe asthma and oxygen compromised blood that left me gasping for every breath. Up until the illnesses, I was a runner and a regular at the gym. The doctor told me to take thirty days off work. In an effort to comply with his recommendations, I quit the consulting job, but there was no one else to run my businesses: my husband, Walt, was a disabled Vietnam veteran, and our son was in grade school. The weight was on my shoulders. I felt like the weight had always been on my shoulders since I was in grade school. I couldn't stop. I didn't know how to stop. But somehow, I knew I had to find the space. An inner prompting led me to sit in my big armchair for an hour every day, stare out the window in silence, and just listen. This was the conscious beginning of my quest.

At first, three minutes of sitting still felt like torture, but I persisted. One morning, after a few weeks of sitting quietly for an hour a day, a strange, almost painful tingling sensation began to creep up my limbs from my toes and fingers. Scared, I asked within, prayerfully, *What is that!* I heard in

---

[6]Abraham Joshua Heschel, *The Prophets* (Peabody, MA: Hendrickson, 2017), 1:16.

response, "Relaxation." As I continued this meditative journey, in time I came to understand that my addiction of choice had been my own adrenaline. If I was constantly working, I could numb the pain and block out the traumas, which also prevented the possibility of healing.

As Bessel Van der Kolk describes in his book *The Body Keeps the Score*, my body was telling me things that I was unable, or more accurately, that I was refusing to hear.[7] I had no breath—I had lost my voice, my own agency. During the weeks and months that followed, I began to connect with my inner voice, my body, and with God, who I thought had abandoned me. The process led me to study theology. I wanted answers, and I wanted them from God and from Scripture, in the original Hebrew and Greek.

In the years since my disability and through my theological studies, life has often grown even darker. By early summer of 2007, I had completed a Master of Divinity degree, undergone major surgery, hit rock bottom financially and emotionally, and was about to start a PhD in theological studies. I was no master of divinity: I was broke, broken, and beating myself up. I had convinced myself that all the problems in my life must be God's will. I was desperately trying to figure out what I must have done wrong, or what was wrong with me for my life to be such a mess. For years, I had been praying to *know* the love of God because, for me, God's love was only a theological construct. I didn't *know* that God loved me. How could I believe in God when I had experienced so much evil, abuse, and loss?

Later that summer during a worship service, my life flashed before my eyes. Science informs us that people who report these flashes are dying, having a near-death experience, or are under severe stress.[8] That fit. A burn pile of "supposed tos" and "shoulds" was amassed over my heart, ready to be lit. For years I had been trying to live while hoping to die. I was secretly jealous at funerals, wondering why I had to stay. I was tired of living a "Whack-A-Mole" carnival game where it felt like every time I lifted up my

---

[7]Bessel A. Van der Kolk, *The Body Keeps the Score: Brain, Mind, and Body in the Healing of Trauma* (New York: Penguin, 2015). See also Gabor Maté, *When the Body Says No: The Cost of Hidden Stress* (London: Vermilion, 2019).

[8]Judith Katz, Noam Saadon-Grossman, and Shahar Arzy, "The Life Review Experience: Qualitative and Quantitative Characteristics," *Consciousness and Cognition* 48 (February 2017): 76-86; Veronika V. Nourkova, "Compressed Life Review: Extreme Manifestation of Autobiographical Memory in Eye-Tracker," *Behavioral Sciences* 10, no. 3 (2020): 1-14, www.mdpi.com/2076 -328X/10/3/60.

head, some unseen hammer would whack me down again. I felt powerless against dark thoughts that compelled me to comply with covert contracts. The malevolent forces I could not then comprehend impelled me to "just be quiet and the pain will go away." Retreating, I submitted to physical, spiritual, and emotional abuses, hoping my acquiescence would make the hurting stop. But it never did. I didn't understand the various forces of evil at work. The subconscious lies I came to accept about myself and the world became the pervading narrative of my day-to-day existence, derailing the boldness intended for me and the wildly beautiful life I was meant to live. Through the lies, I too often allowed evil rather than good to flourish.

That summer morning of 2007, every bad thing that had ever happened to me flashed across the screen of my mind in living color: There were quick clips of my life from my earliest sense of being unwanted, to rejection by my husband, to rejection by my church family. Unique to my experience, however, was an awareness between each scene of walking along a path with a deep chasm on either side. As each hurtful experience knocked me off the path onto one side or the other, I glimpsed the cause behind each blow. Sometimes the cause was someone else's deliberate harmful intention, sometimes it was my own ignorance or naivety, and sometimes it was unintentional but still devastating.

Incredibly, however, with each fall I felt an unseen hand I knew to be God catch me and gently place me back on the path. With each blow, in place of my self-flagellation for being so stupid or worthless, I felt enveloped with an overwhelming love by the hand that caught me. Never did that hand harm me. This centering and impactful experience became an undercurrent guiding my next steps. Even though the journey ahead was steep and filled with challenges, something within my core connected and grounded me in a *knowing* love. I was seen. I was not traveling alone. I was never alone.

During the next six years of work in the doctoral program, my research occasionally hit pause as another clip from my flashback reel replayed in my head. Then, as the silent divine voice disclosed, "*This* is the cause behind that one," I saw the relationship between the evil that happened, its cause, and how my response affected what came next. Gradually a network of connections developed. Evil gained entrance into my life through different sources and means. Some evils entered willfully and intentionally. Other evils entered as a consequence of a chain of actions, and some were simply acts of nature, but how I responded mattered. Through this process, I began to identify distinct, destructive instruments of evil and various operations through which they worked.

The insights sparked an awareness that I, that we, are not alone and are not powerless against the internal and external forces that assault us. In this book, many of the stories behind the scenes from my flashback will be filled out, along with what was learned about the evil behind them and their implications for how to get back on a meaningful path of life.

APPROACH AND GOALS

My life experiences, research, and conversations are the foundation of this book's exploration into demystifying evil. I have engaged a broad range of materials including academic studies and people's stories ranging from ancient history to modern times, on different continents, in different languages, belief systems, and cultures. Universally, I've found that it's hard for people to understand what has happened to them when they encounter evil and why God, gods, people, or the universe allow these serious breaches of goodness.

The fourfold aim of this book is to (1) challenge simplistic answers to the problem of evil; (2) resist passivity or resignation to evil; (3) affirm the goodness and justice of God; and (4) provide tools for transforming the wake of evil into forces for good.

This book is written for those who wrestle with life's hardships and confusion, those who are questioning their faith, and those who have quit believing in or never believed in God but are willing to engage in the conversation about the intersection of God, humanity, good, and evil. That's a broad goal. I continue to engage and wrestle. Mine has not been an easy quest—few are. The hope is that my stories and studies can point to paths that cut through evil and move toward personal empowerment and peace. May the excrements of evil be overturned into manure for fertile soil where goodness can grow.

WHAT'S AHEAD?

While it's presumptuous to pretend that we'll solve every mystery about evil, this book seeks to provide clarity by examining the various ways harm, distress, and other destructive forces work to prevent our flourishing. Five major instruments of evil and/or good are presented that give us insight into how evil enters our lives and how we can alter its impact by the choices we make and the actions we take.[9]

The book of Genesis is the premier account of the beginnings of good and evil. The opening chapters provide a framework for this book by examining the ways good and evil operate. Each of the major instruments, or sources, of evil in the five parts of the book is paired with a corresponding image from Genesis. Discussion of the sources of evil and their operations offers a way to objectively evaluate evil so that we are better equipped to find healing, motivation, and power to transform their devastations into good. The major instruments of evil addressed in this book are as follows:

- action-consequence

- natural forces

- human agency

- nonhuman malevolent spiritual forces

In the final section, we will explore the role of God and Jesus Christ in all of this.

Part one, "Wrestling with Evil," (the part you're currently reading) continues in chapter two, "Distinguishing Between Evil, Suffering, and Pain and the Ambiguity of Evil," along with a cautionary note on the misuse of the terms *evil* and *good*. Chapter three, "Defining Evil—Biblically," provides a definition of evil as the corruption of good, with emphasis on God's creational and relational goodness.

Part two, "Natural Causes: Cosmic Seed and Natural Evil," contains two chapters. Chapter four, "Action-Consequence and the Cosmic Seed," explores the oldest beliefs about the cause of good and evil. This concept is the basis of the adages "you reap what you sow" and "what goes around comes around," and most understandings of karma. The image from Genesis is the seed. Almost all living things on earth come from seed: plants, animals, people, and metaphorically speaking, thoughts, words, and actions. This

---

[9]The ideas for this book arose out of my life and my research: Ingrid Faro, *Evil in Genesis: A Contextual Analysis of Hebrew Lexemes for Evil in the Book of Genesis*, Studies in Scripture & Biblical Theology (Bellingham, WA: Lexham, 2021).

universal expectation can be seen in ancient texts and prayers, in most religious systems, and in New Age vernacular. It makes sense logically, but it doesn't always hold true. Chapter five, "Nature: Are All Natural Forces Natural?" considers the role of nature to gain perspective on the wildness of creation, along with ways in which the willful intent of sentient beings can affect biological and environmental factors to bring good or harm. We'll look at biblical perspectives on the relationship between nature, humanity, and God, and examine the role of physical forces and laws of nature that are part of the ebb and flow of living on this earth.

Part three, "Human Causes: Surprising Ways We Participate in Evil and Good," contains three chapters. In chapter six, "Human Need and Desire: The Misuse of Intended Good," considers the fact that we all have needs and desires, and that they are meant to be good and intended by the Lord! We will conversely examine how our needs and desires can work for us or against us depending on how we respond to them and what we do to fulfill them. In chapter seven, "Self-Sufficiency: The Root of Pride and Insecurity," readers consider how both pride and insecurity are related to self-sufficiency and our need to be in control. This approach either elevates self by squashing others or becomes ineffective by diminishing personal agency by focusing on our inabilities. In their own ways, both responses can contribute to the proliferation of evil, harm, and wrongdoing. Positive expressions of these negative attributes are confidence and humility, which at best, work together in a healthy personality to foster human flourishing. Chapter eight addresses "Human Responsibility and Authority." This may be the most challenging conversation in the book, calling us out of lethargy and passivity toward evil into our God-given vocation to act as his image-bearers. Chapter nine explores "Human Freedom and the Path to Restore the World," beginning with the question of what human freedom is and what it means for the operation of evil and good.

Part four, "Unseen Causes: Spiritual Forces at Work," investigates the participation of nonhuman, spiritual entities that act with purposeful intent in human lives and world systems. Chapter ten addresses "Malevolent Forces and The Rise of the Satan." Although the concept of spiritual forces has been scorned by intellectuals since the Enlightenment, a global perspective together with the acknowledgment that there's more out there than meets the eye will be openly discussed. Chapter eleven, "Demons, Angels, and Other Spiritual Entities," examines scriptural evidence of malevolent and beneficent spiritual beings and their engagement with the physical universe. In chapter twelve, "The Divine Council and the Rules of Engagement," the reality of the divine council is explored, especially regarding their participation in heavenly, human, and world systems. The section on "rules of engagement"[10] provides further explanation of God's response to spiritual conflict and cosmic involvement in the administration of good and evil.

Part five, "God at Work," may raise the biggest questions for most people. In chapter thirteen, "The Power of Mercy and Grace," we look at God's approach to human evil. Chapter fourteen addresses "The Costly Work of Forgiveness" for God and for us. Too often the words "just forgive" or "you have to forgive" are tossed around without understanding the price of the process. Chapter fifteen, "For Those Who Mourn: Turning Ashes into Beauty," concludes our exploration with hope.

Welcome to this journey. I believe you won't be the same by its conclusion.

---

[10]The first to use this military term to refer to God's actions in spiritual conflict is John C. Peckham. See his "Rules of Engagement: God's Permission of Evil in Light of Selected Cases of Scripture," *Bulletin for Biblical Research* 30, no. 2 (2020): 243-60, and *Theodicy of Love: Cosmic Conflict and the Problem of Evil* (Grand Rapids, MI: Baker Academic, 2018).

*Chapter Two*

DISTINGUISHING BETWEEN EVIL, SUFFERING, AND PAIN AND THE AMBIGUITY OF EVIL

To understand the nature of the problem of evil,
we also need to reflect on the nature of suffering.

ELEONORE STUMP

EVIL AND SUFFERING in the world are the basis for most arguments against the goodness, justice, and existence of God. Today's news is filled with suffering and death: another mass shooting, genocide, sex abuse scandals, racially motivated attacks. Globally, tensions between opposing religious, political, and cultural groups break out in violence, kidnappings, and massacres. The human toll can be measured in rising rates of depression, anxiety, suicide, addiction, and abuse. Beyond what we see in the news is the hidden ugliness in homes, schools, workplaces, and neighborhoods, compounding the impact on each of us from everything that could broadly be called evil. The evils around us, and throughout history, seem endless.

DISTINGUISHING BETWEEN EVIL, SUFFERING, AND PAIN

In exploring a definition of evil, it's helpful to first note the distinctions between evil, suffering, and pain.[1] These terms don't always equate with one another and often do not carry the same meaning or weight. Yet, they are intricately interrelated. Each affects the other, but they are not the same.

---

[1] Eleonore Stump, *Wandering in Darkness: Narrative and the Problem of Suffering* (Oxford: Oxford University Press, 2012), 4-13.

Further, there are different types of suffering, afflicted and chosen, and there is negative and positive pain. For example, death could be thought of as evil, but it is possible for a person to die suddenly with only momentary suffering or pain. Pain can be welcomed as good when it drives one to seek medical attention, uncovering a previously unknown illness and leading to a cure. Pain causes a hand to swiftly recoil from heat prior to incurring injury, and this, too, is good. Pain may also lead one to recoil from a potentially harmful relationship before suffering is endured.

In *Wandering in Darkness,* religious philosopher Eleonore Stump explains that suffering implies a loss: an unwanted, unwilling, unwelcomed taking away of something valued, needed, or wanted.[2] Suffering can be born from desire and expectations, but frequently these are subconscious. We often don't know the root of our suffering, our longing, or our felt but unidentified needs. So, whether or not we suffer in a particular instance could depend on our ability to make peace with our circumstances or to find contentment in the midst of loss. When pain is unwanted, unexpected, or mishandled, it usually becomes suffering. For example, the pain associated with muscle ache after a "good" workout or a healthy childbirth is associated with a positive outcome and not perceived as suffering or evil, but as part of the process of an expected good that is willfully endured. Similarly, with delayed gratification the process of waiting may be painful, yet it's considered well worth the delay when one experiences satisfaction from a desired result or reward. The effort involved in education, exercise, investing or saving money, and parenting is perceived as worthwhile and good. These are examples of tasks that require enduring hardship for a period of time, leading to a long-term reward, not evil or suffering.

However, the pain associated with an expected good becomes suffering if the outcome is a stillbirth, disease, financial collapse, or any other hardship or loss correlated with evil. In other words, pain that is not accepted voluntarily and brings an unexpected loss brings suffering. Suffering can be psychological, physical, spiritual, and/or empathic. While we may willingly enter into the pain or suffering that another experiences, we may suffer because we are unable to relieve the pain of the one we care for or love. The

---

[2]Stump, *Wandering in Darkness,* 10-11.

evil that human beings endure constitutes suffering for them because it is contrary to human flourishing or contrary to the core desires of the sufferer, or both.[3] However, there is a good suffering: when a person willfully chooses to suffer along with or in the place of another for the purpose of relieving suffering, or suffering in place of the other in order to prevent or reverse evil with healing and good.

Types of Suffering

Differentiating between suffering as a result of evil and intentional suffering to bring about a positive end result is helpful. Three types of suffering can be distinguished by the nature and source of the suffering:

1. External Suffering—suffering imposed by an unjust and broken world on broken people.

2. Internal Suffering—suffering from internal struggles that places pressure on our choices and character.

3. Intentional Suffering—suffering that arises from willfully laying down our lives for the sake of others, without seeking reward or affirmation.

All three of these can have transformative effects in our lives, but the first two come from brokenness (our own or others) and can lead us to personal wholeness only if we process the internal or external broken parts. The third is chosen suffering from a place of personal wholeness that leads to the wholeness of others.

External suffering is common to all humanity. This includes persecution, affliction, sickness, accidents, and all kinds of evil. This world is not the best of all possible worlds. *This* is not how it's supposed to be (and not as God intended in his good creation). Creation is marred by fragility and taking for oneself at the expense of another. While self-care is important, acting without a moral compass with concern for the part (self, or a single system) at the expense of the whole (others) breaks us apart. If we recognize that all of us are susceptible to harmful thoughts and actions and, to some degree, we're all broken and vulnerable and in need of healing to our body and soul, it's possible to see external suffering as normative but still

---

[3]Stump, *Wandering in Darkness*, 11.

corruptive or evil. Integrality, intraconnectivity is the divine intent, not shattering. We need to expose and fight the brokenness of the external systems that bring suffering while being willing to expose and change our own harmful ideas and behaviors.

Internal suffering involves the feeling of loss, fear of loss, or unfulfilled longings. Suffering often comes from our unmet needs, desires, or expectations. Part of the experience of suffering is the anxiety and torment of thinking of life without something or someone. Internal suffering can come from the fear of losing something or someone. The thought of living without this person, this experience, or this thing can be too painful to imagine. Suffering caused by fear of lack or loss can trap us into clinging to an object, person, or circumstance. It can cause us to manipulate or be manipulated in the effort to control or change a person or an outcome. It's a vicious cycle that robs many of sleep and peace. As the apostle John wrote, "There is no fear in love. But perfect love drives out fear, because fear has to do with punishment. The one who fears is not made perfect in love" (1 Jn 4:18).

Intentional suffering is chosen suffering leading to the wholeness of others. It involves deliberate acts of giving of ourselves and our resources or even laying down our lives for the sake of others. We see this kind of intentional suffering on battlefields, in hospitals, on streets of the poor, and in daily acts of kindness by those who willingly act in the best interest of another at the risk of their own personal loss or harm. This does not mean being a "doormat" or a "garbage can" for other people's anger, cruelty, or problems, but it does involve elevating the needs of others for their wholeness at our own expense. Intentional suffering takes strength, courage, and personal wholeness. Jesus expressed this through the parable of the Good Samaritan and by his words, "No one takes [my life] from me, but I lay it down of my own accord" (Jn 10:18).

Evil, suffering, and pain overlap, but recognizing the distinctions between each can help us identify our feelings and responses.

THE AMBIGUITY OF EVIL

For most, evil is whatever they think is evil, but many draw false conclusions based on their perceptions of their experience. What one calls evil another may call good, especially if they think it is in their personal best interest.

People may think they're doing good things for a person or for the environment but may actually be producing greater harm. This is illustrated well in the books *When Helping Hurts: How to Alleviate Poverty Without Hurting the Poor . . . and Yourself* by Steven Corbett and Brian Fikkert, and *Toxic Charity* by Robert Lupton.[4]

What is considered evil is often defined within a culture and can quickly change based on social norms. For example, a slogan appearing in the Google Code of Conduct from about 2004–2018 read, "Don't be evil."[5] There was no explanation and no definition of *evil*. It was understood as part of the corporate culture at Google that nothing should be done "that in any way can compromise people."[6] Former CEO and executive chairman of Google Eric Schmidt responded to questions about the nebulous nature of this rule in a National Public Radio interview on May 11, 2013, stating, "There's no book about evil except maybe, you know, the Bible or something."[7]

In more global terms, people generally identify evil with moral wrongs such as human trafficking, exploitation of the poor, oppressive governmental regimes, institutionalized evil, war, and abuse. The term *evil* has been used for political purposes as well. President George W. Bush's State of the Union address on January 29, 2002, used the phrase *axis of evil* to describe Iraq, Iran, and North Korea in their use of terrorism and weapons of mass destruction. This phrase became part of the rhetoric used to identify

---

[4]Steve Corbett et al., *When Helping Hurts: How to Alleviate Poverty Without Hurting the Poor . . . and Yourself* (Chicago: Moody, 2014); Robert D. Lupton, *Toxic Charity: How Churches and Charities Hurt Those They Help, and How to Reverse It* (San Francisco: HarperOne, 2012).

[5]Ian Bogost, "What Is 'Evil' to Google? Speculations on the Company's Contribution to Moral Philosophy," *The Atlantic*, October 15, 2013, www.theatlantic.com/technology/archive/2013/10 /what-is-evil-to-google/280573/. See also "Preface," Google Code of Conduct, Alphabet: Investor Relations, http://investor.google.com/corporate/code-of-conduct.html: "Don't be evil. Googlers generally apply those words to how we serve our users. But 'Don't be evil' is much more than that. Yes, it's about providing our users unbiased access to information, focusing on their needs and giving them the best products and services that we can. But it's also about doing the right thing more generally—following the law, acting honorably and treating each other with respect."; Adarsh Verma, "Google Drops 'Don't Be Evil' Motto from Its Code of Conduct," *Fossbytes*, February 26, 2021, https://fossbytes.com/google-drops-dont-be-evil-motto-code -of-conduct/.

[6]Sydney Brownstone, "What Does Google's 'Don't Be Evil' Actually Mean After Snowden," *Fast Company*, August 28, 2014, www.fastcompany.com/3034969/what-does-googles-dont-be-evil -actually-mean-after-snowden.

[7]Peter Sagal, "Google Chairman Eric Schmidt Plays Not My Job," NPR, *Wait Wait . . . Don't Tell Me*, May 11, 2013, www.npr.org/templates/transcript/transcript.php?storyId=182873683.

enemies of the United States and to justify the War on Terror, the attack of Afghanistan, and other military actions taken by the US government.[8] However, as philosopher Susan Neiman points out, the *axis of evil* phrase has not been revisited, reconsidered, or lamented for not being used in reference to other countries that commit acts of mass destruction, such as the bombing of Hiroshima, for example.[9]

Evil may be associated with those who pollute the environment or with acts of nature (which insurance policies have often woefully labeled "acts of God"). An evil person may be thought of as one who holds differing views from another. Someone who claims to be tolerant identifies the evil other as intolerant or ignorant for perceived wrongs such as voting for the "wrong" party, or holding to any number of perspectives a person associates with harm. But, "If evil can't be defined in a way that ensures we will recognize it, what's the point of using the concept at all?"[10]

English philosopher Michael Palmer provides a helpful definition in his *Atheist's Creed*: "I believe that not everything is permissible. For while that which increases happiness is not always a good, that which increases misery is always an evil."[11] Nevertheless, some modern cultures may lack the perspective of a long view of history, or an understanding of evil from ancient times, from sources, including the Bible, which have been formative in the establishment of values and laws for a few thousand years across continents and cultures.

MISUSES OF THE WORDS GOOD AND EVIL

I'm compelled to include a cautionary note that is simultaneously a call to humility in this discussion. Be wary of people who use the terms *good* and *evil* too easily or ascribe them too readily to others. Sometimes good

---

[8]"Bush State of Union address," Transcript of George W. Bush's State of the Union Address January 29, 2002, CNN, http://edition.cnn.com/2002/ALLPOLITICS/01/29/bush.speech.txt/. See also, "This Day in History: George W. Bush Describes Iraq, Iran, and North Korea as 'Axis of Evil,'" *History.com*, January 27, 2020, www.history.com/this-day-in-history/bush-describes -iraq-iran-north-korea-as-axis-of-evil.

[9]Susan Neiman, *Evil in Modern Thought: An Alternative History of Philosophy*, Princeton Classics (Princeton, NJ: Princeton University Press, 2015), 479-87.

[10]Neiman, *Evil*, xiii.

[11]Michael Palmer, *Atheism for Beginners: A Course Book for Schools and Colleges* (Cambridge: Lutterworth, 2013), unnumbered page following the copyright page, caps original.

intentions are nullified by the wake of their effects. For example, the consistently overprotective parent can stunt the child's growth and development into confident maturity. Or a parent may want to toughen up a tender child by being harsh or cruel, only to throw the child into solitude, despair, or seeking love in potentially harmful ways for lack of kindness and affection. Another example is illustrated in *When Helping Hurts*, which explores the harm done by many helping endeavors that end up mirroring forms of colonialism.[12] With good intentions, we may bring more harm than good.

Then there are those who have sufficiently extinguished their conscience and empathy and no longer feel a responsibility for the well-being of another—caring only for their own benefit or the benefit of their inner circle. An inflictor of pain who embarks on a path to bring intentional misery, harm, or torment to a person or a people group with no remorse may ultimately be recognized as evil. This lack of conscience includes harmful actions against or neglect of fellow human beings as well as animals and the natural world.

There is another, often subtle, kind of evil. Those who seek to abuse or oppress others by weaponizing words for the purpose of doing harm: to subdue, to demean, or to silence a person or a people group. The words themselves are an act of evil. If you have been called evil by one who has the power to instill in you guilt, shame, or blame, it is likely a misuse, or indeed, an abuse of that power. It is a verbal act of violence on your soul. In such cases, recognize that you are empowered to identify as evil the words and actions of that person—or collective of persons—who forms a system that abuses or oppresses.

FROM MY STORY: EVIL AS ABUSE

Before my first marriage I was well trained to obey those who I was told had authority over me. That included my pastors and my husband. Two weeks before my wedding, my soon-to-be husband informed me that he had cheated on me and then kicked me. I

---

[12]Corbett et al., *When Helping Hurts*. See also C. S. Lewis, "The Inner Ring," Memorial Lecture at King's College, University of London, C. S. Lewis Society of California, 1944, www.lewis society.org/innerring/.

married him anyway. I didn't tell anyone what had happened because I thought that covering it up was the right thing, as if it was my job to protect him. He was a pastor in training and had one-third of the New Testament memorized. We even started in seminary together. For over six years I never divulged his infidelities or increasing physical and emotional abuses, except once. When he broke my nose, I drove myself to the ER. The doctor urged me not to go home. When I lied and told him I had run into a door, he replied kindly but firmly, "I know that's not true. I can see the imprint of a ring on your nose." So, when I left the ER, I checked myself into a hotel and, for the first time, called our pastor and told him what had happened.[13] His advice was short and swift, "Go home and love your husband!" I obeyed as I was accustomed to do. The violence escalated unchecked, as abuse always does, until he tried to kill me.

One day, without warning or incident, the man who had vowed to love, honor, and protect me, shoved me into the bedroom and pinned me down on our bed with the full force of his weight against my throat. There had been no discussion or disagreement preceding this event. Looking into his eyes for some compassion all I saw were shark eyes, two black holes with no expression; no one was home in his soul. He was a body builder, so I didn't struggle for long. As I closed my eyes, I resigned myself to the inevitable and silently said, "Lord, into your hands I commit my spirit." I fully expected that to be my end. I felt no pain or fear, just peace. At that moment, our doorbell rang. An old friend I hadn't seen for years told me years later that at that time, he couldn't shake the thought that kept coming into his head that he urgently needed to come visit me and my husband, right now. When the doorbell rang, my husband sat up, stopped choking me, got up, answered the door, sent him away, and sat down in the living room as if nothing had happened.

Eventually, I escaped, found a safe place to live, and started going to a counselor for the first time in my life. One of the first questions she asked me was, *Why did you stay?* I was shocked. I didn't even know

---

[13]This church shut down a couple of decades ago after the death of the pastor.

I *could* ask that question, or the many that followed in the coming months and years. I hadn't been asking the right questions. I thought that if I tried harder or if I was smarter, I could figure out how to make him love me or make the abuse stop. I began to believe that maybe I deserved the cruelty. Like most who experience abuse or trauma, I was looking through a broken lens, a distorted perspective. It took some time for me to absorb the idea that the abuse was not my fault.[14] I also had to learn what it means to recover from codependency and to retrain my thinking. The best alternative word for codependent is "self-love deficit disorder."[15]

Sometimes those who remain in abusive situations stay because they think they can figure out how to make things work. They may believe they can change the abuser, or that it's their duty or responsibility to stay. Many who stay in abusive relationships are determined to keep trying to fix the other person or the situation. But the truth is, although we have the ability to influence others, we are not powerful enough to change anyone except our own selves. Everyone must choose their own response to life's hardships. Abusers rarely change.

Statistically, most perpetrators come from families where they witnessed or experienced abuse themselves.[16] Unless an individual makes a conscious, strategic decision to change, those who have been violated as children either *become* violators or select relationships where they will continue to *be* abused as adults. Tragically, my pastor never stepped in to speak with my husband or take steps to protect me. I believe my husband could have been saved from his traumatic

---

[14]One in four women and one in seven men have been victims of severe physical violence by an intimate partner in their lifetime. M. C. Black et al., "The National Intimate Partner and Sexual Violence Survey: 2010 Summary Report," National Coalition Against Domestic Violence, n.d., www.speakcdn.com/assets/2497/male_victims_of_intimate_partner_violence.pdf.

[15]I first heard this term from psychotherapist Ross Rosenberg on YouTube. See also Ross Rosenberg, *The Human Magnet Syndrome: Why We Love People Who Hurt Us* (Eau Claire, WI: Premier Publishing & Media, 2013).

[16]"Boys who witness domestic violence are twice as likely to abuse their own partners and children when they become adults." Domesticshelters.org, "Children and Dometic Violence," January 7, 2015, www.domesticshelters.org/articles/statistics/children-and-domestic-violence. Cf. Murray A. Straus and Richard J. Gelles, *Physical Violence in American Families: Risk Factors and Adaptations to Violence in 8,145 Families* (New Brunswick, NJ: Transaction, 1990), 8, 145.

disorders before he lost his own life in an accident not many years later. Logically, we know that brokenness does not grant the right to abuse others. It's wrong, horribly wrong. But how do we learn to "see" differently? If we've never learned that we're *valuable* and *worthy* of great love and respect, how can we learn what is good or evil, or what these words mean practically and personally? How can we heal and learn how to respond in ways that are helpful and restorative? In the process of healing from abuse, however, we need to identify and call out what is evil.

When I told my parents about my husband's abuse, they just shook their head. But my sister jumped up from the dining room table, ran into the kitchen and yelled at him, "How dare you hurt my sister!" Seeing her response of rage at my abuse paved the way for me to get angry myself and motivated a much-needed courage within me to recognize the tremendous violation of my worth that had taken place. I came to realize that facing and naming the evil *as evil* was an important step in restoration from evil.

My story is a poignant example of calling evil good. I thought I was doing something *good* by trying to protect my husband's reputation. But I wasn't saving our marriage by my silence. Rather, I was sealing in a potentially ongoing generational cycle of abuse. What we permit we condone. I came to learn that it's neither good nor nice to allow evil to run over you. Toleration of evil actions from a person is standing in agreement with the evil, giving free rein to do violence physically, psychologically, emotionally, or spiritually.[17] We must take a stand against abuse in all its forms, and come along side those who are being abused.

Everyone has experienced evil. However, to the person who has been severely broken by evil, evil can feel comfortable and become their norm. Those who have not processed their traumas in the light of what's true can allow the evil propagated against them to be inflicted to other through them. Even though everyone experiences evil and suffering, it never feels right or

---

[17]The U.S. National Domestic Violence Hotline is 800-799-7233 or dial 911. For more information, begin with thehotline.org: www.thehotline.org/identify-abuse/, or www.thehotline.org/get-help/domestic-violence-local-resources/.

normal unless one is so broken by evil that they become someone who inflicts it. When evil or trauma goes unprocessed and unhealed, we may
become its hand. As the saying goes, "Hurt people hurt people." And to
some extent, we are all hurt people, hurting other people. But I am calling
us to become part of the "healed people who heal people." As we grow in our
healing, we join with those who intentionally take on the suffering of others
to destroy the works and effects of evil, untwisting the corruption to bring
about good.

Chapter Three

DEFINING EVIL—BIBLICALLY

Woe to those who call evil good and good evil, who put darkness for light
and light for darkness, who put bitter for sweet and sweet for bitter.

Isaiah 5:20

ANTHROPOLOGISTS CLAIM THAT "there is no universally agreed-upon notion of evil throughout all the various cultures of the world."[1] What people generally consider evil is often best determined by its effect on their self-worth and is, therefore, intricately tied to perceptions of what they see, feel, and believe. However, as Nobel laureate Elie Wiesel writes, "When words have lost all meaning for children, it is a sure sign of disaster."[2] This is true for adults too. How do you talk about or face something you can't define? Defining a word so daunting and conceptual as *evil* is a challenge that must be taken on.

Historically, many societies have drawn their most articulate definition of evil from the Bible. As Old Testament scholar Walter Moberly points out, "The assumption that the Bible has something vitally important to say about the fundamental needs and concerns of human beings draws people to the Bible . . . (for people of faith and) from the perspective of no faith at all."[3]

---

[1]David Parkin, ed., *The Anthropology of Evil* (Oxford: Wiley-Blackwell, 1991), 16.
[2]Elie Wiesel, *A Jew Today* (New York: Vintage, 1979), 156-57.
[3]R. W. L. Moberly, *The Old Testament of the Old Testament: Patriarchal Narratives and Mosaic Yahwism* (Eugene, OR: Wipf & Stock, 2001), 3. Moberly also refers to the narratives of the patriarchs in Genesis as the "Old Testament of the Old Testament," 105, 146. See also Mark J. Boda, *A Severe Mercy: Sin and Its Remedy in the Old Testament* (Winona Lake, IN: Eisenbrauns, 2009), 16: "The book of Genesis functions as the introduction to the Torah, which in turn lays the foundation for the entire Old Testament, in terms of both its story and its theology."

Psychologist and trauma specialist Diane Langberg states, "That which has the capacity to destroy what God has created deserves our serious attention."[4] Therefore, having looked at perspectives and attempts to define evil from our current times, we turn now to how the Bible presents evil and how this compares and contrasts with modern conceptions.

While many definitions and descriptions of evil are offered in this chapter, principally I find that evil is the corruption of goodness. Further, it is fundamentally the corruption of creational and relational goodness.[5] Evil consists of thoughts, actions, or forces that diminish life. Evil takes what is good and twists and defiles it. When it comes to human behavior, evil injects lies to steal, destroy, and kill what was originally good. These behaviors are starting points for the perversion of good. However, evil has a broad range of meaning and comes at us from multiple sources.[6]

CREATIONAL GOODNESS AND EVIL

Interestingly, the Bible doesn't address the philosophical problems of evil or the question of theodicy (essentially, the argument that if God is good and all-powerful, and God created the world, then God is responsible for evil). Rather, the Bible assumes God is good and always does justly (Ps 145:9; Gen 18:25). Its focus is on the fact that there *is* evil and wrongdoing, that we as human beings are supposed to do something about it, and that God wants to work in and through us to overcome it and to transform the impact of evil into something good. The Bible doesn't ask what is evil or why did it happen because it's a given. Rather, it seems to ask, "How will we/I/you respond to evil whenever it strikes in whatever form it takes? Will we let evil define us? Overtake us? Will we let bitterness, resentment, or hatred distort our behavior, or will we master them and work in cooperation with God to overcome and reverse the devastations of evil with good?"[7]Origins and

---

[4]Diane Langberg, *Suffering and the Heart of God: How Trauma Destroys and Christ Restores* (Greensboro, NC: New Growth, 2015), 49.

[5]Cornelius Plantinga defines sin as the vandalism of shalom. See Cornelius Plantinga, *Not the Way It's Supposed to Be: A Breviary of Sin* (Grand Rapids, MI: Eerdmans, 1999), 89.

[6]For my complete study, see Ingrid Faro, *Evil in Genesis: A Contextual Analysis of Hebrew Lexemes for Evil in the Book of Genesis*, Studies in Scripture & Biblical Theology (Bellingham, WA: Lexham, 2021).

[7]Faro, *Evil in Genesis,* 200. See also R. W. L. Moberly, *The Theology of the Book of Genesis*, Old Testament Theology (New York: Cambridge University Press, 2009), 36-41; Walter Brueggemann,

beginnings are important to every story. Most cultures have a narrative of how the world began and how human beings came to be. What we believe about how we got here directs the way we view the world and ourselves. The contrast between the biblical story of how humans were created and other ancient stories of origins have some similarities, but even more important are their distinctions.

The Bible opens with resounding emphasis on the goodness of creation through the symbolic sevenfold repetition of the word *tov* (good). In the first chapter of Genesis, every step of creation begins with God's intention expressed in words (e.g., "Let there be light"), the actualizing of God's words ("and it was so"), and God's evaluation of what was made, "and God saw that it was good."[8] The sevenfold use of "good" in Gen 1:4, 10, 12, 18, 21, 25, and "very good" in 1:31 is an expression of emphasis and completion. This word, *tov* (good), is also used to describe all the trees of the Garden, which were both "pleasing to the sight and good for food" (Gen 2:9). Goodness is a state of being, related to shalom, to wholeness. In the beginning, everything is as it should be: it is good, beautiful, appropriate, and harmonious. Everything that God says and does is consistent with his character. In sum, the narrative tells us that God is good and that all he made and does is in the best interest of his creation and humanity. All that he says and all that he does is consistent with who he is. Yet, the universe is not God, so it is not perfect.

In the narrative of God's final act of creation, he makes humanity in his image and according to his likeness. In this narrative, God created us for the purpose of establishing and maintaining his reign of goodness, fruitfulness, abundance, and wholeness in the earthly realm as his coregents, his viceroys, empowered to act in his name (Gen 1:26-28). The biggest difference between the Bible's account of humanity's creation and that of other ancient narratives is that in other stories of creation, the world was made through warring gods in conflict with each other. In general, only human kings or rulers were made in the image of the gods and empowered to rule in the domain of the gods. In contrast, the biblical story speaks of only one God creating the world and humanity, with *every* human being made in his image and

---

Genesis, Interpretation: A Bible Commentary for Teaching and Preaching (Atlanta: Westminster John Knox, 1986), 12-21.

[8] All biblical quotes are from the NIV unless otherwise indicated.

empowered to rule as his representatives to carry out his goodness in his domain of the earth. Here, every human being, male and female, has special status with God, and God takes personally how we treat one another and his creation (Gen 1:26-28; 5:1-2; 9:5-7; Mt 25:40-45).

However, along with authority, humanity was given the choice to either cooperate with God or to defy him. These two choices are represented by the two trees in the Garden of Eden: the choice of living in thankful cooperative relationship with God for all his goodness, or the choice of doing what seems right in their own eyes, wanting to decide autonomously what's good or evil, and taking to fulfill their own desires. Since humanity chose the latter, as Abraham Heschel said, "There was a moment when God looked at the universe made by Him and said: 'It is good.' But there was no moment in which God could have looked at history made by man and said: 'It is good.'"[9] Evil is more clearly understood in contrast to good. Good is that which promotes flourishing and harmony.

The biblical concept of good (*tov*) is identified as (1) something desirable, abundant, healthy; (2) inner or relational well-being; (3) protection of a person or property, sparing or preserving life; and (4) moral or ethical uprightness, redemption, and forgiveness.[10]

Evil is routinely contrasted with good (*tov*). In the Hebrew Bible, the main word for evil is *ra* (*ra* as an adjective, *raah* as a noun, or *raa* as a verb). A study of this word in context reveals that *ra* carries a wide range of meaning, referring to anything perceived as bad, deficient, harmful, or wicked.[11] It is "related to the concepts of death and cursing, in direct opposition to good, life, and blessing."[12] The biblical concept of evil (*ra*) is identified as (1) something deficient or negative; (2) emotional or relational distress; (3) harm or death to a person or property; and (4) moral failure or wickedness.[13] Good promotes flourishing. Evil consists of actions or forces that hinder flourishing. Evil vandalizes what is good.[14] Tremendous confusion and harmful behavior arise when evil is called good or good is called evil.

---

[9]Abraham Joshua Heschel, *The Prophets* (Peabody, MA: Hendrickson, 2017), 168.
[10]Faro, *Evil in Genesis*, 72-76.
[11]Faro, *Evil in Genesis*, 64.
[12]Faro, *Evil in Genesis*, 196.
[13]Faro, *Evil in Genesis*, 65-72.
[14]Langberg, *Suffering*, 49.

The New Testament has a similar concept of evil. The words used in the Greek usually describe a morally bad person or action but also refer to something that's undesirable, harmful, or painful. A good summary is given by Scott Gleaves, "The identification of something as evil or bad depends on one's perspective with relation to what is considered good or right. The biblical standard of 'good' is established by God (Gen 1:31; 2:9), so anything that deviates from divine expectations of goodness is evil (Gen 6:5; Eph 5:16; 6:13)."[15] Satan is identified as "the evil one," and demonic spirits are called evil.[16] In both Testaments, what is evil is often contrasted with what is just and right.

RELATIONAL GOODNESS AND EVIL

Biblically, the most important relationship is between people and God. From the creation narrative through the entirety of the Bible, God created humanity to be in relationship with God as well as one another. As Jesus poignantly recaps, every law, responsibility, and teaching stems from two commandments: to love the Lord with all your heart, soul, mind, and strength, and to love your neighbor as yourself (Mt 22:36-40; Deut 6:4; Lev 19:18). Further, it is made clear that your neighbor is everyone you meet (Lev 19:33; Lk 10:25-37). In contrast, evil is anything that destroys relationship with God or your neighbor.

A significant finding of my study of the biblical concept of evil is the close connection between evil and sight. In Genesis, evil is most frequently associated with seeing or perception.[17] The correlation between evil and sight begins in the first chapter, with the phrase "God saw that it was good" repeated seven times. This sentence structure occurs again in the third chapter of Genesis when "the woman saw that the fruit of the tree was good" and *she took* from the tree and ate its fruit, in direct contradiction to God's warning that this tree would bring death. The same sentence structure occurs next in the sixth chapter of Genesis, when the sons of God saw that the daughters of men were good (*tov*), *and they took* whoever they wanted.

---

[15]G. Scott Gleaves, "Evil," In *Lexham Theological Wordbook,* ed. Douglas Mangum and Derek R. Brown, Lexham Bible Reference Series (Bellingham, WA: Lexham, 2014).

[16]Satan is referred to as the evil one in Mt 13:38; Jn 17:15; Eph 6:16; and 2 Thess 3:3, and demons are called evil in Lk 11:13; Acts 19:12-16.

[17]Faro, *Evil in Genesis,* 97-132.

God called their actions evil and corrupt. The contrast between the way God sees things and the way people see things continues throughout the Bible. For example, at the end of Judges, when people had become corrupt and were doing horrific evils, the final words are, "Everyone did what was right in their own eyes" (Judg 21:25 NASB95). In 1 and 2 Kings and 1 and 2 Chronicles, the story of nearly every king of Judah concludes with an assessment of whether the king did what was right in the eyes of the Lord or did what was evil in the eyes of the Lord. In other words, the distinction between what is good and what is evil is directly related to whether a person's actions are in alignment with God's perspective or are against God's perspective.

To expand on the concept of evil and perception: people who see themselves as the center of their universe view others through the lens as an entitled person who takes or grasps from others to fulfill a personal desire. Their perspective and consequent actions treat people like objects. Therefore, others are viewed as mere commodities, used to fulfill their own needs. People are seen as objects to be consumed. The result is harm and misery to the used. The hallmark of evil is the association between evil and selfishly taking for oneself without regard for others or God.

Evil is associated with ideas and forces that seek to steal or destroy what rightfully belongs to another. In opposition to viewing self as the center of creation, God's perspective sees every human being and all his creation as highly valuable. Unlike the world power systems where the weak are oppressed to serve the strong, God's intended power dynamic is for the strong to serve and lift up the weak. Jesus dramatically demonstrated this when the night before his crucifixion he took on the role of the lowest servant in any household, took up a towel, and kneeled down to wash the feet of each of his disciples, even the one that he knew would betray him to his death that very night. Then he admonished them, saying,

> "Do you understand what I have done for you?" he asked them. "You call me 'Teacher' and 'Lord,' and rightly so, for that is what I am. Now that I, your Lord and Teacher, have washed your feet, you also should wash one another's feet. I have set you an example that you should do as I have done for you. Very truly I tell you, no servant is greater than his master, nor is a messenger greater than the one who sent him. Now that you know these things, you will be blessed if you do them. (Jn 13:12-17)

When we violate our God-given purpose of serving and protecting all of creation and each person's value, we are doing evil. When we submit ourselves to the desires and will of those who abuse people and power, we are serving evil. When we passively accept the words and actions of those who oppress and silence, we become participants in the corruption of divinely intended justness and rightness.

Biblically, therefore, what is good aligns with God's view of creation—for the world to be a place of harmony and abundance and for relationships to be based on the mutual caring and respect for the dignity and value of every human being. Evil sees and acts contrary to God's perspective and purposes, no matter how good it may appear to us. The ability to see God's way is learned, by cultivating relationship with God through prayer and engaging with Scripture, by faithfully following Jesus Christ, and by listening to God's Holy Spirit. These practices will never contradict each other.

As Heschel observes, "The root of all evil is, according to Isaiah, man's false sense of sovereignty and, stemming from it, man's pride, arrogance, and presumption. . . . There is no limit to cruelty when man begins to think that he is the master."[18] According to the biblical perspective, people's desire for autonomy—to be independent gods who are not answerable to anyone, especially the Lord—will ultimately pervert what is just and right. They will try to either rule over others as sovereign or subject themselves to another as their lord.

How Did Evil Spiritual Forces Enter the World?

A common question is, *When and where did evil spiritual forces enter the world?* Some argue for what is often called "the gap theory," which is belief in a precreation existence of rebellious angelic forces that caused the destruction of the earth, occurring between Genesis 1:1 and Genesis 1:2. Others attribute the entrance of evil to the lies of the serpent in Genesis 3 leading to the rebellion of Adam and the woman. Either way, many scholars point out that even though Genesis 1–2 lacks conflict or a battle motif, there is a fragility to creation due to the immense responsibility God endowed on earthlings as coregents over creation, giving us authority over the

---

[18]Abraham J. Heschel, *The Prophets*, 1st Perennial Classics ed. (New York: Harper Perennial Modern Classics, 2001), 165.

possibilities for evil to enter the world.[19] The language of Genesis 2 also demonstrates that "from the inception the human was mortal."[20] The formation of humanity as both dust and divinity (Gen 2:7) along with the necessity of the Tree of Life and a tree of death (the Tree of the Knowledge of Good and Evil) foreshadow our temporality and the looming risk inherent in the good creation.

I'll not further address the question whether the rebellion of spiritual beings against God occurred prior to the creation of the earth between Genesis 1:1 and Genesis 1:2 (the "gap theory") or after the creation of humanity between Genesis 2:25 and Genesis 3:1 because it's not crucial for our discussion. Scholar G. B. Caird points out, "The Hebrew mind was less interested in the origin of evil than in its conquest."[21] He further observes that "evil can exist as a force in the world only because it is able to take the powers and authorities of God and to transform them into world-rulers of this darkness."[22]

WHERE DOES EVIL GET ITS POWER?

Since I affirm that evil is not the absence of good, but the corruption of good, this points us in the direction of asking where evil gets its power. The answer lies in this: evil derives its force from the power in goodness. For example, consider the strength of the flow of a mighty river, one that is clean and teeming with life. For millennia this river may have cut its way through soil or granite to form its life-giving path through nature. Now suppose a dam is built to contain or stop its flow, but that dam breaks, and the natural flow of the river becomes diverted and floods cities or forests, causing death and destruction. The goodness of the river becomes a force for destruction, death, and therefore evil. The river was good. The diversion of its path caused evil.

God is the ultimate source of goodness, and his will is always for good, life, and blessing to his creation and creatures. God made his creation good,

---

[19]J. P. Fokkelman, *Narrative Art in Genesis: Specimens of Stylistic and Structural Analysis*, 2nd ed. (Eugene, OR: Wipf & Stock, 2004), 12; Jon D. Levenson, *Creation and the Persistence of Evil* (Princeton, NJ: Princeton University Press, 1994), xiv.

[20]Ziony Zevit, *What Really Happened in the Garden of Eden?* (New Haven, CT: Yale University Press, 2013), 124-25, 168.

[21]G. B. Caird, *Principalities and Powers: A Study in Pauline Theology*, The Chancellor's Lectures for 1954 at Queen's University, Kingston Ontario (Eugene, OR: Wipf & Stock, 2003), 10.

[22]Caird, *Principalities and Powers*, 53.

with the inherent ability to replicate itself, like seeds, with life within themselves. He also created nature and bodies and cells with the ability to heal. However, when cells within a body begin to ignore their naturally programmed signals, often due to toxins or other interfering substances within the body, they no longer generate and regenerate along healthy paths in unison with other cells around them, and instead multiply in a disordered way, invading the good space with aberrant cells, causing damage and death to the healthy tissue. The good force of life within healthy cells can be overrun by abnormal cells that "trick the immune system into helping cancer cells stay alive and grow" and even "convince immune cells to protect the tumor instead of attacking it."[23] The cancer cells don't know they're evil. They're not moral agents. However, they work evil by deviating from the power of health and goodness designed into a healthy body and using the perversion of that power to do damage.

Likewise, love and relationships are good, and perhaps the strongest human force to bring healing, help, and wholeness to the lives of individuals, families, and communities. However, when a person believes that they must receive the love or respect of another and tries to take it by manipulation, intimidation, or domination, this is a perversion that can only produce damage, harm, and sometimes death to the object of that person's corrupted version of love.

Some evils that come our way are intentional, others seem random. We can have control over some evils, but others seem to be out of our control. Ultimately, however, the impact of our choices in response to evil determines whether evil prevails or good overcomes it.

---

[23]"What Is Cancer," National Institute of Health: National Cancer Institute, www.cancer.gov /about-cancer/understanding/what-is-cancer#:~:text=Differences%20between%20Cancer%20 Cells%20and%20Normal%20Cells,-Cancer%20cells%20differ&text=For%20instance%2C%20 cancer%20cells%3A,cell%20death%2C%20or%20apoptosis).

Part Two

NATURAL CAUSES

COSMIC SEED AND NATURAL EVIL

Evil is a result of the freedom inherent in all of creation. God did not create evil, but God created all creation in freedom.

KAREN BAKER-FLETCHER

IN THE PROCESS of exploring the ways evil can gain access into our lives, we begin with the most common assumptions based on simple action-consequence and the forces of nature. Many of us struggle to find a reason for everything that happens, and there are many things that don't fit or make sense. First, let's consider how evil can enter our lives as a result of our actions. Choices we make set a trajectory of behaviors that cause consequences we might not foresee or anticipate. Often these events unfold like the opening of a leaf or like the rolling of a thunderstorm. Sometimes they don't involve forethought or awareness of an ultimate outcome. Many people are simply living their lives, thinking about whatever stream of consciousness manifests, without much evaluation of its content. They act without conscientious regard toward the eventual outcome. *Nevertheless,* the accumulation of thoughts leads to behaviors that have a lasting impact.

Second, we explore how nature itself has predictable, normal cycles but can strike with ferocity, bringing harm and suffering without aim or intent. Nature generally falls outside of our consideration of moral evil. However, we'll also examine the complicity of humanity in what is commonly considered "natural evil." Not only do these natural evils occur through the weather, but they also occur in physical bodies, through sickness and disease, and through encounters with animals and insects that cause harm as part of nature without evil intentions.

Chapter Four

ACTION-CONSEQUENCE AND THE COSMIC SEED

No matter what we sow, the law of returns applies. Good or evil, love or hate, justice or tyranny, grapes or thorns, a gracious compliment or a peevish complaint—whatever we invest, we tend to get it back with interest.

Cornelius Plantinga Jr.

The idea that actions have built-in consequences is the most fundamental explanation for the good and the evil that happens to people. This process is widely understood throughout history—from ancient cultures to modern "new age" and scientific reasoning. Concepts such as "what goes around comes around," "you will reap what you have sown," "you'll get what's coming to you," and karma, describe the process of action-consequence.

For a simple example, when I worked as a dietitian, I had conversations every day with people about the role of nutrition in the recovery of their health. Most people who could improve their health through changes to their eating or lifestyle were unwilling to do so. The comment, "But I'd rather die than give up . . .'' was followed by my response, "That's a choice you can make." I've seen people continue unhealthy habits for decades and then question why God let a specific instance of bad health happen. It wasn't God's fault. Often their bad health was a result of bad choices over a long time. Yet, when something went wrong, they looked for someone to blame, and God was the biggest target.

When seeking to dismantle evil and look for areas of causation, a good place to start is ourselves. The choices we make and the subsequent consequences of our actions must be examined for their role in causing good or evil in our lives.

IMAGE OF ACTION-CONSEQUENCE FROM GENESIS: THE SEED

In the first chapter of the Bible, the idea of action-consequence unfolds through the image of a seed. Genesis 1 introduces a core truth: life comes from seed (Gen 1:11-14, 29). Somehow, life is contained in a seed. This is true for plants, fish, birds, mammals, and humans. The seed of an apple planted in fertile ground produces an apple tree. The seed of a bull planted in a fertile cow produces a calf. In Hebrew and in Greek, the word *seed* is also the word for *semen*, and throughout the Hebrew Bible it is translated into English as *offspring* or *descendants*.

After the creation narrative, *seed* appears again after the deception of the serpent, referring to the representatives of malevolent forces as *offspring* of the serpent, as the *seed* of the woman are her *offspring*. This seed of the woman would bring hope to the world through striking the serpent's offspring (seed) on the head: "And I will put hostility between you and between the woman, and between your offspring (seed) and between her offspring (seed); he will strike you *on the* head, and you will strike him *on the* heel" (Gen 3:15 LEB). Seed, therefore, has both a natural and a symbolic reference.

UNIVERSAL UNDERSTANDINGS OF ACTION-CONSEQUENCE

Some of the earliest literature records the belief that good things come to good people, and bad things happen because someone did something bad, or they offended God or the gods. For example, this expectation is expressed in the ancient Babylonian work, *Poem of the Righteous Sufferer*, and in the Sumerian tablet, *Penitential Prayer to Every God*, in which the afflicted begs for mercy and forgiveness from whichever gods he unknowingly offended.[1] As Old Testament scholar Rolf Knierim states, "One does not need a deity in order to realize that an evil act has consequences, and a crime deserves punishment."[2]

Most Buddhist religions embody "the Law of Cause and Effect," also known as karma, meaning action or deed. Karma is a central belief of

---

[1] Amar Annus and Alan Lenzi, *Ludlul Bēl Nēmeqi: The Standard Babylonian Poem of the Righteous Sufferer* (Helsinki: Neo-Assyrian Text Corpus Project, 2010); Joshua J. Mark, "Ludlul-Bel-Nimeqi," in *World History Encyclopedia*, January 20, 2023, www.ancient.eu/article/226/.

[2] Rolf P. Knierim, *The Task of Old Testament Theology: Method and Cases* (Grand Rapids, MI: Eerdmans, 1995), 445. See also Andrew E. Hill and John H. Walton, *A Survey of the Old Testament*, 3rd ed. (Grand Rapids, MI: Zondervan Academic, 2009), 456.

various traditions of Buddhism, and is believed to some extent in Jainism, Hinduism, Sikhism, Taoism, and Falun Gong.[3] Common to these belief systems is the theory of causality. "Cause gives rise to effect—this is an inherent fact of life."[4] As a "Universal Truth . . . every event, action, or moment in this lifetime has its own cause and effect. . . . We all want favorable effects and are afraid of negative outcomes. Once we understand the Law of Cause and Effect, it's only natural to refrain from committing evil, the cause of future sorrow, and to do more good, the cause of future happiness."[5] Accordingly, within this belief system, the Law of Cause and Effect operates with "unfailing precision . . . even the gods cannot alter its path."[6] These religions recognize that multiple causative agents are at work simultaneously, creating intricate patterns and networks of subsequent effects.[7]

While Judaism and Christianity also acknowledge a cosmic system of action-consequence, they also believe in the involvement of a personal God who is capable of forgiving an action and changing its consequence, thus altering the trajectory that is generally deemed inescapable in a purely karmic system.

In modern times, scientific, psychological, and various New Age conceptualizations of action-consequence continue to develop. Visualization is a scientific-cognitive method that engages the mind for performance enhancement in a wide spectrum of fields, from physical sports and muscle development to decision-making and planning.[8] "According to the

---

[3]Max Corradi, "Understanding the Law of Cause and Effect: Karma in Buddhism," *Sivana East*, n.d., https://blog.sivanaspirit.com/bd-sp-law-cause-effect-karma/; Joseph Goldstein, "Cause and Effect: Reflecting on the Law of Karma," *The Buddhist Review Tricycle*, 2008, https://tricycle .org/magazine/cause-and-effect/; "The Selected Buddha's Dhammas: The Law of Cause and Effect (The Law of Karma)," Mahidol University, Wisdom of the Land, www.mahidol.ac.th /budsir/Part4_5.htm.

[4]Master Hsing Yun, *Conditionality: The Law of Cause and Effect: Buddhism in Every Step (A9)*, trans. Fo Guang Shan International Translation Center (2010), 9.

[5]"Law of Cause and Effect—Foundation of Buddhism," in *Tibetan Buddhist Encyclopedia*, February 26, 2016, http://tibetanbuddhistencyclopedia.com/en/index.php/Law_of_Cause_and _Effect_—_Foundation_of_Buddhism.

[6]Hsing Yun, *Conditionality*, 1.

[7]Piyadassi Thera, "Law of Cause and Effect," *Tibetan Buddhist Encyclopedia*, December 30, 2014, http://tibetanbuddhistencyclopedia.com/en/index.php?title=Law_of_Cause_and_Effect.

[8]Lace M. Padilla et al., "Decision Making with Visualizations: A Cognitive Framework across Disciplines," *Cognitive Research Journal* 29 (2018), https://cognitiveresearchjournal.springeropen .com/articles/10.1186/s41235-018-0120-9. See also Tim Blankert and Melvyn R. W. Hamstra,

International Coaching Academy's neuroscience and visualization research paper, 'if you exercise an idea over and over [in your mind], your brain will begin to respond as though the idea was a real object in the world.'"[9] The brain does not distinguish between actively imagining something and experiencing it.

Popular versions of this practice are reflected in "the Law of Attraction."[10] This concept has gained traction as the power of "manifestation." Oprah Winfrey promoted this in an interview with LinkedIn's former CEO: "You control a lot by your thoughts and we control a lot by our joined thoughts . . . by what I [and we] believe. . . . When I started to figure that out for myself, I became careful of what I think and what I ask for. . . . I was like what else can I do? What else can I manifest? Because I have seen it work. I have seen it happen over and over again."[11] The fact that "thoughts can become things" is core to Rhonda Byrne's popular book and movie *The Secret*.[12] As she describes, "The law of attraction is a law of nature. It is as impartial and impersonal as the law of gravity is. It is precise, and it is exact."[13] These practices tap into action-consequence as a core design of creation, functioning like the scientific mysteries of quantum physics and string theory and to some degree, the basic principles of belief that work regardless of a person's faith or lack of faith in God. A key distinction between *The Secret* and biblical faith is the goal of the person. Byrnes addresses the reader as "You."

"Imagining Success: Multiple Achievement Goals and the Effectiveness of Imagery," *Basic and Applied Social Psychology* 39, no. 1 (2017): 60-67; Cathryne Maciolek and Mandy Lehto, "Visualize It: The Technique Used to Win the Game, Get Rich, and Fight Illness," *Psychology Today*, November 8, 2011, www.psychologytoday.com/us/blog/the-psychology-dress/201111/visualize-it.

[9]Bianca Weiland, "The Science Behind Visualization," *Activacuity*, January 24, 2016, www.activacuity.com/2016/01/the-science-behind-visualization/. See also Bala Kishore Batchu, "Research Paper: Neuroscience behind Visualization," *International Coach Academy*, December 3, 2013, https://coachcampus.com/coach-portfolios/research-papers/bala-kishore-batchu-neuro-science-behind-visualization/, 3.

[10]Andrew Shorten and Paul Gunter, "What is the Law of Attraction? Open Your Eyes to a World of Endless Possibilities," *Greater Minds*, www.thelawofattraction.com/what-is-the-law-of-attraction/.

[11]Kimberly Zapada, "How to Manifest Anything You Want or Desire: Yes, That Even Includes Love . . . and Money," *Oprah Daily*, December 20, 2020, www.oprahdaily.com/life/a30244004/how-to-manifest-anything/.

[12]Rhonda Byrne, *The Secret* (New York: Atria, 2006). Also see Dr. Joe Dispenza, *Becoming Supernatural: How Common People Are Doing the Uncommon*, 2nd ed. (Carlsbad, CA: Hay House, 2019). See also Paulo Coelho, *The Alchemist: A Fable About Following Your Dream* (San Francisco: HarperOne, 2014), 22.

[13]Byrne, *Secret*, 44.

Although she doesn't explicitly state it, You has a god-like quality, to attract to Yourself what You want. Much of the emphasis of those she quotes is on feeling good. While feeling good is important, this is detached from the goal of a person whose desire is to cooperate with the Creator God to fill the universe with goodness for all people and all creation.

The idea that thoughts and words can become reality, like seeds producing plants, is fundamental to a biblical understanding of faith. When Jesus explains to his disciples the parable of the farmer planting seeds, he describes the seed as the word (*logos*) of God, or the word of the kingdom planted in people's hearts and minds (Lk 8:11; Mt 13:18; Mk 4:13-20). Then he describes the various ways that God's word, as a seed planted in people's hearts, can be ineffective due to problems, pain, distractions, and harmful choices, compared to those who experience the good seed/word growing into maturity and fruitfulness through nurturing and protecting it.

SEED AS WORDS PRODUCING ACTIONS AND CONSEQUENCES

Seed is used in both Testaments as a metaphor for words that are spoken that take root as ideas and grow into fruitful or unfruitful outcomes. The seed of thought planted in the fertile ground of the mind produces corresponding actions, and these actions bear consequences. Elmer Martens notes, "The link between an act and its consequence is so tight that whatever follows from an evil act is an implementation of what is implicit already in the act itself. The result of an act is embedded in the act itself just as the fruit is embedded in the seed."[14]

This concept is built into the words of the Hebrew language of the Old Testament. Just as a seed contains the genetic material to produce the plant already encoded within, words contain the power to create ideas that become behaviors with expected results, unless there is an intervention to change their outcome.

When discussing the concept of *seed* as words producing actions that bear consequences, it's vital to point out that *the legal basis for God's blessings and judgments is rooted in the relationship established between Creator, the*

---

[14]Elmer A. Martens, "Sin, Guilt," in *Dictionary of the Old Testament: Pentateuch*, ed. Desmond Alexander and David Baker (Downers Grove, IL: InterVarsity Press, 2003), 771. See Hos 8:7; 10:12-13.

cosmos, and humankind. Personal accountability is built into the biblical system of creation and covenant relationships. From a Christian perspective, God as the Creator of the world has a vested interest in the well-being of the universe and everything in it. While God cares deeply (more than any of us) about the whole creation, *he gives particular attention to human beings because he made and commissioned us to govern his creation as his representatives.* God, as Creator, covenanted with humanity to care for and provide for the cosmos, with the caveat that they live in accordance with his design and word.[15]

Chief Rabbi Jonathan Sacks expresses the foundational belief that the "reciprocal nature of justice" is reflected in the literary structures of Scripture. Built into the narrative and sentence structure of biblical Hebrew is "one of the Torah's most profound beliefs; namely, the reciprocal nature of justice. Those who do good are blessed with good. Those who do evil, suffer evil. What happens to us is a mirror image of what we do . . . mirror-image symmetry is the literary equivalent of a just world."[16]

If God is indeed the Lord of lords and Creator of all creation, as the Bible claims, he has the right to say how things are supposed to go down here, whether we like it or not. Most people don't like it. The choice in the Garden and the choice that most people make actively or passively is to be their own god and to do whatever they want, whenever they want, and however they want. From the biblical perspective, this is the essential plot conflict of the world. Nevertheless, whether or not we like it or want it, there are natural and divine consequences to our freely made choices and to our actions.

As God created seeds to have life in themselves and to produce according to their kind, in the same way our thoughts produce actions that bear consequences. This process is in alignment with the seed principle built into the fabric of the universe.

The consequence of the refusal to govern according to God's creational purposes by doing harm to his world—and especially to people—is expressed in God's words to Noah and his sons, "And your lifeblood I will require; from

[15]For an in-depth analysis of this statement, see Daniel I. Block, *Covenant: The Framework of God's Grand Plan of Redemption* (Grand Rapids, MI: Baker Academic, 2021).
[16]Jonathan Sacks, *Koren Shalem Siddur, Ashkenaz,* Bilingual edition (Jerusalem: Koren Publishers Jerusalem, 2017), xxiii.

every animal I will require it. And from the hand of humankind, from the hand of *each* man to his brother I will require the life of humankind. '*As for* the one shedding the blood of humankind, by humankind his blood shall be shed, for God made humankind in his own image'" (Gen 9:5-6 LEB). The word translated *require* in this verse means that God requires an accounting and recompense for harming the life of any human because each one is made in his image. Sooner or later, God requires restitution for every wrong done.

The language of the flood narrative in the Bible demonstrates God's covenant commitment to the well-being of the world and the correlation between actions and divine consequences. Daniel Block notes, God's "cosmic interest pervades the flood account."[17] Genesis 6 begins with an ancient evil of "the sons of God" leading to the Nephilim. The "sons of God/gods" were most likely nonhuman, spiritual entities who rejected the order that God had established in creation by wanting to mate with humans. "The sons of God saw that the daughters of humanity [*adam*] were good [*tov*]."[18] The result was a cataclysm of evil and most likely cohabitation between spiritual entities and human beings in rebellion against God.[19] "The LORD saw how great the wickedness of the human race had become on the earth, and that every inclination of the thoughts of the human heart was only evil all the time" (Gen 6:5).

The story of the flood hints that God was patient with the rebellion, first giving a warning to humanity through Noah to stop corrupting the earth, while Noah built a large boat on dry land.[20] The people did not respond to the warning and continued to degenerate. The justice of God's actions can be seen more closely by looking at the Hebrew, where the consequences of bad choices come in "precise symmetry of crime and punishment."[21]

The punishment fits the crime, so to speak, with lexical precision through double entendre: two meanings used for the same word.[22] The Hebrew root

---

[17]Block, *Covenant*, 16.

[18]My translation from Genesis 6:2a.

[19]For starters, see Michael S. Heiser, *The Unseen Realm: Recovering the Supernatural Worldview of the Bible* (Bellingham, WA: Lexham, 2015), 92-109.

[20]See also 2 Pet 2:5.

[21]J. P. Fokkelman, *Narrative Art in Genesis*, 36, 37, 41.

[22]See, for example, Koch, "Is There a Doctrine of Retribution in the Old Testament?" 75. This was explored last century by Karl Fahlgren in his dissertation at Uppsala University in Sweden. Through lexical analysis, he "discovered that a whole series of Hebrew roots were . . . used to

words are used in this narrative to describe both the action and its consequence. Genesis 6:11-13 states that the land became *corrupted* (*shakhat*) because all living things *corrupted*, or *destroyed* (*shakhat*), the land by filling it
with *violence* (*khamas*), or complete lawlessness. The Hebrew word *shakhat*
is translated as *corrupt* or *corrupted* when referring to humanity's violent
lawlessness, and *shakhat* is translated as *destroyed* when referring to the consequence of their actions that God brought on them. In other words, the root
word for the corruption done to the earth by all living things is the same root
word used to describe the consequence, usually translated as *destroy*. As God
explained to Noah, all people and living creatures had *corrupted* or *destroyed*
(*shakhat*) his good creation by their violent disregard for life and nature, so
therefore, God would *bring about their corruption*, or *destroy* (*shakhat*) them,
by washing away the pollution of their violence with floodwaters, uncreating
the land as a reversal of the good creation in Genesis 1 (Gen 6:9-13). What
the living things had done to the earth would come back on them. Because
of the destruction they brought on creation, creation would destroy them.
There is symmetry of action and consequence in the original language.

Therefore, a logical question to ask about the corruption and destruction
is, *How does God feel about what happened in the flood narrative?* God is
described in the narrative as grieving over the evil and what became of his
good creation and humanity. The word used in Genesis 6:6 to describe what
God felt in his heart is *pain* (*atsav*). This word for pain comes from the same
root word used to express humanity's pain (*atsav, itsavon*) in Genesis 3:16-17,
describing both the labor pain to produce children and the labor pain to
produce food out of hardened ground. God suffers with our suffering. He is
grieved and feels pain over our wrongs and afflictions.[23]

---

describe both an action and its consequences." For example, the Hebrew word *ra* can mean both
"ethically depraved" and also "bringing misfortune"; and . . . *Hamas* means both "violent deed"
and "destroying (oneself)." Klaus Koch, building on Fahlgren's work, demonstrates the concept
that actions have "built-in consequences which God simply sets in motion." His action-
consequence model has been rightly criticized as an oversimplification of the model of retribution, because this agency does not operate alone, by any means. Nevertheless, Hebrew is full of
double entendres—two meanings for the same verbal root. For another example, *guilt* (*asham*)
and *iniquity* (*avon*) are used to describe both the wrong of the action and its consequence in
terms of *punishment* or, as a guilt offering.

[23]See also Is 54:7-9. Claus Westermann also points out the "crime and punishment" theme in
Gen 1–11: Claus Westermann, *The Promises to the Fathers: Studies on the Patriarchal Narratives*
(Philadelphia: Fortress, 1980), 54.

Therefore, scholar Rolf Knierim observes that the "sentence of death by flood for humanity's social and ecological violence is a legal decision. It is based on the illegality of violence, which is textually grounded in creation."[24] Daniel Block finds that the land itself is witness to God's covenant and responds to violations done by those who God appointed as earth's caretakers and stewards—namely, us.[25] Nature, as God's witness, responds to humanity's lawlessness. A cosmic connection between moral evil and natural disasters exists. The biblical text demonstrates that, like seeds, God's justice works in concert with people's freely made choices. Action-consequence in Scripture can be described as God *"facilitating the completion of something which previous human action has already set in motion."*[26]

The role of human choices in action-consequence cannot be understated. Life is not haphazard or random. As another example, the importance of human choice is emphasized in Deuteronomy, as Moses recounts the history of God's people and their covenant relationship with him. Toward the end of his speech, Moses reminds them of the choice they must make moving forward: "This day I call the heavens and the earth as witnesses against you that I have set before you life and death, blessings and curses. Now choose life, so that you and your children may live and that you may love the LORD your God, listen to his voice, and hold fast to him. For the LORD is your life" (Deut 30:19-20). The decisions they make will affect their offspring, their *seed*. The choice they are called to make is just like the first one in the Garden of Eden. This multiple-choice test has only two options: (a) choose life or (b) choose death. He gives them the answer: it's (a). Choose life (i.e., choose to believe, follow, and obey God and his word) so that you and your *seed* will live well.

Moses continues from there to reiterate God's justice to his covenant people according to action-consequence. "For I know that after my death you are sure to become utterly corrupt [*shakhat*—there's that word again from Gen 6] and to turn from the way I have commanded you. In days

---

[24]Knierim, *Task of Old Testament Theology*, 432.
[25]Daniel I. Block, "What Do These Stones Mean? The Riddle of Deuteronomy 27," *Journal of the Evangelical Theological Society* 56, no. 1 (2013): 23-24, 27n76, 29.
[26]Klaus Koch, "Is There a Doctrine of Retribution in the Old Testament?," in *Theodicy in the Old Testament*, ed. James L. Crenshaw, Issues in Religion and Theology (Philadelphia: Fortress, 1983), 57.

to come, disaster [the Hebrew word is evil, *raah*] will fall on you *because* you will do evil [*raah*] in the sight of the LORD and arouse his anger by what your hands have made" (Deut 31:29). Notice the cause and effect at play in what he says. Evil will come on them because of the evil that they will do.

Choices made that produce consequences are part of the plot throughout the Bible. For example, Judges 2:11-23 describes a downward cycle of bad choices. The people forsake their covenant with God and serve foreign gods, such as the Canaanite god Baal (with idolatry, ritual prostitution, and child sacrifice). Then God steps back from protecting them and they are invaded. When they cry out to God for help, God sends deliverers (called judges) to help them and restore peace to the land. But when the people become comfortable, they abandon God again and return to serving other gods with their ritual practices. This cycle repeats again and again. But a time comes when they cry out for God's help and he steps back from sending deliverers, allowing them to be attacked without God's interference to protect them. By the end of Judges, the people have spiraled downward through increasingly degrading behaviors until they are as corrupt as Sodom (Judg 2:11-23; 17:1; 21:25).

The Prophets repeat the theme of personal and national accountability.[27] For example, the prophet Hosea recounts the covenantal violations of Israel and Judah toward God, opening with, "The nation continually commits spiritual prostitution by turning away from the LORD" (Hos 1:2 NET). Scholar Jerry Hwang points out the growing urbanization and proliferation of a ruling class at the time of Hosea, which led to the systematic and systemic "unholy trio of money, sex, and power." These "three Is' of injustice, immorality, and idolatry" became embedded in Israel's institutions. They worked in tandem with one another to demoralize its people and commodify their land for the benefit of an upper-class, urbanized power elite.[28] In response to the power brokers' actions that defied God's creational and covenantal requirements for how to treat people and land, Hosea states that the elite "do not take heart

---

[27]Isaiah introduces an understanding of the action-consequence early, declaring "Woe to the wicked! Disaster is upon them! They will be paid back for what their hands have done" (Is 3:11). Obadiah moans, "As you have done, it will be done to you; your deeds will return upon your own head" (Obad 15). Ezekiel declares the same, "I will surely bring down on your head what you have done . . . you will bear the consequences" (Ezek 16:43, 58).

[28]Jerry Hwang, *Hosea: A Discourse Analysis of the Hebrew Bible*, ed. Daniel I. Block (Grand Rapids, MI: Zondervan Academic, 2021), 24-25.

[that] all their evil I have remembered. . . . When they sow wind, then they reap a whirlwind" (Hos 7:2; 8:7).[29] In the Hebrew, the word *sow* is the verbal form of the word for seed. Hwang explains that the pairing of sowing seed and reaping a harvest "expresses Hosea's signature link between sinful act and creational consequence. As elsewhere in the prophetic book, the justice of YHWH plays out in the realm of creation's inbuilt mechanisms of morality more than through a juridical act of retribution (cf. 1:4; 4:9)."[30] Klaus Koch states similarly, "The actions of the people have determined their destiny . . . *actions have built-in consequences and it is in this vein that he proclaims the onset of disasters.*"[31] Like the physical laws of the universe, and like the growth of a seed, God determined that the trajectory of human behaviors would produce outcomes as consequences that only the mercy and grace of God can stop or reverse.

For one more example, Psalm 7:14-16 precisely summarizes the relationship between a person's actions and the consequent results:

> Whoever is pregnant with evil
> > conceives trouble and gives birth to disillusionment.
> Whoever digs a hole and scoops it out
> > falls into the pit they have made.
> The trouble they cause recoils on them;
> > their violence comes down on their own heads.

The psalmist first metaphorically compares the operation of evil to sperm implanted in a womb, which grows, develops, and produces an offspring of deceit. He then describes that one who digs a ditch with the intent to harm another will eventually fall into the trap he has set. The principal of action-consequence proliferates throughout the Old Testament.

ACTION-CONSEQUENCE IN THE NEW TESTAMENT

The New Testament echoes and builds on the basic metaphor of planting seeds and harvesting a crop. Psalm 7:14 and the letter of James express a similar understanding. James warns that no one should say that when they're tempted to do something that God is the one tempting them.

---

[29]Hwang, *Hosea*, 12.
[30]Hwang, *Hosea*, 219.
[31]Koch, "Is There a Doctrine of Retribution in the Old Testament?," 66.

Because "God *cannot be tempted* by evil, and he himself tempts no one. But each one is tempted *when he* is dragged away and enticed by his own desires. Then desire, *after it* has conceived, gives birth to sin, and sin, *when it* is brought to completion, gives birth to death" (Jas 1:13-15 LEB). The apostle Paul uses imagery of sowing seed and reaping to encourage people to continue doing what is good, "Do not be deceived: God is not to be mocked, for whatever a person sows, this he will also reap. . . . And let us not grow weary in doing good, for at the proper time we will reap, *if we* do not give up" (Gal 6:7-9 LEB).

Servants are also encouraged that God sees their actions and the actions of those they serve. "Because you know that the Lord will reward each one for whatever good they do, whether they are slave or free" (Eph 6:8). In other words, if they are mistreated, God will hold their masters or employers responsible and will pay them back at some point. Jesus speaks of this in the parable of the beggar Lazarus, who was mistreated by a wealthy man day after day, in which the wealthy man was told after he died, "Remember that in your lifetime you received your good things, while Lazarus received bad things, but now he is comforted here and you are in agony" (Lk 16:25). While in the Bible justice is expected to be given and to be sought out in this life, there is the assurance that if this does not happen in this life, justice will be meted out in the next.

The expectation that bad things happen because a person must have done something bad is also evident among Jesus' disciples. When they saw a man who was born blind, "His disciples asked him, 'Rabbi, who sinned, this man or his parents, that he was born blind?'" Here, Jesus overturns this common belief, saying "Neither this man nor his parents sinned . . . but this happened so that the works of God might be displayed in him" (Jn 9:2-3).

Further, Jesus points out that horrible things can happen without an action-consequence rationale when he speaks of the Galileans whose blood Pilate mixed with their pagan sacrifices, or the tower in Siloam that fell and killed eighteen people (Lk 13:1-5). He gives no explanation for the intentional act of murder or for the tragic accident. Instead, he reminds us that all of us will die, and we should be more concerned about turning our lives to God in this life. In the Sermon on the Mount, Jesus teaches the importance of forgiveness when we are wrongfully treated, and to love our enemies

(Mt 5:10-12, 38-48). Turning the other cheek could be viewed either as passivism or as the ultimate act of defiance by restraining power and refusing to repay evil for evil. Jesus the Christ lived and died for this ultimate act, taking on himself the weight of all injustice, oppression, sin, and evil on the behalf of humankind while being perfectly innocent.

The apostles Peter and Paul also speak of not repaying evil for evil but rather doing what is good for the other and return a blessing (Rom 12:17; 1 Thess 5:15; 1 Pet 3:9). This teaching, like the Joseph story, seeks to reverse the effects and perpetuation of evil through beautifully subversive acts of goodness, mercy, and grace. However, if the doer of the wrong or the evil refuses to accept mercy, justice must be meted out. A system can have justice without mercy but cannot have mercy without justice.

FROM MY STORY: MY EXPERIENCE OF ACTION-CONSEQUENCE

By the time I was sixteen years old, life had taught me that the only reason anyone was ever kind to someone else was to get something from them. At that age my big sister said to me, "I think you're going to die of old age at twenty-five." I remember thinking to myself, *I sure hope so.* I didn't want to live in a world void of love or care. By age seventeen my body was complying with my predominant thoughts of death. I physically degenerated from athletic to barely able to walk. My bones softened and my spine could be moved by a simple push. I was in constant pain, and slept on the floor for support, praying to die. The doctors were unable to determine a cause, and the increased dosages of painkillers did not alleviate the pain.

I didn't know that my body was complying with my internal language, the seed I had sown, wishing to die. Amazingly, before that year was up, in desperation I went to a Young Life meeting—a place where people talked about Jesus. There I met Donna, a college student who was helping with the meeting. I don't remember anything she said, but I do remember looking into her eyes as she spoke with me, and through her eyes I encountered something I had never seen before. Love. I saw the love of God in her eyes. I left the meeting and wept all the way home and for hours that night. Through the tears I

heard a silent voice speaking to my heart about how my bitterness
was killing me—about forgiveness, compassion, and that I too could
be forgiven of my bitterness. I did not feel a tinge of guilt or shame,
but rather, I was washed and immersed in a presence of Love. As I
silently spoke with this presence, I was invited to release my bitterness
so that Jesus could remove it from me. Have you ever pulled a weed
from loose soil and had that great feeling of seeing the entire root
come out? As I lay on the floor, it felt like a giant hand had grabbed
hold of something in my heart and began to gently pull. From the tips
of my toes and fingers, I could imagine what the earth would feel as
the tiny tendrils of the roots of a weed were extracted from the soil.
This sensation continued through my body until the last of it was
pulled from my heart and disappeared. Peace, a supernatural peace,
filled the void, and I slept.

My body also began to heal. Part of the process was natural. Part of
it was miraculous. Within a few weeks after encountering Jesus, I went
to a prayer meeting where a couple of new young friends prayed for
me. As I stood up after their prayer, strength flooded my body, all pain
left, and my bones were no longer soft. I wanted to live and not die!
Later in life, struggles and abuse would strike again, challenging my
will to live a few more times before I learned to understand the
sources of evil and how I could reframe my past and change the
consequences of evil's operations.

Although the principle of action-consequence is operational, it is not
always realized in people's lives. In other words, although the most common
expectation is that trouble will be returned for trouble, or that disaster will
ricochet back on a person due to evil actions, there are many passages and
entire books in Scripture, especially Job and Ecclesiastes, that point out that
often this expectation does not happen. Over thirty chapters of the book of
Job repeat the ancient Near Eastern expectation of suffering for sin or
wrongdoing, as Job's three "friends" build up their case and their anger
against him for not admitting what he did wrong to deserve all the troubles
that came on him. However, Job is justified, and God asks him to pray for
his friends who spoke and acted wrongly.

Although one's attitude and state of mind generally give birth to actions, it is the thoughts and the actions that bring about the consequences of good or bad. Humanity is expected to resist thoughts of doing wrong to others (Gen 4:7). We are portrayed as having the ability to rise above our thoughts when they are destructive. Good and right behaviors are considered a human ability and responsibility. We are urged by Scripture, "Do not conform to the pattern of this world, but be transformed by the renewing of your mind. Then you will be able to test and approve what God's will is—his good, pleasing and perfect will" (Rom 12:2). We are to recognize that words, both thought and spoken, planted in our minds and hearts grow and produce the content that is in them. Words, like a cosmic seed, have the power to create worlds. Therefore, pay attention to what is spoken to you, over you, or at you. Evaluate the words that you hold in your head. Listen to your internal dialogue, especially when you're triggered, and ask if you're cultivating words that are untrue or harmful. Become a steady gardener of your inner life so that your outer life can flourish.

Chapter Five

NATURE
ARE ALL NATURAL FORCES NATURAL?

We all long for Eden, and we are constantly glimpsing it: our whole nature at its best and least corrupted, its gentlest and most human, is still soaked with the sense of exile.

J. R. R. Tolkien, *The Letters of Tolkien*

We are stardust . . . We are golden, caught in the devil's bargain, and we've got to get ourselves back to the garden.

Joni Mitchell, "Woodstock"

Natural disasters have ravaged the world and shattered countless lives. Recently I watched *The Impossible*, a movie about the true story of a family on vacation in Thailand who survived the Indian Ocean tsunami on December 26, 2004. Waves over one hundred feet high pounded the coast of Banda Aceh and devastated the coastal areas of Thailand, Indonesia, Sri Lanka, Maldives, and India, causing damage as far away as East Africa and killing nearly a quarter million people. The visuals are difficult to watch, much less to imagine living through the devastation. Pundits, preachers, journalists, and religious leaders sought to publish reasons for the disaster, as people tried to make sense of the unthinkable horrors that occurred.

Just as we tend to search for meaning on a massive scale when tragedies like a tsunami hit, we do so on a small scale every day as we seek to understand

and to avert harm. The event may be as small as helping a terrified friend get a mouse out of her kitchen or helping replace a neighbor's roof that has been torn off by a tornado, to organizing relief crews to help hurricane victims. In all these cases, those negatively affected by nature have experienced harm even though moral intent cannot be attributed to acts of nature. While this chapter primarily looks at the interconnectivity between nature and both human and nonhuman forces of evil, the ultimate goal is that we might rise above the disasters to prevent them and to help when they do happen.

Though created by God, nature is wild and free and capable of causing harm without evil intent. Nevertheless, humanity as God's appointed representative is held accountable to steward creation, spread goodness, and bring healing and restoration when nature brings evil to living beings.

IMAGE FROM THE BEGINNING OF GENESIS:
THE SEA MONSTERS (*TANNINIM*)

A common question among Christians is whether "natural evils" were included in God's good creation.[1] From a biblical worldview, wild animals, storms, movements of the stars, tides, shifting tectonic plates, and laws of nature such as the laws of gravity, entropy, and thermodynamics are part of a good creation. Yet, natural forces can cause harm without evil or willful intent.

The biblical imagery of *sea monsters*, or *large sea creatures* (*tanninim*), points to the potential wildness or danger of nature in creation. Genesis 1:21 reads, "So God created the great creatures of the sea [*tanninim*] and every living thing with which the water teems and that moves about in it, according to their kinds, and every winged bird according to its kind. And God saw that it was good." The *tanninim* were part of the good that God created in the beginning, along with the fish and the birds, and God blessed them (Gen 1:21-22). However, later on in the Hebrew Bible, *tanninim* are often portrayed as symbols of chaos or destruction (Is 27:1; 51:9; Ps 74:13). Yet, in Psalm 148:7, the *tanninim* are told to "praise the LORD" along with all the rest of God's creation including "lightening and hail, snow and clouds," and "stormy winds that do his bidding."[2]

---

[1] For example, see Jim Stump, "Naming Natural Evils: Is the Coronavirus Evil?," *Sapientia Henry Center Trinity University*, November 6, 2020, https://henrycenter.tiu.edu/2020/11/naming-natural-evils/.

[2] *Tannin*, also glossed as "sea dragon," "serpent," and "crocodile," is often associated with the sea (*yam*) and is generally considered distinct from leviathan. For discussion on *tanninim*, see David

CONCEPT OF NATURE IN THE OLD TESTAMENT

The Bible generally uses the term creation rather than nature. "By creation the Bible understands the whole range of existing things, from humans to ants, not excluding the abyss and Leviathan," as Roland Murphy notes.[3] Creation, then, is a broader term than nature, encompassing humans and extending to the unseen spiritual realm of created beings. God created the heavens and the earth, the seen and the unseen realms, in an ontological oneness. The Hebrew narrative of Genesis 1–2 brings all beings and entities into a relational union. First, God created humanity in unity with himself and his divine counsel, "Let us make humankind in our image and according to our likeness" (Gen 1:26 LEB). God's purpose for creating human beings continues in the passage: in order that they may rule as his earthly representative. Old Testament scholar Sandra Richter explains:

> Both the biblical text and its ancient Near Eastern counterparts make it clear that for humanity to be named a ṣelem (image) is for humanity to be identified as the animate representation of God on this planet. In essence, woman and man are the embodiment of God's sovereignty in the created order. Here male and female are appointed as God's custodians, his stewards over a staggeringly complex and magnificent universe, *because* they are his royal representatives.[4]

Not only are humans tasked with the role of stewardship on this earth, but the interconnection of the earth, humanity, and animal life is demonstrated from the beginning in the Bible. The importance of unity among a diversity of beings is illustrated by the Hebrew words of the biblical narrative. According to Genesis 2:7, the earthling (*adam* in Hebrew) was formed from the earth (*adamah* in the Hebrew), so that humanity's oneness with the ground is established from the beginning: the *adam* was formed from and is one with the *adamah*—we are one in earthly substance. The animals

---

Toshio Tsumura, "The Creation Motif in Psalm 74:12-14? A Reappraisal of the Theory of the Dragon Myth," *Journal of Biblical Literature* 134, no. 3 (2015): 547-55; Philippe Guillaume, "Animadversiones: Metamorphosis of a Ferocious Pharaoh," *Biblica* 85, no. 2 (2004): 232-35; David A. Diewert, "Job 7:12: Yam, Tannin and the Surveillance of Job," *Journal of Biblical Literature* 106, no. 2 (1987): 203-15; John Day, "God and Leviathan in Isaiah 27:1," *Bibliotheca Sacra* 155 (1998): 423-36.
[3]Roland E. Murphy, "Wisdom and Creation," *Journal of Biblical Literature* 104, no. 1 (1985): 6.
[4]Sandra L. Richter, *Stewards of Eden: What Scripture Says About the Environment and Why It Matters* (Downers Grove, IL: IVP Academic, 2020), 17.

and birds were also formed from the ground (*adamah* in Genesis 2:19). Not only are humans, animals, and birds interconnected to the *adamah*, but we are all referred to as "living beings" or "living souls" (*nephesh hayah*, Genesis 2:7, 19). God created all things in oneness, intended to be in unified relationship. All of nature was created to flourish in harmony, from plants to creatures large and small, simple and complex; and all were to relate to one another and to God in this state of being called "blessed." Let's take a moment to contemplate the beauty and goodness of creation before we move on to "natural evils."

The Wonder and Order of Creation[5]

Daily, we witness the order and regularity of nature with the confidence that the laws of gravity, magnetism, and so on, will function as intended, that is, that the earth will rotate around the sun, that seeds planted under the right conditions will grow, and so forth. We also witness the stranger things of science, such as quantum physics and string theory, which further underscore the entanglement of all life and particles. The laws of nature are part of God's good creation. Because of the dependability of these laws, a person stepping off a cliff will fall, and the one who touches a live wire will receive a shock. Tides will rise and fall. Tectonic plates will shift and collide. The sun will shine, and the rain will fall on the just and the unjust alike. And this is all part of God's good creation.[6] The movements of the stars and planets can be calculated with precise accuracy. The mathematical swirl of galaxies such as the Milky Way matches the curving spiral of every nautilus seashell and the horns of a ram. Spirals occur throughout nature more than any other shape. The logarithmic spiral of the galaxies and the nautilus is approximately the same as the spiral of the seeds of a sunflower, the curve of tusks and horns, fossils of the extinct ammonites, cyclones, and even the calculation of the "exponential rates of decay of radioactive atoms."[7]

The amazing precision amid the extravagant creativity with which God created the universe—or multiverse—is awe-inspiring. Some of the most

[5]"The Wonder and Order of Creation" is a lightly edited excerpt from Ingrid Faro, "The Question of Evil and Animal Death before the Fall," *Trinity Journal* 36 (2015): 12-13.
[6]See Hugh Ross, *Hidden Treasures in the Book of Job: How the Oldest Book in the Bible Answers Today's Scientific Questions* (Grand Rapids, MI: Baker Books, 2014), 53-104.
[7]Eli Maor, *E: The Story of a Number* (Princeton, NJ: Princeton University Press, 1994), 66-68.

profound scientific discoveries throughout history have been made by people with a deep faith, people for whom scientific discovery was intricately connected with seeking to know God and the ways of God better. Einstein's colleague Sir James Jeans declared, "the Great Architect of the Universe now begins to appear as a pure mathematician . . . the universe begins to look more like a great thought than a great machine."[8] It is often this sense of awe that has both fueled creative scientific ventures of discovery and has maintained a posture of humility between scientists and theologians. As William P. Brown points out, however, "In this time of culture wars, political incivility, and polarized discourse, . . . fear and fatigue have all but displaced love and wonder."[9] Retaining a sense of wonder and humility is required as we ponder the wisdom of God's design in creation.

WISDOM IN CREATION

The traditional Jewish understanding of creation is that through wisdom God brought order to the "disorder of raw creation."[10] Scholar James Barr notes, "Genesis is interested in an organized world, as against a chaotic world."[11] The Bible contains a large amount of Wisdom literature. Proverbs 3:19; 8:22-26 say that God created the heavens and the earth with wisdom. The rabbis integrate these passages in Proverbs with Genesis 1:1 producing the Midrashic (ancient Jewish commentary) understanding that "In wisdom God created the heavens and the earth," so that the laws of nature preceded the entrance of light and were manifested in all the works of creation.[12] The laws of nature in the universe were set into motion as part of God's good design, as his well-laid-out plan.[13] My friend told me about a friend of hers, an atheist Chinese scientist, who came to believe in the God of creation when

---

[8]James Jeans, *The Mysterious Universe*, ed. Vesselin Petkov (Montreal, QC: Minkowski Institute, 2020), 122, 137.

[9]Brown, "Wisdom's Wonder," 13.

[10]Faro, "Question of Evil and Animal Death," 11.

[11]James Barr, "Was Everything That God Created Really Good? A Question in the First Verse of the Bible," in *God in the Fray: A Tribute to Walter Brueggemann*, ed. Tod Linafelt and Timothy K. Beal (Minneapolis: Fortress, 1998), 62.

[12]For an excellent discussion on this issue, see Murphy, "Wisdom and Creation," 3-11.

[13]Michael D. Swartz, *The Signifying Creator: Nontextual Sources of Meaning in Ancient Judaism* (New York: NYU Press, 2014), 14-16.

he observed that we study nature and use the laws that govern the physical universe, but we can't create or alter any of them.

The Scriptures use nature to teach spiritual truths and to help us apply these truths to living life in the world.[14] Theologian Jürgen Moltmann notes that "Theological traditions talk about a twofold knowledge of God: the knowledge derived from creation, and the knowledge derived from Scripture. . . . The *theologia naturalis* that is accessible in the history of sin and death is a recollection of the primordial knowledge of God."[15] Psalm 19 declares that nature speaks, providing all with some knowledge of God, who is understood to have created the laws to govern the physical world. This psalm places creation parallel to the Torah, i.e., God's commands and instructions, which gives wisdom to the simple (Ps 19:8). Everything was created through knowledge, understanding, and wisdom, which are key character traits of God, and important characteristics that God wants humans to gain. In God's original intentions for this world, Richter points out that "Here there would always be enough. Progress would not necessitate pollution. Expansion would not require extinction. The privilege of the strong would not demand the deprivation of the weak. And humanity would succeed in this calling because of the guiding wisdom of their God."[16]

Creation is the context and background for God's instructions for how humans are supposed to see and manage the world, which was designed to be flourishing, abundant, blessed, and good. Human violations of the creational order and refusal to serve as stewards for the good of all God's creation has resulted in "life-denying consequences in the physical world."[17] James Bruckner points out that before the Old Testament Law and Ten Commandments were given, the legal precedents of death, disorders, and sicknesses were based on the relationship established between the Creator

---

[14]Faro, "Question of Evil and Animal Death," 193-213.

[15]Jürgen Moltmann, *God in Creation: A New Theology of Creation and the Spirit of God* (Minneapolis: Fortress, 1993), 57.

[16]Richter, *Stewards of Eden*, 20.

[17]James K. Bruckner, *Implied Law in the Abraham Narrative: A Literary and Theological Analysis* (Englewood Cliffs, NJ: Sheffield Academic, 2002), 199-201, 335. See also, Knierim, *Task of Old Testament Theology*, 430. Knierim, in line with Bruckner's work on "implied law" states, "Murder is not the only time the death sentence is applied legally. The deity's sentence of death by flood for humanity's social and ecological violence is also a legal decision. It is based on the illegality of violence."

0

and created, with humanity bearing divinely endowed accountability for our actions.[18]

Some scholars take this a step further in finding that the land itself is witness to God's covenant and responds to violations by those whom God appointed as earth's caretakers.[19] The Bible speaks of the earth as an active, living participant that sees and responds to what humans do. For example, after Cain murdered his brother Abel, the Lord[20] (Yahweh) called him out and said, "Your brother's blood cries out to me from the ground" (Gen 4:10).[21] The land is said to have "vomited out its inhabitants" when they defiled it by their vile treatment of others (Lev 18:25, 28; cf. 10:2). The Lord calls heaven and earth to bear witness to the covenants and agreements made between God and his people, and to the choices they make (Deut 30:19). And the New Testament's commentary on Genesis 3:17 describes the whole creation as groaning in pain because of humanity's failure to follow God and steward his creation as it waits like a woman in labor for God's children to step into their image-bearing responsibility (Rom 8:19-22).

God maintains a relationship with all his creation. The laws of nature that proceed from divine wisdom are the building blocks of God's good design. He took personal care to make and care for the earth as a parent. Philosopher Eleonore Stump points out that "From the beginning of creation, then, and from the outset of God's conversation with Job, God is portrayed as a parent."[22] God speaks as a mother when describing giving birth to the earth: "Who shut up the sea behind doors when it burst forth from the womb, when I made the clouds its garment and wrapped it in thick darkness" (Job 38:8-9).[23] God is also described as a mother who gave birth to his people: "Can a mother forget the baby at her breast and have no

---

[18]Bruckner, *Implied Law*, 202.
[19]Block, "What Do These Stones Mean?," 23-24, 27n76, 29.
[20]Most English translations use Lord (in small caps) to translate the Hebrew word Yahweh. In this book I alternate between using Lord and Yahweh.
[21]Mari Jørstad, "The Ground That Opened Its Mouth: The Ground's Response to Human Violence in Genesis 4," *Journal of Biblical Literature* 135 (2016): 705-15. Jørstad argues that with humanity's connection with the ground (*adam-adamah*) and stewardship-rulership fiat in Gen 1:28, Gen 4:10 "presents the ground as an agent responsive first and foremost to God's will, thus resisting and frustrating human disobedience and violence."
[22]Stump, *Wandering in Darkness*, 187. She further points out that in Job 38–41, God speaks in second person, personally, not at a distance.
[23]See also Job 38:28-29.

compassion on the child she has borne? Though she may forget, I will not forget you!" (Is 49:15).

Physicist Hugh Ross further points out that "every act of God is optimally designed for the maximum benefit of Earth's life and for humanity in particular . . . [however] there is much that humans in their sin have done to degrade this optimization."[24] The effects of the laws of nature can be helpful or harmful. But nature in itself lacks the intentionality to do evil. Rather, humans impose evil on nature. For example, gravity is good. It serves many cosmic purposes as a basic law of nature, and in a most simplistic, practical sense, keeps us from flying off into space. But if a person steps off a cliff or a building, the effects of gravity will cause them to fall downward, possibly bringing injury or death. Shifting tectonic plates can trigger earthquakes and tsunamis, but they also stir up valuable nutrients from the sea. More importantly, life might not have been possible on earth without them. Hurricanes in and of themselves are good. For example, they help regulate the temperature of the planet. But when a hurricane hits a mobile home park built along a coast of Florida, it will likely cause harm and death. There is a degree of stability and order to the laws of nature that we rely on, which Michael Murray terms *nomic regularity*.[25] Nature, in general, cannot be good or evil, since it has no moral compass. What makes natural disasters "evil" is not that they occur or that nature itself is evil, but that the *effect* of nature can bring harm when it is on a collision course with living creatures.[26]

Further, some natural disasters can be linked to a breakdown of moral order.[27] Human irresponsibility and ignorance contribute to the harmful impact of some natural disasters, such as greed-based food production that contaminates crops and animals, and heavily processed foods that increase human illness, disease, and death. Also, "because of human

---

[24]Hugh Ross, "Physics of Sin," *Reasons to Believe,* January 1, 2002, www.reasons.org/articles/the-physics-of-sin.

[25]For further explanation and a more philosophical discussion, see Michael Murray, *Nature Red in Tooth and Claw: Theism and the Problem of Animal Suffering* (Oxford: Oxford University Press, 2011), 130-65. Terence E. Fretheim, *Creation Untamed: The Bible, God, and Natural Disasters* (Grand Rapids, MI: Baker Academic, 2010), 27. Fretheim notes, "This potential for 'natural evil' was present from the beginning of the creation."

[26]Murray, *Nature Red in Tooth and Claw*, 148; Terence Fretheim, *Creation Untamed*, 7; Faro, "The Question of Evil and Animal Death," 200.

[27]Faro, "The Question of Evil and Animal Death," 200.

abuses, mosquitoes now inhabit virtually 100 percent of Earth's land-masses. Before humans arrived, they occupied just 10 percent."[28] Indeed, *a relationship of cosmic connection can be discerned between moral evil and some natural disasters due to human greed.*

Human culpability in doing evil to creation that precipitates some natural disasters is in stark contrast with the good stewardship appointed to humanity by divine fiat.

HUMAN RESPONSIBILITY FOR GOODNESS IN THE COSMIC TEMPLE[29]

Humanity was given tremendous freedom along with the responsibility to carry out God's intention for creation.[30] Jewish theologian Marvin Sweeney also points out the creation narrative's emphasis on human responsibility. In the opening two chapters of the Bible, God sets the example and model for humanity to emulate with "the obligation to create order and holiness in an otherwise chaotic world."[31] The Garden of Eden represents the temple as the symbol of divine order in the cosmos, "which comes to expression in the natural world of agriculture and life, the human world of politics and protection from enemies, and the moral world of human, ethical, and ritual action that renders the world of creation as holy."[32] At least, this was the plan.

Understanding human accountability in conducting God's mission is core to interpreting the entire biblical text from Genesis through Revelation. Christopher Wright summarizes humanity's role as "our committed participation as God's people, at God's invitation and command, in God's own mission within the history of God's world for the redemption of God's

---

[28]Ross, "Physics of Sin."

[29]The following section includes edited excerpts from Faro, "Question of Evil and Animal Death," 13.

[30]Craig G. Bartholomew and Michael W. Goheen, *The Drama of Scripture: Finding Our Place in the Biblical Story*, 2nd ed. (Grand Rapids, MI: Baker Academic, 2014), 22.

[31]Marvin A. Sweeney, *TANAK: A Theological and Critical Introduction to the Jewish Bible* (Minneapolis: Fortress, 2011), 56. See also Levenson, *Creation and the Persistence of Evil*, 112-14.

[32]Sweeney, *TANAK*, 16. For further references on the Garden as temple, see all the essays in Mark J. Boda and Jamie Novotony, eds., *From the Foundations to the Crennellations: Essays on Temple Building in the Ancient Near East and Hebrew Bible*, Alter Orient Und Altes Testament 366 (Münster: Ugarit-Verlag, 2010) and John H. Walton, "Creation in Genesis 1:1–2:3 and the Ancient Near East: Order Out of Disorder After Chaoskampf," *Calvin Theological Journal* 43 (2008): 57.

creation."[33] Gregory Beale's *The Temple and the Church's Mission* demonstrates that the Garden of Eden was the first temple, or Holy of Holies—the place of God's dwelling. Adam, and thereby humanity, was mandated not only to serve and guard it, but also "to extend the geographical boundaries to the Garden of Eden until Eden extended throughout and covered the whole earth."[34] God gave humanity the role and the right to spread God's presence from the Garden to the rest of the world. Jewish scholar Umberto Cassuto further explains the origin of evil:

> The primary purpose of the Torah in these chapters [Genesis 2–3] is to explain how it is that in the Lord's world, the world of the good and beneficent God, evil should exist and man should endure pain and troubles and calamities. The answer given here to the burning question of the origin of evil in the world is this: although the world that issued from the hand of the Creator is, according to the testimony of the previous section, good—yea, very good—yet man corrupts it by his conduct and brings evil into the world as a result of his corruption.[35]

Therefore, the reason creation's original goodness and flourishing has not spread throughout the earth is because people reject God and his divinely ordained mission given to every human in creation.[36]

This process of spreading shalom and repairing the world (*tikkun olam*) is lost on us if we, as God's appointed coregents, do not recognize and step into our God-given authority and responsibility to be shepherds of the earth. In the big picture, nature responds to our actions. God, who commanded the light to shine in the darkness, called us to be his light in this physical universe, and to extend the Garden to the rest of the world, bringing order and preventing chaos.[37] "Humans were created to bring the spiritual into the physical, and thereby to transform the earth into the dwelling place of God. From the beginning, the creation of humanity is to bring God's ways, God's

---

[33]Christopher J. H. Wright, *The Mission of God: Unlocking the Bible's Grand Narrative* (Downers Grove, IL: IVP Academic, 2006), 22-23.

[34]Gregory K. Beale, "Eden, the Temple, and the Church's Mission in the New Creation," *Journal of the Evangelical Theological Society* 48 (2005): 10-11.

[35]U. Cassuto, *A Commentary on the Book of Genesis (Part I): From Adam to Noah* (Skokie, IL: Varda Books, 2012). 71.

[36]See Wolfhart Pannenberg, *Systematic Theology*, trans. Geoffrey W. Bromiley (Grand Rapids, MI: Eerdmans, 2009), 3:162.

[37]Faro, "Question of Evil and Animal Death," 30.

plans, and God's presence into this world in relationship with God, and to thus transform the earth into his sanctuary."[38]

NATURE AND CREATION IN THE NEW TESTAMENT

The New Testament confirms humanity's role to bring God's "kingdom" (his government and his ways) into the physical realm of the earth. Jesus, as the ultimate image of God the Father, fulfilled this role in multiple ways. The opening words of the Gospel of John connect Jesus with God as Creator:

> In the beginning was the Word, and the Word was with God, and the Word was God. He was with God in the beginning. Through him all things were made; without him nothing was made that has been made. In him was life, and that life was the light of all mankind. The light shines in the darkness, and the darkness has not overcome [or understood] it. (Jn 1:1-5)

This declaration places the opening three sentences of Genesis as a reference to the Trinity, in which God in the beginning acts in conjunction with the Spirit, and speaks light into existence through his Word (Gen 1:1-3). John declares that Jesus was that Word in each act of creation.

Jesus described himself as being one with God and doing the works of God (Jn 10:30; 14:9; 5:19). In fact, Jesus uses this as a basis for people to believe in him, saying, "Do not believe me unless I do the works of my Father. But if I do them, even though you do not believe me, believe the works, that you may know and understand that the Father is in me, and I in the Father" (Jn 10:37-38).

The works Jesus did demonstrate God's rulership over creation. They are meant as an example to us of the authority that God intended his image-bearers to wield over creation to bring the cosmos into harmony and obedience to him.

While living on this earth, Jesus validated his power and mastery over the forces of nature: Weather, food, the wind, the waves, fish (gathering them into nets, and bringing a gold coin), sickness and diseases of all kinds, birth

---

[38]Faro, "Question of Evil and Animal Death," 195. See also G. K. Beale, *The Temple and the Church's Mission: A Biblical Theology of the Dwelling Place of God* (Downers Grove, IL: IVP Academic, 2004), and Gordon J. Wenham, "Sanctuary Symbolism in the Garden of Eden Story," in *"I Studied Inscriptions Before the Flood": Ancient Near Eastern, Literary, and Linguistic Approaches to Genesis 1–11*, ed. Richard S. Hess and Tsumura (Winona Lake, IN: Eisenbrauns, 1994), 399-404.

defects (blindness, deafness), accidents (healing the ear of the high priest's servant that Peter cut off), death (others and his own), plants (fig tree), food (multiplication of bread and fish), water (turned into wine), spiritual entities (malevolent demonic forces), and even fire on the Day of Pentecost (demonstrating the tangible presence of the Holy Spirit of God) are all under the authority of Jesus.

Jesus authorized and commissioned his followers to exercise power in his name: "Heal the sick, raise the dead, cleanse those who have leprosy, drive out demons. Freely you have received; freely give" (Mt 10:8).[39] New Testament scholar Craig Keener documents the phenomenon of miracles in his book *Miracles: The Credibility of the New Testament Accounts*. He further shows that these miracles have continued in every generation through the followers of Jesus, as detailed in *Miracles Today: The Supernatural Work of God in the Modern World*.[40] The works of God through Jesus Christ and those who follow him cannot be waved off as myth or fabricated stories.[41]

In Jesus' final conversation with his disciples, he passes on to them, and to us, the original mandate that *we are to do the works of God*, saying, "Very truly I tell you, whoever believes in me will do the works I have been doing, and they will do even greater things than these, because I am going to the Father" (Jn 14:12). These works entail the daily care for this earth that God entrusted to our stewardship, as well as not limiting God to what may seem impossible to us through our finite logic and abilities. This is part of the "good news" of the kingdom of God.

For example, when the apostle Paul was taken as a prisoner by ship to Rome because of his faith in Jesus, the vessel encountered harsh storms and violent winds for many days. But an angel from God told him that he and the lives of all the people onboard the ship would be spared (Acts 27:14-23). Paul told this to the men on the ship and he was unafraid. They became shipwrecked on the island of Malta but no human lives were lost. The indigenous people on

---

[39]See also Lk 9:2; 10:9; Acts 5:16; Jas 5:14-18.

[40]Craig S. Keener, *Miracles: The Credibility of the New Testament Accounts* (Grand Rapids, MI: Baker Academic, 2011), and *Miracles Today: The Supernatural Work of God in the Modern World* (Grand Rapids, MI: Baker Academic, 2021).

[41]See also Randy Clark, "A Study of the Effects of Christian Prayer on Pain or Mobility Restrictions from Surgeries Involving Implanted Materials" (DMin diss., United Theological Seminary, 2013).

Malta were kind to the refugees from the ship and made them a fire because of the cold. As Paul gathered sticks and set them on the fire, a viper came out and fastened on his hand. The people, on seeing the poisonous "snake hanging from his hand, they said to each other, 'This man must be a murderer; for though he escaped from the sea, the goddess Justice has not allowed him to live,'" and they expected him to fall over dead (Acts 28:4-5). But when he shook the viper from his hand and suffered no ill effects, they changed their minds and decided he must be a god. But Paul pointed them instead to Jesus and proceeded to heal the sick people on the island (Acts 28:7-10).

Perhaps this, along with many other stories from the book of Acts and the early church prompted the longer ending to be added to the Gospel of Mark:

> He said to them, "Go into all the world and preach the gospel to all creation. Whoever believes and is baptized will be saved, but whoever does not believe will be condemned. And these signs will accompany those who believe: In my name they will drive out demons; they will speak in new tongues; they will pick up snakes with their hands; and when they drink deadly poison, it will not hurt them at all; they will place their hands on sick people, and they will get well."
>
> After the Lord Jesus had spoken to them, he was taken up into heaven and he sat at the right hand of God. Then the disciples went out and preached everywhere, and the Lord worked with them and confirmed his word by the signs that accompanied it. (Mk 16:15-20)

Humanity has been called and entrusted to do far more than we are doing in the realm of nature.

New Testament scholar Douglas Moo demonstrates that because humanity has chosen to ignore or defy God, this planet has been "unable to attain the purpose for which it was created."[42] The New Testament asserts,

> For since the creation of the world God's invisible qualities—his eternal power and divine nature—have been clearly seen, being understood from what has been made, so that people are without excuse. For although they knew God, they neither glorified him as God nor gave thanks to him, but their thinking became futile and their foolish hearts were darkened. (Rom 1:20-21)

---

[42]Douglas J. Moo, "Nature in the New Creation: New Testament Eschatology and the Environment," *Journal of the Evangelical Theological Society* 49 (2006): 461, quoted also in Richter, *Stewards of Eden*, 20.

God makes himself known. But when people willfully disregard God, his response is their freedom: "God gave them over . . . God gave them over . . . God gave them over . . ." (Rom 1:24, 26, 28). In other words, as C. S. Lewis wrote, "There are only two kinds of people in the end: those who say to God, 'Thy will be done,' and those to whom God says, in the end, 'Thy will be done.'"[43]

Therefore, both Testaments point to God's creation of a good earth, and God's mandate that human beings would have authority and responsibility to care for creation by spreading his presence and goodness for the flourishing of the planet and all creatures in it. God did not rescind that mandate. We can do more, and we can do a whole lot better.

THE BEST OF ALL POSSIBLE WORLDS: A NEW HEAVEN AND NEW EARTH

Voltaire assumed that this present earth was the best of all possible worlds and thus rejected the possibility of a good and just God who would allow natural disasters and suffering. However, according to the biblical record, this is not the best of all possible worlds. The best possible world is that which is to come.

Long before naturalism or the theories of evolution, the ancient biblical scholars proposed that this present world is in process, and that this process has something important to do with the role of humanity.[44] The Old and New Testaments attest to the creation of a new heavens and a new earth in which the old passes away.[45] Creation was "subjected to futility" not as a punishment, but due to the failure of its stewards (humanity) to fulfill our mandate to care for it and for one another, and to spread goodness throughout the world. Therefore, the earth is in a "gestational period," as philosopher Jim Stump describes, "not yet born into what it is ultimately intended to be."[46] As Romans 8:19 explains, creation is waiting for the

---

[43]C. S. Lewis, *The Great Divorce* (San Francisco: HarperOne, 2015), 72.

[44]Russell D. Moore, "Heaven and Nature Sing: How Evangelical Theology Can Inform the Task of Environmental Protection (and Vice Versa)," *Journal of the Evangelical Theological Society* 57, no. 3 (2014): 573-81; "The Purpose of Creation: 'Today the World Was Born,'" *Sichos in English*, Timeless Patterns in Time, n.d., www.chabad.org/holidays/jewishnewyear/template_cdo/aid/4456/jewish /The-Purpose-of-Creation.htrr.

[45]For example, Is 11:6-9; 25:8; 65:17-25; Rev 21:4.

[46]Stump, "Naming Natural Evils." See also Alexander Coe Stewart, "Heaven Has No Sorrow That Earth Cannot Feel: The Ethics of Empathy and Ecological Suffering in the Old Testament," *Canadian Theological Review* 4, no. 2 (2015): 19-34.

children of God to step up into our original calling. The struggle of creation is connected to our struggle as humans because we were made as one together. "God created a place that needed to be subdued, a place where his image bearers would have a job to do. We are supposed to have an influence on creation, to cooperate with God in setting it free."[47]

In this future best of all possible worlds, God will dwell in the midst of his people, "They will be his people, and God himself will be with them and be their God. 'He will wipe every tear from their eyes. There will be no more death' or mourning or crying or pain, for the old order of things has passed away" (Rev 21:3-4). This present creation along with humanity will be resurrected (see Rom 8:18-21).[48]

The last chapter of the Bible returns to the imagery from Genesis 2 of the rivers and the Tree of Life for healing in the Garden of Eden:

> Then the angel showed me the river of the water of life, as clear as crystal, flowing from the throne of God and of the Lamb down the middle of the great street of the city. On each side of the river stood the tree of life, bearing twelve crops of fruit, yielding its fruit every month. And the leaves of the tree are for the healing of the nations. No longer will there be any curse. (Rev 22:1-3)

Scripture brings the reader and the story of nature full circle regarding the ultimate end and new beginning of creation. For those who believe these words, we have the responsibility to care for this planet and all its inhabitants. The coming new earth also gives hope that although there is much pain, suffering and natural evils, there is a future "best of all possible worlds" in which we can participate.

As stated at the outset of this chapter: although natural evils abound and creation can cause devastation without evil intent, nevertheless, humanity as God's appointed representative is held accountable to steward creation care, spread God's goodness, and subdue creation's wildness when it brings harm to living beings. While many have asked why God allows evil, the biblical narrative asks humanity: Why do you tolerate and perpetuate evil every day?

---

[47]Stump, "Naming Natural Evils." See also Pannenberg, *Systematic Theology*, 3:645.
[48]Richter, *Stewards of Eden,* 127-29.

Part Three

HUMAN CAUSES

SURPRISING WAYS WE PARTICIPATE IN EVIL AND GOOD

*God's supremacy over the universe is inseparably
bound up with the lordship of man.*

<small>G. B. CAIRD</small>

*It is not just that every human person is a sinner. It is also the case that the
totality of our economic relationships with each other and of our ecological
relationship to the earth itself have all been perverted and twisted.*

<small>CHRISTOPHER J. H. WRIGHT</small>

<small>WHILE THE PREVIOUS CHAPTERS</small> explored the role of natural conse-
quences and natural forces in the operation of evil and our implicit accountability, we now focus directly on humanity's explicit responsibility in the
workings of good and evil, and the gray areas in between where we struggle. In

response to the question of how a good God can allow atrocities when he has the power to stop them, we examine the ways humanity abdicates our God-appointed responsibility to maintain goodness, order, harmony, and justice, and opens the door for evil to enter the world.

Chapter Six

HUMAN NEED AND DESIRE
THE MISUSE OF INTENDED GOOD

You can't always get what you want, but if you try,
sometimes, you might find you get what you need.

Rolling Stones

We all have needs and desires. The need to deal with this reality is one reason there are laws regulating behaviors. It's also a reason that most major religions either establish rules of conduct to control the way people pursue what they want or teach paths to eliminate feelings of desire altogether. Further, most economic systems are based on the study of what people want and are willing to pay, which is used to determine the value of goods and commodities. *Commodity* is an interesting and important term in this discussion. For when relationships or resources are viewed in terms of supply and demand to meet needs or desires, they become objectified or monetized as a product or service.

God created humanity with needs and desires for which he intended to provide abundantly and in a timely fashion. Therefore, having needs and desires is part of God's good creation. However, seeking to meet our perceived needs and desires becomes evil when we turn away from God for their fulfillment and look instead to use others as a means of fulfilling our own personal wants and cravings. Attention is diverted from caring for creation and serving the weakest among us, to caring for ourselves and taking from the weakest. Evil, then, consists of turning the cosmos into a commodity instead of building community for the common good.

When we try to fulfill our needs and desires apart from God, we open the door to evil. Additionally, part of the creational intention was for the trio of God, male, and female to work together in spreading the goodness of God to creation and to prevent corruption and evil from entering the cosmos (Gen 1:26-28).

Life lived in the pursuit of desires can bankrupt the heart or the pocket-book. Unmet needs or the loss of something or someone we care about can be a source of pain, suffering, or regret. Desire as unrestrained passion leads to chaos. Unrequited "love" or unrestrained jealousy can explode into emotional or physical damage. Willful endeavors to satisfy one's personal needs or desires can move a person to harm themself or someone else by trying to press fulfillment of what they want. This can be as simple as forcing affection or gifts on a person, to something as harmful as rape or any other kind of physical and emotional violence. Either way, it can get ugly, dangerous, and even deadly.

However, needs and desires can also bring about important and beautiful results. The need to create and the desire to inspire can produce master-pieces. The desire for delicious food can lead to new recipes and production of helpful food sources. The needs of others can move us to incredible feats of kindness and generosity. Recognizing and responding with compassion to the needs of those around us can build community. Taking into consideration one's own necessities and wants, along with those of others, can promote harmony and fruitful outcomes in relationships, community, and economic development.

Our thoughts and behaviors often focus on our real and perceived needs and desires. Much of our daily lives revolve around trying to satisfy these. This includes what we eat, where and how we live, the way we buy and dispose of things, the social media or chats we engage, the shows we watch, the work and hobbies we do, and the people we choose to be around.

IMAGE FROM GENESIS: ALL THE TREES IN THE GARDEN

The role needs and desires play in our lives is portrayed in the imagery of *all the trees* in the Garden of Eden. The passage reads, "The LORD God made all kinds of trees grow out of the ground—trees that were pleasing to the eye and good for food . . . And the LORD God commanded the man [*adam,* or earthling], 'You are free to eat from any tree in the garden'" (Gen 2:9, 16). The Garden is the idyllic portrayal of life as it's meant to be and one day will be. Everything needed for a good life and contentment was provided. There was an abundance of food, water, beauty, the potential for safety and peace, and access to a tree that provided health and life. There was meaningful work to serve and to protect the Garden (Gen 2:15). The concept of work as painful toil, labor, or drudgery was not present in this Garden. Needs were satisfied in terms of food, water, beauty, and eventually human companionship. Even gold was in the Garden, which is called *good* (Gen 2:12). And the trees not only provided *good* food but were beautiful and pleasing to look at (Gen 2:9).

SOMETHING "NOT GOOD" IN THE GOOD GARDEN

However, the narrative of Genesis 2 also points out that in the Garden, something was "not good" (*lo tov*). It was "not good" to be alone (Gen 2:18). The phrase *not good* only occurs once in the Hebrew of the entire book of Genesis. This was not evil; rather, it was a need *not yet fulfilled.*[1]

Having needs and desires is not evil or bad. Needs and desires are part of God's good design. To illustrate, you could consider it *not good* to be very hungry while you're waiting for a feast to be served. But it's *not evil* because there is an anticipation of something good! In contrast, to be very hungry during a famine or with no resources to get food threatens your health and potentially your life. That is *evil*. Therefore, the experience of needing and desiring companionship not yet provided by God, is called "not good" by the Provider himself, the source of all good things. In Genesis 2:18, the LORD God said he would provide a companion, a person of strength corresponding to him (we'll look at these words in detail shortly). Surprisingly, the aloneness identified was not *immediately* satisfied. Even in the very good Garden where there was no lack of provision, the human had to wait, had to be alone for an unidentified period of time, anticipating the companion that would resolve the need for intimacy and satisfy what was not good.

Before providing the *adam*, the needed co-image-bearer, the text tells us that the provider paraded past the *earthling* all forms of animals and birds,

---

[1]Ingrid Faro, *Evil in Genesis: A Contextual Analysis of Hebrew Lexemes for Evil in the Book of Genesis*, Studies in Scripture & Biblical Theology (Bellingham, WA: Lexham, 2021), 101-2.

and gave him the job of identifying and naming them![2] But none of these acts resolved the *not good* of being alone. Why wouldn't God immediately provide what was necessary for a good life? Here's an explanation: God wanted the *earthling* to participate in the process of identifying his need and what would rightly fulfill it.

This process can be seen in the sequence of events in Genesis 2:18-20. God first paraded past *adam* the animals and the birds to observe and name. This gave him the chance to see for himself and figure out that, *nope, the giraffe doesn't meet my need for companionship. Nor does the ostrich or the goat.* It was not until an undisclosed number of animals had passed by and been observed that God brought the woman. For when the one "built" from his "side" appeared, he broke out in exuberant poetry, the first recorded words uttered by a human in the Bible, "Now this is bone of my bones and flesh of my flesh!"

Furthermore, in Hebrew, the words in Genesis 2:18-25 underscore the intended unity of man and woman in three ways to demonstrate that humanity is designed to function in harmony together. First, this companion is referred to as an *ezer knegdo*, a strong corresponding help (Gen 2:18, 20). The Hebrew word *ezer* is generally translated into English as *helper*, which is a weak translation. In English, the word *helper* is thought of as "one that helps, especially: a relatively unskilled worker who assists a skilled worker usually by manual labor."[3] Can I emphasize enough that *that is not* the meaning of the Hebrew word *ezer*! Rather, in the Hebrew Bible, *ezer* is used 76 percent of the time to refer to God or to Yahweh as our helper.[4] Contextually, in light of Gen 2:15, this indicates that the work given the *earthling*—to serve and protect the Garden—was to be done together with the woman in the priestly task as cogovernor and cokeeper, and as a co-image-bearer (Gen 1:26-27).

---

[2]I use *adam* or "the *adam*" here instead of "Adam" or "man" because the translation of the Hebrew word *adam* into the Septuagint (the Greek translation of the Hebrew Bible from about 200 BC) varies. It begins as *anthrōpos* in Genesis 1:26-27; 2:5-15; Genesis 2:16 transliterates the Hebrew as *Adam*; Genesis 2:18 switches back to *anthrōpos*—human; Genesis 2:19-25 and Genesis 3 switch back again to the transliterated Hebrew into Greek as *Adam*. In other words, the Septuagint translates *adam* as *anthrōpos* or *human/humanity* in Genesis 2:7, 8, 15, 18. And it transliterates *adam* as "Adam" in Genesis 2:16, 19, 20, 21, 22, 23; 3:1 [2:25 MT]; 3:8, 9, 12, 17, 20, 21, 24.

[3]*Merriam-Webster*, "helper (n.)," www.merriam-webster.com/dictionary/helper.

[4]Sixteen times out of the twenty-one times the word occurs it refers to God or Yahweh as a *helper/help*. For example, Deut 33:7, 26, 29; Ps 40:17; 70:5; 121:1, 2; 124:8; 146:5.

Second, this companion is "built" from the "side" of *adam*. Most translations of Genesis 2:21-22 say that the LORD God "took one of the man's ribs and then closed up the place with flesh. Then the LORD God made a woman from the rib [*tsela*] he had taken out of the man." However, in the whole Hebrew Bible, the word *tsela* is only translated into English as *rib* in Genesis 2. Everywhere else it is translated *side*. There are other words in Hebrew to refer to the sides of various objects. But in this instance, the word for *side* is intentional. In "the nearly forty other occurrences it is used specifically to refer to the sides of the ark of the covenant, the sides, or chambers of the temple, the sides of the tabernacle, or sides of the altar before the tabernacle."[5] In order for the sides of the ark of the covenant or the sides of the tabernacle or the temple storerooms to hold them up they had to be equal in strength and proportion. They had to fit and function together. This word draws attention to the picture of male and female being "built" to stand together in unison with equivalent strength and purpose, representing a place where the glory and presence of God is made tangible in the earth. In the Garden, *adam* was invited into the process of figuring out the solution to aloneness in order to understand God's purposes for companionship. Adam had to wait for God to provide a well-suited, strong companion and not take or settle for something *not good* just to quickly fulfill what was lacking for life to be good.

Sometimes people do not receive what we need because we don't yet understand what we *truly* need, and therefore resign ourselves to a false provision which will not and cannot satisfy. Therefore, we can end up with something that, from a biblical perspective is "evil," harmful, and not part of God's good design for our life. It takes time and patience, waiting and evaluating, along with learning and growing in wisdom to discover what's important and what we truly need. If we're willing to keep learning through trial and error and plenty of mistakes and missteps, we may find what we most deeply need and long for.

The third Hebrew word that points to the unity between all humanity as male and female, as well as to the kind of unity intended in the marriage

---

[5]E.g., of the Ark (Ex 25:12, 14; 37:3, 5); of the tabernacle (Ex 26:20, 26, 35; 36:25, 31); of the altar Ex 27:7; 38:7); side walls or structures of the temple (1 Kings 6:5, 8; 15; Ezek 41:5, 9, 11); or side chambers of the temple (Ezek 41:6-8). See Faro, *Evil in Genesis*, 102n18.

relationship, appears in Genesis 2:23: "The man said, 'This is now bone of my bones and flesh of my flesh; she shall be called "woman" [*ishah*], for she was taken out of man [*ish*].'" Note the linguistic connection between these two words: *ish-ishah* is similar to the *adam-adamah* connection in the Hebrew. Furthermore, the phrase *flesh and bone* is synonymous with kinship language in the Hebrew Bible.[6] According to Genesis 1:26-28, all humanity is family, or kin.[7] The peaceful Garden scene closes with the words, "And so it was that the two of them were naked, the *adam* and his wife/woman [*ishah*], and they had no shame between themselves" (my translation). In other words, they had nothing to hide from each other and they had no ulterior motives. What we most deeply long for is intimacy—to be seen and known by another. The counterfeit is sex without union of heart. Sex without intimacy is an addictive drug that temporarily treats the underlying pain of aloneness but leaves one even more isolated and in need of core companionship.

"The only possibility we have of catching a glimpse at ourselves is through the eyes of another,"[8] writes Karen Barad. None of us can actually physically *see* our face or look into our own eyes, except through a mirror (or in ancient times, reflected in water, or a sheet of metal). Other people are our mirror—eyes reflecting into our souls. Yet, few people (if any) really see us, hear us, or know us. But this is what we long for. This is the companionship we need. We cannot truly know ourselves in isolation. As psychologist Curt Thompson puts it, "there's no such thing as an individual brain."[9] We only grow to know ourselves as we connect with others. He goes on to speak of how we become transformed through "collaborative interaction, with one

---

[6]See Catherine L. McDowell, *The Image of God in the Garden of Eden: The Creation of Humankind in Genesis 2:5–3:24 in Light of the Mīs Pî, Pīt Pî, and Wpt-r Rituals of Mesopotamia*, Siphrut: Literature and Theology of the Hebrew Scriptures (Winona Lake, IN: Eisenbrauns, 2015), 138; Gordon John Wenham, *Genesis 1–15*, Word Biblical Commentary (Grand Rapids, MI: Zondervan Academic, 2014), 70; Faro, *Evil in Genesis*, 147n36. Tracing the term for *flesh and bone* throughout the Old Testament and the New Testament reveals that it always refers to kinship and family. (The term for *flesh and blood* in both the Old Testament and the New Testament refers to our humanity.)

[7]See previous note.

[8]Karen Barad, *Meeting the Universe Halfway: Quantum Physics and the Entanglement of Matter and Meaning* (Durham, NC: Duke University Press, 2007), 11.

[9]Curt Thompson, *Anatomy of the Soul: Surprising Connections Between Neuroscience and Spiritual Practices That Can Transform Your Life and Relationships* (Carol Stream, IL: Tyndale Refresh, 2010), 137.

person empathically listening and responding to the other so that the speaker has the experience, perhaps for the first time, *of feeling felt by another.*[10] Nothing is more freeing and fulfilling than a tested relationship where nothing is concealed from the other, where there is no darkness, blame, or fear. One of my favorite definitions of love is a covenant commitment to the well-being of another. That's a take I got from Daniel Block's studies in the Torah.[11]

Sometimes I imagine a world where there are no hidden motives. That will be a good world. That is one of the aspects I treasure most when thinking of the new heavens and earth—no more pain or sorrow inflicted on one another or on ourselves. But we are far from the Garden. From Genesis 3 and throughout history, people tend to look at others and the rest of creation to fulfill personal wants and needs. Humans and things are generally viewed and used in a utilitarian way as a commodity rather than appreciated for their own intrinsic value and worth. Therefore, we often approach others clothed with the appearance we want them to see, concealing our thoughts and intentions that we may try to hide even from ourselves. Unless we're willing to acknowledge our capacity for inflicting harm as well as good, we will conceal the darkness within until it consumes us or others.

Needs and desires are intended to be good as they help us learn to recognize our motives and to wait or work patiently, and observantly, for the fulfillment of what is "not good," while looking expectantly to the trusted Creator. I have come to see and believe that when I hold my hands open, something good is happening in the observing and waiting that cannot happen if I rush, push, or take what I want when I want it. Impatience, frustration, anger, and bitterness work rottenness in our hearts.

We can learn to silence the voices that relentlessly urge us to "Take what you want! You *need* it. Take it now!" When we push away the pressure to grasp, and instead quiet our mind, we can develop a stillness of soul that moves us toward peace and wholeness. The process of waiting, watching, and learning leads us to discover what we need to know about our inner self

---

[10]Thompson, *Anatomy of the Soul*, 137.
[11]Daniel Isaac Block, *How I Love Your Torah, O Lord! Studies in the Book of Deuteronomy* (Eugene, OR: Cascade Books, 2011), 83.

and our true needs. In trusting God with a conscious expectation of good, even in the midst of need and want, we can rest even in our lack, no matter what the present circumstances.

NEEDS, DESIRES, AND THE ROOTS OF TEMPTATION

If someone had asked me some years back what I thought was the first time God commanded something in the Bible, I would have thought it was when God said, "Do not eat of the Tree of the Knowledge of good and evil." But I'd have been wrong. The first time the word *command* (*tswh*) is used is when "the LORD God commanded the earthling saying, 'From all the trees of the Garden, eat freely!'" (Gen 2:16, my translation), using strong emphatic language. It's like saying, "Look around at everything I have given you! Eat! Enjoy it all!" What a great commandment! God wants us to enjoy the beauty and the bounty he has given us. Enjoyment and gratitude are central to Garden living. Joyful generosity and expectant trust in the goodness of the Creator fills this first command. Contentment springs up when we adjust our daily lenses *first* toward thankfulness and seeing the beauty around us.

This is a basic concept in psychology and counseling. It's central to breaking addictions and transforming depression. Research and many people's personal experiences point to the importance of gratitude. The warning *against* failing to thankfully receive the goodness and beauty around follows in Genesis 2:17. Yes, there was that one forbidden tree. Access in the Garden had already been given to the tree of life so they could stay healthy. But among the thousands (millions?) of freely accessible trees, why restrict that *one* tree of the knowledge of good and evil with the warning that if they ate from it, they would certainly die?

While wanting and waiting are part of God's good creation, all legitimate human needs and desires were intended to be freely provided by a personal God with the one requirement of wholly trusting him and thankfully partaking of his abundant goodness. Although a need can be identified as "not good," neither the wanting nor the waiting is evil, or bad. However, as seen in Genesis 2:17, taking for oneself illegitimately to satisfy one's own desires is unauthorized, and initiates a process of inner, and eventually outer, decay.

"All the trees" in the Garden represent the bounty of God in creation. God wants us to enjoy all the goodness of life. When we fail the "command" to take pleasure in all the beauty and wonderful things God has legitimately given us, we fall prey to gnawing, nagging compulsions for what could destroy us. The call to "trust in the LORD with all your heart and lean not on your own understanding" leads us on a path of peace within ourselves and with others (Prov 3:5).

The New Testament continues the theme of trusting God's goodness and provision.

HOW THE NEW TESTAMENT TALKS ABOUT NEEDS AND DESIRES

In Jesus' famous Sermon on the Mount, he teaches us to not worry because God knows our needs and he wants to provide for us if we'll take the time and effort to seek him and set our priorities in order. Jesus sounds like he's giving a current commentary on the first command in Genesis 2:16 to fully enjoy God's bounty:

> Therefore I tell you, do not worry about your life, what you will eat or drink; or about your body, what you will wear. Is not life more than food, and the body more than clothes? Look at the birds of the air; they do not sow or reap or store away in barns, and yet your heavenly Father feeds them. Are you not much more valuable than they? . . . But seek first his kingdom and his righteousness, and all these things will be given to you as well. (Mt 6:25-33)

The call from Jesus is like the one in the Garden: be thankful in the present, focus with gratitude on what you have, and trust God to provide what he knows you need in the future.

Additional language used in the New Testament is "casting our anxieties on the Lord," and seeking God and his way first. For example, "Do not be anxious about anything, but in every situation, by prayer and petition, with thanksgiving, present your requests to God. And the peace of God, which transcends all understanding, will guard your hearts and your minds in Christ Jesus" (Phil 4:6-9; see also 1 Tim 6:6-19; 1 Pet 5:6-7). The importance of contentment and leading a life of goodness, care, and love is emphasized rather than stressing over needs or striving after riches. Let me tell of a time I learned about contentment.

FROM MY STORY: NEEDS, DESIRES, AND A KEY TO HAPPINESS

The lesson of gratitude from "all the trees of the Garden" came alive for me during the years of my second husband's illnesses. As his pain and accumulation of medical and mental conditions worsened, he became more volatile and understandably unkind. I felt alone in caring for him, our young son Walter, our household, and managing the two businesses I ran. My own health began to deteriorate with severe asthma and agglutination of my red blood cells, which further hampered the transportation of oxygen in my body. I was angry, bitter, exhausted, and breathless, taking steroids, and using inhalers. Many nights I would cry alone in our bed as my husband lay on the sofa either medicating or writhing in pain. Most of the time there was nothing I could do to resolve either our miseries or our son's efforts to navigate it all.

Then, early one morning I cried out to God, complaining heavily because of a recent verbal assault from my husband. I knew it came from his pain and was not personal, but I felt abandoned. Then, the calm, silent voice I had come to recognize as God spoke quietly to my spirit, "Give me your anger." I took off on my own verbal rampage at God, listing all the reasons why I had every right to be angry. The still voice said again, "Give me your anger." As I was about to go off again, I heard, "Your anger is killing you." This time he had my attention. I knew this was true. I was about to say, "I don't know how!" when suddenly a Great White Light shined above me, and I saw the outline of a throne, with Jesus standing next to the throne. The brightness of his being made it impossible to see him, except for his arms with pierced hands outstretched to me. He compassionately spoke, "Ingrid, I died for you anger. Give me your anger."

Overwhelmed with the power of his love, I used my arms to gather up all my anger in a huge bundle and threw it at heaven, shouting silently, "Here! Take it!" As I released my bundle of anger into the light it felt like a giant dam broke lose within my body and my blood rushed freely from my heart to my toes like a powerful wave. Then the wave came back up to my lungs and with it, a huge breath of air.

I breathed deeply in and out for the first time in many months. Warmth and healing flooded my body and soul, and that same powerfully gentle voice said these simple words: "Would you like to know the key to happiness?" I know that sounds like the title to a corny movie, but it was very real and true.

As I listened, God explained to me that when he gave the Tenth Commandment at Sinai in the wilderness, "You shall not covet," marriages were arranged, and many people did not have the freedom they wanted or that he wanted for them. Nevertheless, he wanted and expected them to be happy, even in the wilderness. Even under those harsh circumstances, happiness was possible. God told me that I was coveting—desiring a different husband. Not anyone else in particular, but not the one I had. My anger, discontentment, and bitterness had been tearing my body apart. Then God told me the three keys to happiness. First, he said, "Look for beauty all around you. Every day, find as many things as you can to be thankful for, including any small thing your husband does that is kind or thoughtful or useful. Look for something beautiful, anything at all, no matter how small. Notice beauty and be thankful for it. Hold onto these. As you focus on being thankful, you will find yourself gradually becoming content. As contentment grows inside you, you will discover that you are happy."

These simple steps transformed my life. I've learned to look for beauty around me every day and notice any small act of kindness. I've learned the ancient Jewish tradition of the centering prayer of giving thanks first thing in the morning before I get out of bed or do anything else (the "Modeh Ani"). I thank God for my breath and my life, and add words of thanks for specific gifts, and even my troubles and stumblings, saying that I trust even these to be turned into good for myself and those around me.[12] As I change my thinking, first from within, my outer circumstances gradually transform organically. Over time, these habits of the mind are like planting and watering a field of good seed.

---

[12]Omer Adam sings the extended version of the "Modeh Ani" prayer created by Avi Ohayon (lyrics) and Asaf Tzruya (music). Translation by Robbie Gringras for Makom, the Israel Education Lab of the Jewish Agency for Israel, www.youtube.com/watch?v=npRw36_Ftmc.

The cultivation of thankfulness grows into contentment, which can blossom into happiness, even in the midst of unchanged circumstances. Enjoying and being thankful for "all the trees of the Garden," all the good things in this life, continues to protect me from chasing after those things that I thought I needed or desired that would lead me into places of darkness and despair.

Along with thankfulness, I also learned a most valuable lesson from my son around the same time. When he was just seven years old, life in our home was always serious. So, he sat me down on his bed one day and said in his most mature voice, "Mom, we have to laugh at least once every day, even if you have to tickle me." These are some of the wisest words I've ever heard. And I've continued the habit of daily laughter every day since.

Having needs and desires is intended to be good and positive, not harmful or draining. As we learn to live each day with thankfulness for all we have and focus on the beauty in our lives, we can grow in contentment even in times of hardships and needs. This does not mean succumbing to evils, oppression, or the abuses of others. But it does mean refusing to allow suffering to define our identity, determine our destiny, or control our lives. God intends to work amid our situations to transform our unmet needs and desires, and even the evil and harm of our circumstances, into opportunities for goodness, justice, and righteousness to flow out from them, even if it is not in our lifetime but for the next generation.

We can't change the past, but we can reframe the past and the trajectory of our future with the decisions we make today. Troubles and loss are unavoidable. Although cruelty happens, these words of the psalmist have often helped believers hold steady in times of hardship: "*I would have despaired* unless I had believed that I would see the goodness of the LORD in the land of the living. Wait for the LORD; Be strong and let your heart take courage; Yes, wait for the LORD" (Ps 27:13-14 NASB95).

Chapter Seven

SELF-SUFFICIENCY
THE ROOT OF PRIDE AND INSECURITY

*The root of all evil is, according to Isaiah, man's false sense of sovereignty
and, stemming from it, man's pride, arrogance, and presumption. . . . There
is no limit to cruelty when man begins to think that he is the master.*

ABRAHAM JOSHUA HESCHEL

PRIDE IS LISTED among the seven (or eight) deadly sins, or capital vices,
since the time of the desert monks in the third century AD. In Christian
circles, the sin of pride is reviled. Synonyms that accompany pride include
arrogance, conceit, self-importance, egotism, and some might throw in nar-
cissism for good measure. Of course, there's the positive side where you're
proud of someone or yourself for standing up to wrongs, for having the
courage or tenacity to see something through, for doing something helpful
and positive, or for accomplishing a worthy achievement. But in the conversation about evil, we'll look at pride considering its potential for harm to self
and others.

The flip side of pride is insecurity. Synonyms for insecurity include ti-
midity, reticence, self-abasement, and self-doubt. There's not a positive side
to insecurity but it's generally more socially acceptable. Sometimes insecurity is mistaken for humility, but this is an error. Humility is a right assessment of one's strengths and weaknesses in which one neither peacocks
nor grovels. However, the pride of self-aggrandizement and the insecurity
of self-abasement are two sides of the same coin: a placement of value centered on oneself—either an exaggerated or a diminished self-perception.

At the center of pride and arrogance is choosing to believe that one's own wisdom and knowledge, one's own reasoning powers, are superior to trusting in the wise words, direction, and provision of a good, almighty Creator and Father. At the center of fear and insecurity is also self-centeredness that focuses on one's own *inabilities* to sufficiently provide, protect, or accomplish one's needs and desires. Arrogant pride and anxious fears both arise from this stance of self-reliance. Both are positions of autonomy that shut God out of the picture, or at least try to push him into the shadows of our thoughts and actions.

If we think of evil as the corruption of creational and relational goodness, then the evil here is turning inward toward self, instead of upward toward God and outward toward creation and others. The evil we bring may not feel malevolent, but the effect is seeking to elevate our self through prideful egotism or to belittle our self through insecure excuses. We focus our efforts on our own abilities or deficiencies. Both pride and insecurity, then, are positions of autonomy, making ourselves gods, which close the door to God, who is good and has a vastly bigger picture that he longs to accomplish in and through us.

IMAGE FROM GENESIS: THE TREE OF THE KNOWLEDGE OF GOOD AND EVIL

The biblical imagery in Genesis for self-sufficiency is the tree of the knowledge of good and evil (Gen 2:9, 17; 3:3-7). The risk God knowingly took when creating humanity with the ability to make choices was that we could choose against him and decide that *our* wisdom is better for us than his.[1] Whereas "all the trees of the Garden" represent our liberty to choose from the vastness of God's abundant provision, the tree of the knowledge of good and evil represents the limit to our liberty—the choice between autonomy or trusting our Creator. God gave us the freedom to make our own choices, even deadly ones. The tree of knowledge together with the tree of life represent two great conflicting desires of humanity: God-filled life versus independent selfhood.[2]

---

[1]See also George W. Coates, "The God of Death: Power and Obedience in the Primeval History," *Interpretation* 29, no. 3 (1975): 227-39.
[2]Coates, "God of Death," 119.

The tree of life is widely used outside of the Bible to represent humanity's quest for immortality.[3] But there is nothing like the tree of knowledge of good and evil outside the Bible, and it is not mentioned in the Bible again outside of Genesis 2–3.[4] "Yet, it is this tree upon which the biblical story of humanity hangs."[5]

In the Garden, the consequence for choosing independence apart from the Creator is given with the warning that this action results in death, or being cut off from the tree of life and alienated from God (Gen 2:17). Like cut flowers—they look alive for a while but not for long. The process of death sets in as soon as they are cut from the root, their source of life. Genesis 2–3 begins in the very good Garden and ends with expulsion to a life of labor and toil outside the Garden.

FROM MY STORY: THE PRIDE OF INSECURITY

How people develop pride or insecurity is related to who or what they trust the most. Through my own fears and perfectionism, I grew to recognize that both are rooted in self-sufficiency and related to how we perceive and use our freedom as human beings. I used to be terrified of speaking in public. This phobia is more common than the fear of "death, spiders, or heights . . . (and) affects about 73 percent of the population. The underlying fear is judgment or negative evaluation by others."[6] Knowing this did not alleviate my inward-looking

---

[3]Peter T. Lanfer, "Allusion to and Expansion of the Tree of Life and Garden of Eden in Biblical and Pseudepigraphal Literature," in *Early Christian Literature and Intertextuality*, vol. 1, *Thematic Studies*, ed. Craig A. Evans and H. Daniel Zacharias, Library of New Testament Studies 391 (New York: T&T Clark, 2009), 96-108; Kenneth Mathews, *Genesis 11:27–50:26: An Exegetical and Theological Exposition of Holy Scripture* (Nashville: Holman Reference, 2005), 202; A. S. Yahuda, *Language of the Pentateuch in Its Relation to Egyptian Part 1* (London: Kessinger, 2003), 19; Roland E. Murphy, *The Tree of Life: An Exploration of Biblical Wisdom Literature* (Grand Rapids, MI: Eerdmans, 2002).

[4]Ingrid Faro, *Evil in Genesis: A Contextual Analysis of Hebrew Lexemes for Evil in the Book of Genesis*, Studies in Scripture & Biblical Theology (Bellingham, WA: Lexham, 2021), 10-11.

[5]Faro, *Evil in Genesis*, 11; Howard M. Wallace, *The Eden Narrative*, Harvard Semitic Monographs 32 (Atlanta: Scholars Press, 1985), 116.

[6]John Montopoli, "Public Speaking Anxiety and Fear of Brain Freezes," National Social Anxiety Center, February 20, 2017, https://nationalsocialanxietycenter.com/2017/02/20/public-speaking -and-fear-of-brain-freezes/; Vickram Tejwani, Duc Ha, and Carlos Isada, "Public Speaking Anxiety in Graduate Medical Education—A Matter of Interpersonal and Communication Skills?," *Journal of Graduate Medical Education* 8, no. 1 (2016): 111, www.ncbi.nlm.nih.gov/pmc/articles /PMC4763377/. Fear of speaking in public, or "Public Speaking Anxiety" (PSA), is classified as

insecurities. I remember the first time when, as a PhD student, I was invited to speak to a group of two hundred people. All my notes were carefully prepared. A quiet voice inside tried to encourage me to speak from just an outline of my notes, but I said, "No way!" I was glued to the page with an occasional furtive glance at the audience. My voice felt compressed, like it barely reached the microphone. The words were good, but the delivery couldn't have been less engaging. Around the same time, I was asked to teach my first graduate class in biblical Hebrew. This was something I had hoped to do for years during my master's program, and I was thrilled at the chance. But during the first two weeks of classes, I was terrified that I would get something wrong, or fail to explain something well (i.e., look like an idiot). Because of these incidents and an upcoming conference paper that I was to present, I asked God for help, lots of it! Fear had paralyzed me my whole life.

As I prayed, the first thing that came to mind was the story of the religious leaders asking Jesus, "Teacher, which is the greatest commandment in the Law?" Jesus replied: "'Love the Lord your God with all your heart and with all your soul and with all your mind.' This is the first and greatest commandment. And the second is like it: 'Love your neighbor as yourself.' All the Law and the Prophets hang on these two commandments" (Mt 22:36-40). And there was the most important part of my answer—love. Love your students. Love the people you're speaking to. Love, *agapaō* in the Greek, is a verb that involves taking an active interest in the other. Focus on caring about them and bringing something worthwhile to meet their needs rather than focusing on your need or desire to sound smart or to be right. I realized, It's not about you! It doesn't matter if you make a mistake or don't know everything. It's not about your success. It's about them.

Turning the attention away from myself to others transformed my inwardly focused fear to outwardly focused excitement to see what God was going to do and how people might benefit from what God had given me the opportunity to learn and share. Knowing that I have

---

a social anxiety disorder in the DSM-5 (*Diagnostic and Statistical Manual of Mental Disorders*; American Psychiatric Association).

> limits to my knowledge and abilities, like everyone else, gives me the
> humility to listen and learn from others as I teach, speak, and learn from
> my own mistakes without fear or embarrassment. Knowing that I care
> more about reaching others than trying to prove how smart or capable
> I am gives me the confidence that when I get something wrong I will
> learn something new. There will always be smarter, more capable
> people. Letting go of comparison or competition, I'm free to enjoy the
> greater gifts of others while giving all I've got and making relational
> connections in the process. When I do make a mistake or when someone
> else makes a mistake, and when we even fail or sin badly, I've learned to
> say, "Congratulations! You've learned something new!" The paradigm for
> growth is not "Succeed or Fail." Rather, it is "Succeed or Learn."

THE LURE OF SELF-SUFFICIENCY

As we follow the plot from Genesis 2–3, the story moves from the beauty, abundance, and relational intimacy of the Garden to the intrusion of a serpent, "the mouthpiece for a Dark Power."[7] Why was the serpent in the Garden, and how did it get in? In Genesis 2:15, many English versions translate the Hebrew in agricultural terms, saying that the LORD God put the *adam* in the Garden of Eden to cultivate and work it, or to care for it and maintain it (*leovdah ulshomrah*). But, in the rest of the Hebrew Bible, these two words *serve* (*abad*) and *protect/guard* (*shamar*) are only used together in reference "to 'serving and guarding/obeying' God's word" or "to priests who 'serve' God in the temple and 'guard' the temple from unclean things entering it (Num 3:7-8; 8:25-26; 18:5-6; 1 Chr 23:32; Ezek 44:14)."[8] In other words, these are priestly terms used together specifically to protect sacred space from disobedience, defilement, or contamination.

If there was no threat in the good Garden, there was no reason for God to tell the earthling "to serve and protect" or "work and guard" the Garden. A dark force was lurking around, and instead of the humans guarding the sacred space, they made the choice to engage the intruder's slander of God

[7]C. John Collins, *Genesis 1–4: A Linguistic, Literary, and Theological Commentary* (Phillipsburg, NJ: P&R, 2006), 171.
[8]Gregory K. Beale, "Eden, the Temple, and the Church's Mission in the New Creation," *Journal of the Evangelical Theological Society* 48 (2005): 6-8.

and entertain its proposal to disobey God. This malevolent creature twisted God's words so that their desire was turned away from "all the trees of the Garden" that God gave them, and focus instead on the one tree, *the only boundary,* God placed before them, which led to the earthlings' unauthorized taking of *the only thing* God withheld for their good.

There's an interesting use of the Hebrew word "desirable" in Genesis 2 and 3 that gives further insight into how one's perception of their desires works hand–in–hand with self-sufficiency. The word "desirable" in Hebrew is *nekhmad*, from the Hebrew root word *khamad*. In Genesis 2:9, all the trees in the Garden were called good for food and desirable (*nekhmad*) in appearance or pleasing to the sight. But in Genesis 3:6, after the woman entertained conversation with the serpent, instead of her seeing *all* the trees in the Garden being desirable in appearance and good for food (Gen 2:9), *now* her attention and desire shifted to the one restricted tree. Now the tree of the knowledge of good and evil became "good for food and . . . *desirable (nekhmad)*" to make her wise.[9] The perception of her own needs and desires shifted from what God had provided in *all* the trees of the Garden as desirable to the sight, to the *one* and only restricted Tree of Knowledge, which was now desirable to make her independently wise.

Beyond offering wisdom, the serpent promised that their "eyes would be opened." This promise was more than simply fulfilling a desire to know what is good and evil. Further excavation reveals that she and the man wanted more than wisdom: they wanted to be gods. In the ancient Near East, the phrase "your eyes will be open" refers to Egyptian and Mesopotamian divinization ritual of making an idol a god.[10] Prompted by the serpent, the couple now looked at the tree solely for what they thought it would give them: divinization, becoming a god. Moved by the serpent's words that God had lied and withheld something good from them, they became discontent with what they had and who they were created as image-bearers. They wanted to wield power. With the serpent's assurance that they

---

[9]Further, the same root word for "desire" (*khamad*), later appears in the tenth commandment, "You shall not covet" (*takhmod*).

[10]Catherine L. McDowell, *The Image of God in the Garden of Eden: The Creation of Humankind in Genesis 2:5–3:24 in Light of the Mīs Pî, Pīt Pî, and Wpt-r Rituals of Mesopotamia*, Siphrut: Literature and Theology of the Hebrew Scriptures (Winona Lake, IN: Eisenbrauns, 2015), 169.

would not die, they developed an appetite for what they had now come to believe they wanted—not to serve God—but to *be gods*.

The same root word for "desire" (*khamad*) used in Genesis 2:9; 3:16 later appears in the tenth commandment, "You shall not covet" (*takhmod*). At the heart of self-sufficiency and coveting is a belief that God is not enough—that God has not provided enough—that God is withholding something that must be taken for one's own personal happiness and well-being. God's goodness of character must therefore be doubted and his warning of consequences for misplaced choices must be disobeyed. When we come to believe that God has denied us a needed good, we also believe that we have the right to take for our self what we think we need. Self is set up as provider and judge of what is good and right. As the ensuing narratives of Genesis indicate, faithful loyalty holds to the belief that God keeps covenant and will provide what we need and what he has promised, even when circumstances appear to be contrary to this belief.

The tree of the knowledge of good and evil represents the desire for personal knowledge in order to be in charge of what's right and wrong and to be the judge of what's good or bad, independently from God's wisdom. After all, who wants to serve a higher up if you can be your own boss? Right? Even if you have no idea how to run the universe or even your own life, the urge to be the autocrat of our own kingdom runs deep. Unbridled pride or insecurity drives us toward self-sufficiency, which then becomes the means of serving a master other than God. That was the serpent's goal all along, for the dark forces moving through the serpent's speech wanted to be gods themselves with earthlings as their servants.

THE SERPENT'S GRAND PLAN TO RULE THE WORLD

The serpent who plotted the temptation had a larger agenda that the earthlings did not know. Subtly, if the earthlings followed the serpent's carefully couched command, they would be obeying and therefore serving the voices of spiritual forces which had turned in opposition to God. That was the malevolent plan. We may think we can be gods, but the reality is, as Bob Dylan rightly sang,[11]

---

[11]Bob Dylan, "Gotta Serve Somebody," www.bobdylan.com/songs/gotta-serve-somebody/.

You're gonna have to serve somebody
Well, it may be the devil or it may be the Lord
But you're gonna have to serve somebody

When we obey someone, in a sense, we become their servants. As stated in the Bible, "Don't you know that when you offer yourselves to someone as obedient slaves, you are slaves of the one you obey" (Rom 6:16). As independent as we may think we are, from a biblical perspective we either serve the King of kings and Lord of lords, or we serve someone else. There are only two kingdoms in this world: the kingdom of God, and every other kingdom. All other kingdoms are subjects of the ruler of this world (Jn 12:31; 14:30; 2 Cor 4:4). God wants us to obey him, since God *alone* is good and capable of always using power for good.

For an outside spiritual force to usurp the authority God gave to humanity as image-bearers, this entity would have to get them to obey its voice instead of God's. Through the serpent's cleverly crafted speech, the woman and the man "who was with her" (Gen 3:6) listened to the words of the serpent and were convinced to see the tree differently: not as a tree of death as God had said, but as the most desirable tree in the whole Garden. This tree became the one thing they had to have. The serpent implied that God had restricted access to this tree in order to withhold something good. Therefore, God was not *really* good, and not to be trusted, that something she needed and desired was being wrongfully denied. The serpent mixed a truth with a lie. First, it was true that seeking wisdom independent from God's wisdom would make them like "a god." But the serpent lied when it declared, "You will not certainly die!" (Gen 3:4). Blinded to the abundance and beauty that surrounded the couple, now only *this* tree became desirable and good.

By desiring the knowledge and freedom to do what was right or wrong in their own eyes rather than attending to what was right or wrong in God's eyes, "their eyes were opened" to this new possibility that self-determination provided.[12] This is how temptation works. When we look away from the good things we have and instead focus on the one thing that we don't have,

---

[12]For more on the phrase, "their eyes were opened," see McDowell, *Image of God in the Garden of Eden*, 169.

that becomes the one thing we *must* have, and we may be willing to forfeit all the goodness in our life to obtain the one thing that will ultimately bring about our destruction.

Two Sides of Self-Sufficiency: Pride and Insecurity

Humanity was intended to partner with God to satisfy our unmet needs and desires and help meet those of others around us. We tend to be fearful or worried that our seemingly ever-expanding range of needs and desires will remain unmet, unfilled, and unsatisfied. Wanting desperately to be in control of all aspects of our lives, we seek the power and ability to see all and know all. But, of course, this is not possible. When our focus turns away from thankfulness for the abundance of all things to the frustrating desire to be in charge, we come to believe that God is unfaithful, insufficient, uncaring, or inattentive. Ultimately, we believe the lie that God is not good enough to care about me, not powerful enough to provide for me, and therefore, not trustworthy to follow, wait for, or trust. Our internal thoughts might be encapsulated by something like this:

> I am big; I am strong and important; I take charge of every situation; my ideas and strategies matter more than anyone else.

Or,

> I am small; I am weak and insignificant; I didn't try because I didn't think it would matter or make a different.

Facing inward, *I* easily becomes the focus of my attention, and I can easily exhaust myself or others in the process of trying to fulfill my self-perceived needs and desires. The consequence of self-reliance leads us to take for ourselves and assume a position of independence from God. If unaware of the unseen realm, we may come to believe that we have obtained all our accomplishments, resources, and possessions by our own intelligence, power, and abilities. Or we may sink into the morose dread that our own abilities, intelligence, and power are insufficient, and we despair.

Worries, anxieties, and burnout can serve as internal signals that we are trusting our own abilities more than looking expectantly and wisely to God for direction, strategies, help, and provision. I include the word *strategies* because God neither pushes buttons to send you help nor gives you a money tree. God works through people and circumstances and involves us in the process through prayer and through (wise, bold, and faithful) actions. This process generally takes time and cooperation. The liberty we grasp for becomes our captor when used for self-centered gain. Often, even our benevolence feeds our need to feel good about ourselves—powerful enough to help someone in need and gain the approval of others.

Nevertheless, the fact that people often genuinely do good things for others for selfless reasons points to an inherently divine quality that is part of who we are as well. We are a mix of positive and negative intentions, dust and divinity, formed by the choices we freely make.

New Testament's Call to Confident Humility and Inner Rest

The ultimate example of what it means to be God's representative is Jesus Christ, who declared, "Anyone who has seen me has seen the Father" (Jn 14:9). Although he spoke and acted with full authority, he stated specifically that he never acted out of self-sufficiency, but only spoke and did what God his "Father" showed him or told him (Jn 5:19-20; 8:28; 12:49; 14:31). He exemplified confidence with humility and goodness without abusing his power. This Jesus, who spoke and acted boldly against the pride and hypocrisy of religious leaders, served, and cared for all who came to him in sincerity. Indeed, Jesus invited all who would listen: "Come to me, all you who are weary and burdened, and I will give you rest. Take my yoke upon you and learn from me, for I am gentle and humble in heart, and you will find rest for your souls. For my yoke is easy and my burden is light" (Mt 11:28-30).

Internal burdens can stress us out because we're thinking and working so hard to keep all the pieces of our lives together. We're anxious about how we'll get each one of our needs met. We worry about what people think of us, how we can achieve more, be more successful, look good enough, meet a deadline, complete a project, be safe emotionally or physically, not look stupid or foolish, and so on. All our efforts to control the outcomes of our life are exhausting. We need rest. And even when we try to rest, often it's only so that we can do more work, complete more tasks, meet more deadlines, or please more people. So, we try to entertain ourselves, or distract or medicate ourselves into a false feeling of pseudo-rest that only masks our weariness.

External burdens that exhaust us include a hostile home or work environment, discrimination, destabilizing economic and social pressures, diseases, pandemics, and various kinds of abuses. Jesus said that "in this world you will have trouble" (Jn 16:33). The word for trouble (*thlipsis*) means difficulty "that inflicts distress, *oppression, affliction, tribulation . . . from inner or outward difficult circumstances.*"[13] Jesus concludes his statement about trouble by encouraging us to look to him for assurance: "Take heart! I have overcome the world."

Christ's encouragement to take on his yoke and learn from him is an invitation to peaceful purpose, partnering with God to trust that he is with us in our internal and external circumstances. We hear the prophets and Jesus rail against injustice and oppression of the poor and the marginalized. God calls us to do justice and love mercy, to help the poor, to give generously of our substance and our souls to those in need. And for those of us in need and exhausted, we can look to the Lord for wisdom and a strategy. Some of us need to not be too proud to seek and/or accept help from others. We may need to find people who will stand with us in our times of hardship, to help us heal, get divine strategies, and rise up to act. Whatever the source of exhaustion, anger, bitterness, or anxiety, recognize these feelings as red flags that something needs to change. Pray, ask, seek, knock, and take action. As Psalm 23:4 tells us, don't lie down in the valley of dark shadows, and do not be afraid of evil, but know that the Lord is with you to bring you through the hardest of places.

Ponder Jesus' words again, "Come to me . . . and I will give you rest. Take my yoke upon you and learn from me." He tells us that rest can come by taking on *his* yoke with him, a symbol of burden-bearing. The word *rest* means "to cause someone to gain relief from toil, . . . *cause to rest, give* (someone) *rest, refresh, revive.*"[14] Unrest can come from pushing or striving. Jesus doesn't tell us to quit or to stop trying—rather, he invites us to quit plowing through life alone, to yoke up with him and, importantly, to learn from him. To repeat his words, "for I am gentle and humble in heart, and you will find rest for your souls. For my yoke is easy and my burden is light." The

---

[13]Fredrick W. Danker et al., *A Greek-English Lexicon of the New Testament and Other Early Christian Literature* (Chicago: University of Chicago Press, 2000), 457.

[14]Danker et al., *Greek-English Lexicon of the New Testament*, 69.

words he uses to describe himself as gentle and humble pertain to "not being overly impressed by a sense of one's self-importance."[15] He wasn't trying to prove anything or impress anyone. He wasn't seeking acclaim, ascendency, or acceptance. He was neither filled with pride nor insecurity, so he did not exert effort to push himself in front of others or to hide from them. His soul was at peace. He was at rest within himself. He did not weary himself with striving, toil, or struggle and was not burdened with anxieties. Therefore, his yoke was easy, and his burden was light. We too can find rest when we're no longer striving to press, push, or pull to prove that we're more (or less) than we are.

Pride puffs out the chest at anyone who stands in the way of completing a goal or task and says, "Listen to me! Don't you know who I am!" Pride can cause us to care more about living up to an expectation (ours or illusions of others), or about receiving praise, admiration, and recognition from our peers, critics, or influential people. In this world's pressure pot, we can easily become focused on what others think rather than on what God thinks of us and the purposes for which he created us.

Insecurity shrinks away from conflict, opportunities, or challenges and sends an accusing inner voice that says, "Who do you think you are? Just shut up!" This prevents us from fulfilling our God-given abilities, aspirations, or purposes. How often have we made or heard excuses like, "But I'm not qualified; I'm not strong enough; I don't have enough experience, or training, or education; I'm too young, too old, too broken." When we focus on the perceived "not enough" in our self we lose sight of the "more than enough" of God at work in us and through us.

God is the one who qualifies us (Col 1:12), and his strength is demonstrated in our weakness (2 Cor 12:9). The only perfect person that God ever worked through was Jesus Christ of Nazareth. Yet, look at all God has done through each broken and flawed human being who simply said "Yes" to God. Our work is to simply follow him. When we fall, he helps us up and we continue our journey with him. This is the story of every prophet, and each of us who chooses to follow Christ.

The New Testament is filled with practical but seemingly contradictory advice that makes perfect sense within a life of faith. Here are some examples:

---

[15]Danker et al., *Greek-English Lexicon of the New Testament*, 861.

Help each other out and take responsibility for your own actions. Don't think too highly of yourself. Examine your own actions and be proud of what you accomplish without comparing or competing with someone else (Gal 6:2-5).

Don't worry about being insufficient in any situation but look to God for his grace and power to be at work in you and through you. Then you can boast and be glad when your weakness is showing in the midst of hardships, pressures, and difficulties because when you are trusting in God's strength, you become strong even in your weakness (2 Cor 12:9-10).

Don't think too highly of yourself but be realistic about your gifts and abilities. Realize that every person has their own talents and capacities. One is stronger in one area, and another is stronger in another area. Appreciate what each one has to offer and work together, because God has given each person special gifts and functions so that you can learn to serve together. Whatever aptitudes you have, use them boldly while you recognize and encourage the gifts that God has given others (Rom 12:3-8).

Jesus presents the most effective leadership as counterpower and points to the strength in humility. "The greatest among you will be your servant. For those who exalt themselves will be humbled, and those who humble themselves will be exalted" (Mt 23:11-12). And he set the ultimate example (Phil 2:6-11).

The New Testament clarifies simply that God's perspective of power is opposite to the world's political, financial, and religious power dynamics. From the biblical perspective, those with the greatest power and advantage are the servants of others, lifting up those with the least opportunity. The greatest strength comes from the deepest trust and dependency on God. Honor follows true humility. Our weakness can become the greatest strength through partnership with God as his wisdom and strength flow through us. We can work in rest, and rest in work. Freedom comes through faithful trust in God.

MY STORY: SELF-SUFFICIENCY AND FREEDOM

When I was a wife, mother, successful businesswoman, and in a leadership position in my church, I had confidence in who I was and in my accomplishments. You could call it pride, but I wouldn't have thought of that as a negative. My identity was grounded in my roles and the general sense of approval I got from where I fit in and what I had achieved. Still, I struggled because of my husband's deteriorating health and my past trauma. But then, one by one, each of my roles and achievements were pulled out from under me: my husband died; my son rebelled by dropping out of high school, moving away from home before he was seventeen; my businesses failed due to a trusted employee's betrayal; I pulled out of ministry and lost my home along with everything I had ever earned, invested in, or worked for. My identity was shattered. For a couple of months, I was homeless, and for a few years, all I earned went out to pay other people's health insurance claims since they had lost their coverage due to my business losses and betrayal. I traded or pawned most of my remaining belongings to provide for essential needs until there was nothing to spare and no reserves.

On one significant day during this time, I was at the grocery store counting the cash I had left to buy food. I had begun letting my appearance go and slumping in my stance. The weight of my shame hung over my shoulders. I was embarrassed by who I had become, and felt degraded by my vulnerability and lack of value to the world. Standing in the grocery aisle, I held two cans of soup in my hands, trying to decide which one to buy. The one I liked better was ten cents more, but I had to guard every penny and I couldn't decide what to do.

As I hovered over them, a silent voice interrupted my thoughts and asked abruptly, "Who are you?" I was startled, recognizing the voice of God the Father speaking to my heart. The voice came again, stronger, "Who are you?" I became instantly aware of my appearance and the bend in my self-perception. Then the voice lovingly commanded me, "Hold your head high! You're the daughter of the Most High King!" In that instant, my identity was reconfigured. In that moment, I knew that the titles and accomplishments of the past no longer mattered, and I became grounded in the truth that I am deeply loved and belong to the family of God. This became an unshakable core identity, deeper than any I had lost or would ever gain again. This identity no one can take from me, and only One could give to me. I straightened up, lifted my head, and began to reconfigure my life in light of my dignity and worth as God's beloved daughter.

Gradually, as I learned to live in this understanding, my confidence began to rebuild. I could be humbly honest about my losses without any sense of humiliation. I could be secure in knowing that I was not alone in the recovery and rebuilding of my life and circumstances. It's been a lengthy process and not an easy one. But it has been well worth it to get to know both God and my own true self better. Resilience, grit, and confidence have come because I know that I am not what I do but who I am: a beloved child of God. No matter how high or how low my life's circumstances bring me, my value is rooted in knowing God loved me first, always will, and is with me to help me through each challenge and opportunity if I only let him and do not insist on being the god of my own life. God is always present and available to guide me and give me his wisdom and peace when I humble myself to listen, receive his strength, and stand against the evil and darkness that attack my life and those around me. Confidence, humility, and inner freedom to trust in God gradually replace pride, insecurity, and the bondage of trying to be in control of my own image and little world. I have rest in Jesus Christ.

HUMAN RESPONSIBILITY AND AUTHORITY

The possession of great power necessarily implies great responsibility.

William Lamb (and Spider-Man)

Man's coexistence with God determines the course of history.

Abraham Joshua Heschel

THE CRUX OF THE HISTORY OF THE WORLD is centered on what humanity does with the power God gave us in creation. Humans drop the ball on responsibility in a couple of different ways. One way is to believe in God but live as if there is no God and as if we will never be held accountable for our self-determined actions. A second way is to believe that everything that happens is God's will and therefore succumb to the whims of power, as if God ordained even the most heinous evils. From the opening of the Bible to the last chapters, humanity is mandated to listen to the Lord, to know his word, and to gather the courage to carry out his will in the earth. The question for each of us is whether we will use our God-given responsibility and authority to extend God's goodness and harmony wherever we have influence, or whether we will either capitulate to evil as if it's God, or seek to expand human sovereignty to our ultimate demise.

From a biblical perspective, the only good thing we can do is to carry out God's purposes, and the only way God's purposes are fulfilled is through our cooperation with God and his will. Biblically, everything else is evil. Jesus said, "No one is good—except God alone" (see Mk 10:18;

Mt 19:17; Lk 18:18-19). Therefore, the only way we can *be* good, and the only thing we can *do* that is good is by doing what God is doing, that is, to do God's will. Humanity's responsibility and divine authorization as God's image-bearers and governors of the cosmos are to seek God and act so that his kingdom is realized in our circumstances: "Your kingdom come, your will be done, on earth as it is in heaven" (Mt 6:10). This prayer Jesus taught informs us that when we respond in obedience and faithful loyalty to God's will as decreed in heaven, the authority of heaven backs our words and actions, empowering God's will to be done on earth. The richest description of what it means to be a human being is most beautifully developed from a biblical and ancient Near Eastern understanding of being created in the image of God.

IMAGE FROM GENESIS: HUMANITY MADE IN GOD'S IMAGE

The concept of humanity's vital role of taking responsibility and authority for what happens on this earth is rooted in being created in God's image and likeness:

> Then God said, "Let us make humanity in our image, according to our likeness, so that they may rule over the fish in the sea and the birds in the sky, over the animals and over all the earth, and over all the creatures that move upon the earth."
>
> So God created humanity in his own image,
> in the image of God he created them;
> male and female he created them.
>
> And God blessed them and God said to them, "Be fruitful and multiply and fill the earth and subdue it. Rule over the fish in the sea and the birds in the sky and over every living creature that moves upon the earth." (Gen 1:26-28, my translation)[1]

Thousands of pages have been written about the *imago Dei*, the image of God.[2] Ancient listeners and readers of these words understood their Hebrew (Semitic) associations and related ancient context, which became obscured

---

[1]See also Gen 5:1-2; 9:5-7.

[2]Summaries of the concept of the image of God, including various interpretations and further resources on the history of interpretation, can be found in Claus Westermann, *Genesis 1–22*, trans. John J. Scullion, Continental Commentaries (Minneapolis: Augsburg, 1984), 147-55; Catherine L. McDowell, *The Image of God in the Garden of Eden: The Creation of Humankind in Genesis 2:5–3:24 in Light of the Mīs Pî, Pīt Pî, and Wpt-r Rituals of Mesopotamia*, Siphrut: Literature and Theology of the Hebrew Scriptures (Winona Lake, IN: Eisenbrauns, 2015), 117-77; Jon Levenson, *Creation and the Persistence of Evil: The Jewish Drama of Divine Omnipotence* (San Francisco: Harper & Row, 1988), 111-20.

by modern Eurocentric philosophical ideas. Reengagement with archaeology in ancient Israelite and Near Eastern sites has brought profound insights into the meaning and implications of the image of God.[3]

In ancient Mesopotamia and Egypt, kings and governors had statues of
themselves erected at the entrance of walled cities and in the lands where
they ruled. For example, many have seen pictures of the huge statues of
Ramses II at key locations, such as in Memphis, which is the ancient capital
of Aneb-Hetch of Lower Egypt, and at Abu Simbel near Aswan, Egypt, along
the Nile River. Statues of kings and governors were often accompanied by
inscriptions that read something like this: "Wherever you see the statue of
this king (or this governor) the laws of this ruler must be respected and
upheld by all; the way you treat this image is the way you treat the ruler of
this land; anyone defacing this image will be defaced; anyone destroying this
image will be destroyed!"

The classic example is the bilingual inscription that includes a list of
curses brought down on anyone vandalizing or destroying the statue that is
the "image" and "likeness" of the Assyrian ruler Had-yit'î found at Tell
Fakharieh.[4] In biblical terms, considering the prohibition against idols and
carved images in the Ten Commandments, *humanity* is God's "statue"—the
image of God. The Hebrew text of Genesis 1:26 informs us that humankind
was created in God's own image *for the purpose of* ruling the physical universe as God's coregent.[5] Humankind was created as the embodied

---

[3]W. Randall Garr, *In His Own Image and Likeness: Humanity, Divinity, and Monotheism* (Boston: Brill, 2003), 95-176, 219, 222; McDowell, *The Image of God in the Garden of Eden*. See also Jon Levenson, *Creation and the Persistence of Evil: The Jewish Drama of Divine Omnipotence* (San Francisco: Harper & Row, 1988), 112-14. For an excellent discussion on the image of God, see Richard E. Averbeck, "Wisdom from the Old Testament," in *Why the Church Needs Bioethics: A Guide to Wise Engagement with Life's Challenges*, ed. John F. Kilner (Grand Rapids, MI: Zondervan, 2011), 34-36.

[4]W. Randall Garr, "'Image' and 'Likeness' in the Inscription from Tell Fakharieh," *Israel Exploration Journal* 50, no. 3 (2000): 230. See also A. R. Millard and P. Bordriiul, "A Statue from Syria with Assyrian and Aramaic Inscriptions," *Biblical Archaeologist* 45, no. 3 (1982): 135.

[5]Daniel E. Fleming, "Religion," in *Dictionary of the Old Testament: Pentateuch*, ed. T. Desmond Alexander and David W. Baker (Downers Grove, IL: InterVarsity Press, 2002), 119; Averbeck, "Wisdom from the Old Testament," 134. (The *weyiqtol*, or, simple *waw* on a jussive, often implies purpose or result.) See also Arnold, *Genesis*, 45n67: "On the basis of numerous parallels from both Egypt and Mesopotamia, it has become clear that the phrase is related to royal language, in which a king or pharaoh is the 'image of (a) god.' Thus humans are created to function as the divine image through the exercise of 'dominion' and 'rule,' which of course is reinforced by the statement 'and let them have dominion over' (v. 26). This statement in v. 26 should be interpreted

representative of God and his ways in the physical world. The opening chapter of Genesis makes clear that all of humanity, male and female, is God's image, and if someone mistreats any one of God's "statues" (his image), God takes it personally!

Randall Garr provides linguistic and literary depth to this passage by examining the texts from the ancient Near East. Humanity was put on earth to represent God's rule, his kingdom, and his form of government in the earth. As sovereign corulers with God, we are responsible for carrying out God's justice and sovereign will.[6] In this sense, he explains, humans are a "theophany" created for "a special binding relationship" with God.[7] Catherine McDowell further explains that humans are appointed by God to act on his behalf, obeying and adjudicating his laws and justice.[8]

Just as kings in the ancient Near East set up statues along the boundaries of their land to show the extent of their domain, God set humanity as living statues to move freely throughout his creation, made to represent his government and maintain his intended order and harmony.[9] Genesis 1:26-27 tells us that humans, male and female, were meant to exercise God's dominion over the earth.[10] Biblically, failing to carry out God's mission as his ambassadors is evil because it is contrary to the good purposes he intended in creation and relationship.

This contrasts significantly with other ancient stories of how humans came into being.[11] For example, common to the Sumerian story of *Enki and Ninmah*, the Mesopotamian *Epic of Gilgamesh*, the Babylonian *Enuma Elish*,

---

as a purpose clause, expressing the motivation behind God's creation of humans in his image: 'in order that they may have dominion over.'"—that is, the imperfect of *radah* with waw conjunctive to connote purpose; see B. T. Arnold and J. H. Choi, *A Guide to Biblical Hebrew Syntax* (Cambridge: Cambridge University Press, 2003), 20. The image of God is about the exercise of rulership in the world. See also Moshe Zucker, ed., *Saadya's Commentary on Genesis* (New York: Jewish Theological Seminary of America, 1984), 257-58.

[6]Garr, *In His Own Image and Likeness*, 219. See Tell Fekheriye (alternate spelling) statue of Hadad-Yith'l, a local Syrian (Assyrian) king.

[7]Garr, *In His Own Image*, 222.

[8]McDowell, *Image of God in the Garden of Eden*, 122.

[9]Allen Ross, *Creation and Blessing: A Guide to the Study and Exposition of Genesis* (Grand Rapids, MI: Baker, 2009), 113.

[10]Christopher J. H. Wright, *Old Testament Ethics for the People of God* (Downers Grove, IL: IVP Academic, 2004), 119.

[11]For example, see Jon D. Levenson, *Creation and the Persistence of Evil: The Jewish Drama of Divine Omnipotence* (San Francisco: Harper & Row, 1988), 117.

and the Greek *Theogony*, humans were generally said to be made of clay (and sometimes an additional element, such as the blood of a god) by one or more of the gods during a bloody conflict between the gods. Their purpose was to do useful work for the gods that the gods did not want to do themselves. Humans were noisy, annoying, and expendable. Their value was in their ability to produce or entertain. Only kings or rulers were made in the image of the gods, and humans were their subjects on behalf of the gods.

However, in the creation narrative in Genesis 1–2, God created all humans as his own royal family, established us as responsible for shepherding the world, and gave us the authority to carry out his mission. Every human was family, royalty, and priest.[12] There was no conflict or war between competing gods. Humans were a forethought in creation, not an afterthought. That was and continues to be God's plan. People were to learn from God and to faithfully uphold his good rule in all realms of life, establishing peace and flourishing for every person and all creation. The stronger helped and served the weaker. God did not retract this creation mandate of responsible authoritative stewardship. It was not removed after the fall or after the flood, as shown by Genesis 5:1-2; 9:5-12.[13] After the flood, Genesis 9:6 states, "Whoever sheds human blood, by humans shall their blood be shed; for in the image of God has God made mankind." In other words, to strike another human is to strike at God.

All wrongs done to others God takes as a personal affront, and from God's perspective, this is evil, harmful, and deleterious to life. God holds each person accountable for the way we treat his creation, especially fellow human beings. In God's eyes, every human being has dignity and worth, and he expects us to share his perspective.

Further insight into humanity's value and purpose is described in Genesis 2:7, "Then the LORD God formed an earthling from the dust of the earth and breathed into his nostrils the breath of life, and the earthling became a living being."[14] John Walton points out that "throughout the ancient Near East, an image was believed to contain the essence of that which

---

[12]McDowell, *Image of God in the Garden of Eden*, 175.
[13]Eugene H. Merrill, "Image of God," in *Dictionary of the Old Testament: Pentateuch*, ed. T. Desmond Alexander and David W. Baker (Downers Grove, IL: InterVarsity Press, 2002), 444.
[14]This is my translation to capture the relationship between the Hebrew word *adam* (human, person) and *adamah* (earth, ground).

it represented. That essence equipped the image to carry out its function."[15] The purpose in recording the act of "breathing into" was to communicate the imparting of essence. For people living in ancient Egypt and Mesopotamia, the concept of putting a deity's essence inside of an inanimate object was common.

Through rituals, a statue, which was usually an image made of clay, wood, or stone, was filled with the essence of a god to empower and equip it to fulfill the functions for which it was made. Herbert Livingston records, "After an image was fashioned, it was put into service by means of a 'mouth-washing' ceremony. It was then alive. Daily they had to be washed, dressed, and perfumed with proper rites. Food and drink offerings had to be given to them; music and dancing had to amuse them."[16] In contrast, when Yahweh God breathed his breath of life into the nostrils of the *adam,* the human became a living being, filled with Yahweh's essence (Gen 2:7). God's plan was that whenever we look at another human being, we would understand that we are looking at God's image-bearer. No human being had less or more value than the other because we were all intended to be God's living representatives.

However, in ancient Egypt and Mesopotamia, the next step in the common *mīs pî pīt pî and wpt-r* ritual was "the opening of the eyes" ceremony. In this procedure, the statue or image *became a god*, endued with special powers of its own. This language can be heard in Genesis 3:5-7 when the serpent urges the humans to go beyond God's intention for them in order to become independent gods themselves: "Your eyes will be opened, and you will become like God [or, a god], knowing good and evil."

Every human being bears the image and likeness of God. But the desire in human hearts is to be gods, not like God: to be independent and in control without responsibility to God for our actions. The history of the world demonstrates that we as humans have not done well at being the masters of our own destiny. Nevertheless, God designed that his will be accomplished through humans willing to listen and act. This is reflected in Psalm 8:

---

[15]John H. Walton, "Genesis," in *Zondervan Illustrated Bible Backgrounds Commentary Volume 1: Genesis, Exodus, Leviticus, Numbers, Deuteronomy* (Grand Rapids, MI: Zondervan, 2009), 20.

[16]G. Herbert Livingston, *The Pentateuch and Its Cultural Environment* (Grand Rapids, MI: Baker, 1987), 109. For details on the "washing of the mouth" and "opening of the eyes" rituals see especially McDowell, *Image of God in the Garden of Eden*, 43-114.

What is mankind that you are mindful of them,
>   human beings that you care for them?
You have made them a little lower than the angels [Hebrew: *Elohim*/*elohim*]
>   and crowned them with glory and honor.
You made them rulers over the works of your hands;
>   you put everything under their feet. (Ps 8:4-6)

Although we have been crowned with glory and honor, when God is rejected, we commonly default to becoming subjects under the rulership of other human beings. We hope to find protection under the pseudo-power of another equally created human or we attempt to subject other equally created humans under our own power. Whether a person tries to rule over others or be ruled by a seemingly more powerful human, God's rule, wisdom, and instruction are rejected as a result. As Abraham Heschel observes, "It is the bitter irony of history that the common people who are devoid of power and are the prospective victims of its abuse, are the first to become the ally of him who accumulates power. Power is spectacular, while its end, the moral law, is inconspicuous."[17]

The temptation of autonomy tends to be too great for earthlings to resist. Knowledge is power. We all want to eat from the Tree of Knowledge in hopes that it will give us independent power and control, which we think will enable us to know what we need to know and do what we want to do without having to trust or rely on anyone else, especially God! Jewish philosopher Martin Buber expresses that in the Garden, "Man has . . . become 'like God,' in that now, like him, he 'knows' oppositeness; but he cannot, like God, rise superior to it."[18] When we are in situations where we feel out of control, we tend to behave in ways we wouldn't under other circumstances. We need but look around us at any moment and recognize that we as humans have not cared well for each other—all brothers and sisters by blood—and have neglected creation.

In sum, being created in God's image and likeness is primarily a physical matter, not in terms of looking like God in some physical way, but rather that we are physical beings who stand as God's mobile statues, so to speak, in a physical world. In fact, he originally placed us in the Garden of Eden

---

[17]Heschel, *Prophets*, 160.
[18]Martin Buber, *Good and Evil* (Upper Saddle River, NJ: Pearson, 1980), 92.

because it was meant to be our throne room—the Holy of Holies within his very good creation. And as his statues, our purpose is to stand for him, for his authority, and on behalf of his divine intentions amid the whole of creation. We are called to "rule" as coregents. This is our function. Our responsibility is to uphold God's goodness, justice, and creative design, and to do it well.[19] The creation narrative in Genesis 1:1–2:3 closes with God resting, not because he is tired, but because he completed the "very good" work of creation. As Heschel puts it, "God's role is not spectatorship but involvement. He and man meet mysteriously in the human deed."[20] Having appointed humanity, male and female, as his "royal stand-in," with "his transfer of power" to oversee the fulfillment of abundance and peace throughout the earth, God takes his royal repose.[21]

THE IMAGE OF GOD IN THE NEW TESTAMENT

This mysterious meeting between God and humanity continues in the New Testament. History is bloody. Millennia have passed with most people spitting in God's face by abusing their fellow human beings and demonstrating their failure to understand who they are meant to be and who God is. Yet, God never withdrew his creation mandate for humans to rule over his creation. From the earliest writings, we see that humans subjugated and killed those they considered weaker or less important or subjected themselves to the evils of others due to fear of reprisal or to apathy, while those who stood up to power were often silenced. This can be seen from the writings of the Prophets in the Old Testament to the life of Martin Luther King Jr. May there be many more who arise today who refuse be silent. The New Testament continues the hope and voice of the prophets in the Old Testament calling for oppression to cease and for justice for every human being.

Jesus spoke of the standard raised by the prophets who expressed God's anger at the cruelty and evil humanity imposed on itself. As Heschel puts it, "To us a single act of injustice—cheating in business, exploitation of

---

[19]Richard E. Averbeck, "Having a Baby the New-Fashioned Way: An Old Testament Perspective" (Trinity Evangelical Divinity School, Deerfield, IL, April 21, 2009), 19.
[20]Heschel, *Prophets*, 13.
[21]Levenson, *Creation and the Persistence of Evil*, 116-117. See also Ps 89.

the poor—is slight; to the prophets, a disaster. To us, injustice is injurious to the welfare of the people; to the prophets, it's a deathblow to existence; to us, an episode; to them, a catastrophe, a threat to the world."[22] Jesus expresses God's grief mingled with his anger toward the callousness of those entrenched in religious, political, and monetary systems that exploit the poor and the powerless. He flips tables, confronts their leaders, and rails against those who try to kill him for his compassion, especially for the marginalized.

In every instance recorded in the four Gospels, when someone came to Jesus for help, healing, or deliverance, he never turned them away. He always met their needs. Jesus never looked down on anyone except to reach out his hand to lift them up. Even on the night he was betrayed to be crucified, he took on the role of the lowest slave in any household and washed the dirty, dusty feet of his disciples, teaching his disciples that he set the standard for them and all who will follow him. They were not to be like those who lord their power over others and live to be served, but they were to follow his example as he came to serve and to give his life as payment for the legal death sentence decreed for treason against God. So are we to lay down our lives for others (Jn 13:12-17; Mt 20:25; Mk 10:42). Jesus is the good Shepherd and looking at him we see God's will spoken and enacted (Jn 12:45; 14:9; 1:17).

He is described as "the image of the invisible God, the firstborn [or pre-eminent one] over all creation. For in him all things were created: things in heaven and on earth, visible and invisible, whether thrones or powers or rulers or authorities; all things have been created through him and for him" (Col 1:15-16; also 2 Cor 4:4; Heb 1:1-3). This Jesus, who makes God fully known by his presence and his actions, affirms that God takes personally the way we treat every person, and that we will be judged by our compassion (Mt 25:31-45).

No matter how kind we may be on any given day, we have all marred and neglected someone who looked to us for kindness, protection, or provision. In this sense, we are all complicit. Along the chain reactions of life, whether quick fashion that enslaves, pornography that traffics, comfort and culinary choices that destroy, or politics that kill, we have all participated in systems

---

[22]Heschel, *Prophets*, 4.

that exploit and take lives. For God the Father, and for Jesus, every exploitation is a disaster—a blow to his face, his body, and his heart.

No matter how good a person's words may sound, or how virtuous their actions may appear, there are ultimately only two kingdoms and only two wills that matter: God's versus anyone else's. Jesus expressed it this way: "Not everyone who says to me, 'Lord, Lord,' will enter the kingdom of heaven, but only the one who does the will of my Father who is in heaven. Many will say to me on that day, 'Lord, Lord, did we not prophesy in your name and in your name drive out demons and in your name perform many miracles?' Then I will tell them plainly, 'I never knew you. Away from me, you evildoers!'" (Mt 7:21-23). Jesus himself set the example for human expectations in his earthly life, telling us that he does nothing from his own will, but only does what he sees and hears God the Father doing. He showed that he always does what pleases God when he declared, "For I have come down from heaven not to do my will but to do the will of him who sent me" (Jn 6:38; cf. Jn 5:30; 8:28-29). Further, "'My food,' said Jesus, 'is to do the will of him who sent me and to finish his work'" (Jn 4:34).

When we align ourselves with God's kingdom and God's will, the goodness and justice of heaven flow to earth. This does not mean that there is no opposition or that the work is easy. This is evident in Jesus' life as well. The night before his crucifixion, in the Garden of Gethsemane, he fell on his face and prayed, saying, "My Father, if it is possible, may this cup be taken from me. Yet not as I will, but as you will" (Mt 26:39). The mission of obedience was not just for Jesus. For he told his followers that "As the Father has sent me, I am sending you" (Jn 20:21). We can have the same confidence Jesus had that God hears our prayers. As his beloved disciple John said, "This is the confidence we have in approaching God: that if we ask anything according to his will, he hears us. And if we know that he hears us—whatever we ask—we know that we have what we asked of him" (1 Jn 5:14-15).

When these passages and ideas first came to me, they sounded too big, too impossible. But that's because we're used to thinking small in terms of our own capacity, abilities, and will. When the LORD told Sarah, Abraham's wife, that she would have a baby in her old age, he asked her "Is anything too hard for the LORD?" (Gen 18:14). Or as the angel said to Mary when she was told she would give birth to the Son of God, "No word from God will lack the capacity to complete it" (Lk 1:37, my translation). When we take on the yoke of life with Jesus, we are partnering with God to accomplish his good will and purposes.

FROM MY STORY: TRANSFORMATION

In summer 2008, after years, decades, of being run over, backed up, run over, backed up, repeat, I had developed a defeatist attitude toward the struggles and traumas in my life. I didn't want to live but I didn't want to take my life either. I was the poster child of theological and personal lethargy toward evil. My husband, Walt, had succumbed to his illnesses five years earlier, and I knew how cruel suicide was, leaving those left behind to slowly dig through the shrapnel of pain and guilt. I didn't want to talk about the pain I had experienced, and I didn't consider doing so a necessity, since I simply accepted it as the inescapable fact of my life. What was there to talk about? From an early age I found that if I put on a smile, people were less likely to ask personal questions for which I had no answers or the desire to process. Covering the pain with a smile-mask also kept them from avoiding me, so I didn't feel like a pariah either. I could mingle and be around people, remaining relatively invisible without being totally isolated. Conceptually, I developed what I came to call a "Whack-A-Mole" theology.[23] It seemed to me that every time I ventured to rise up or try something new, something would always go wrong and knock me down. For example, while I was beginning my second year of a master's program in seminary, my husband died and life continued to fall apart.

After what seemed like a lifetime of things going wrong no matter how hard I tried, I blamed all the problems on God but was not willing to throw away my belief in God. My mantra had become, "The Lord gives, the Lord takes away, blessed be the name of the Lord," which sounds pious but was simply a religious cry of unresolved pain. An overwhelming sense of repeated losses led to passive acceptance of

---

[23]"Whack-A-Mole" is a carnival game that contains holes in a plastic board through which little plastic moles pop up their heads. The participant's job is to hold a hammer and knock each one back down into their hole every time they pop up.

hardship as the normative way of life. I didn't consider any options but to curl up and brace myself for the next set of punches when they came around again.

Then, I got the urge to visit an old friend named Gayle that I hadn't seen in years. I heard that her husband had recently died and thought it would be good for us to reconnect. She was one of those people known for her bluntness and lack of filter, which can be either intimidating or refreshing. As we sat in her living room sharing stories, she suddenly interrupted me, looked intently into my eyes, and shot out two rapid-fire questions: "What's happened to you? Do you believe that everything that happens is God's will?" Taken aback, I stumbled for words and then stammered out, "Yes, I do." She shot back definitively, "I do not!" Her words hit me with the force of a firmly planted wallop across my face, or perhaps defibrillation, or a bucket of ice water dumped over my head. It was as if her words woke me out of a deep slumber. In that instant, I knew I had to change my passive acceptance of the hardships in my life and the view of both my role and God's role in the operation of evil.

Importantly, for starters, I got mad. The good mad of waking up and realizing I had been robbed and that something positive could be done about it. Clinical psychologist and holocaust survivor Edith Eger writes, "There's no forgiveness without rage."[24] I understand that now. Sometimes moving forward begins with anger that shakes us out of the negativity of victimhood. The burst of realization rose from deep within that there was something I could have done to stop much of the wrong in my life, and for the wrong I could not stop, there was much I could do in the aftermath to change its impact.

That moment transformed me from a beaten dog to a warrior with a mission. I was determined that the spiritual forces of darkness would regret ever laying a hand on me and those I love. Every evil deed done to me and every harm that I participated in actively, ignorantly, or passively, would be turned around and used for good in my life and in the lives of those affected by them. I would become a relentless force

---

[24]Edith Eva Eger, *The Gift: 14 Lessons to Save Your Life* (New York: Scribner, 2020), 201.

for goodness, justice, and transformative love. I began to join in The Lord's Prayer, which begins, in my own words, "May God's kingdom come and God's ways be accomplished here on earth through me as he purposes and directs from his heavenly realm" (Mt 6:9-10). My primary job became to understand the good plans intended by God in heaven and to bring them to pass on earth.

The process of conquering my fears and finding my voice in obedience to God's will and Word has been far slower and more challenging than I imagined, yet worth every effort. I stopped wanting to escape and die. I understand the words of rabbi Tzvi Freeman, "By transforming who we are today, we rewrite our own past and author a whole new world."[25] There is so much to live for, so much to see, and so many opportunities to bring change, healing, and joy. In Edith Eger's book *The Gift*, she writes, "As an Auschwitz survivor, I am here to tell you that the worst prison is not the one the Nazis put me in. The worst prison is the one I built for myself."[26] Although we do not forget our sufferings, we can find release from the bondage of the evils and traumas we experience to live full, enriched lives. I see myself as a child of the resurrection: life can emerge from death and ashes.

God never withdrew the role he assigned to humanity, but we have abused our authority and legally given it away. Blaming God or anyone else does not negate our God-given charge. The responsibility to make choices and the power to carry them out is part of what makes people human, created in the image of God—distinct from all other creatures. God knew that humans would fail in our assignment. God knew before creation that human beings would not represent him well or use our God-given power rightly. He knew that humanity would need someone to show us how to do this—someone to help us carry out God's plan. God knew that people would make a royal mess of things; a mess so huge that only God in his own person and power could solve it. Even before humanity's first big mess, God knew that his provision for redeeming humankind would be *himself*, embodied and bloodied, resurrected and ascended, in the person of Jesus.

---

[25]Tzvi Freeman, "Editing the Past," *Daily Dose of Wisdom* (blog), accessed February 16, 2023, www.chabad.org/library/article_cdo/aid/985005/jewish/Editing-the-Past.htm.
[26]Eger, *Gift*, 3.

Chapter Nine

HUMAN FREEDOM AND THE PATH TO RESTORE THE WORLD

God's supremacy over the universe is inseparably
bound up with the lordship of man.

G. B. CAIRD

WHY WOULD A GOOD GOD CREATE a world in which humans can make choices that could corrupt goodness and destroy the cosmos? Since the Bible sets boundaries, many people see God as a killjoy: "Don't do that!" "Don't touch that!" How are we to think about laws and rules? Religions as well as governmental systems have laws about what people can and can't do. These are both appreciated and resented. We resist what we think will be a "no" to what we want, and we begrudge what we perceive as limits to our liberty. We want to be in charge of our own lives and choose what we will or won't obey.

This brings us to a fundamental misunderstanding about freedom. As clinical psychologist Edith Eger notes, "The foundation of freedom is the power to choose."[1] Or as Michael Heiser states, "evil is the perversion of God's good gift of free will."[2] Sometimes when we're doing what we think we're not supposed to do, it feels like we're doing what we want to do.[3] That

---

[1] Edith Eva Eger, *The Gift: 14 Lessons to Save Your Life* (New York: Scribner, 2020), 3.
[2] Michael S. Heiser, *The Unseen Realm: Recovering the Supernatural Worldview of the Bible* (Bellingham, WA: Lexham, 2015), 66.
[3] Wording extracted from Esther Perel, "Rethinking Infidelity . . . a Talk for Anyone Who Has Ever Loved," TED Talk, 2015, www.ted.com/talks/esther_perel_rethinking_infidelity_a_talk_for _anyone_who_has_ever_loved.

feels like freedom, but often that's only a trap. The word *freedom* comes from Middle English and principally meant *generosity* or *benevolence*. This is opposite to what people in current Western culture associate with freedom. "When we say of someone that he 'loves freedom,'" literary scholar David Jeffrey points out, "we mean personal liberty, autonomy, independence. The modern understanding is largely self-directed, the older one largely other-directed."[4] The original concept of freedom was *other-directed*.

The current Western concept of freedom is focused on personal wants, needs, and unrestrained feelings. A world filled with largely self-satisfaction-seeking earthlings creates chaos and compounds harm to others. It can never produce a peaceable society. Choosing what is good for the one that is also good for the other is the concept of loving your neighbor as yourself. Love of God, love of others, and love of self is intended to be mutually compatible, and the only possible way of living in harmony.[5]

Furthermore, when someone is truly free, no one can take it from them. There arises from within an overflow of presence and power that works to set others free from their personal and situational bondages. True freedom rejoices in seeing others whole. Freedom does not grab for power—it releases it to empower others. Freedom produces an unrestrained joy of internal peace no matter what the external circumstances and provides the fortitude to persist in seeking to set free those who are captives to personal bondage or systemic oppression. Freedom brings the wisdom to do what is good not solely for self-centered purposes but for the good of all creation. Obedience to God is not legalism or bondage. It is the loving response to Love that wants us to live a life of unrestrained joy in communion with Love himself and all his creation. To want freedom simply to fulfill one's own needs or desires at the expense of others makes self the consumer and the other a commodity. This is evil.

IMAGE FROM GENESIS: THE TWO TREES
IN THE MIDDLE OF THE GARDEN

The two trees in the Garden of Eden represent our two choices—reliance on God or reliance on ourselves. In other words, we make the choice of who we

---

[4]David Jeffrey, "Prejudice and Pride: Classical Education and the Modern Scholar," *Christianity and Literature* 27, no. 2 (1978): 55.
[5]See the two great commandments (Mt 22:36-40; Deut 6:5; Lev 19:18).

will trust the most in our life and, therefore, whose words we will follow: God's words or human ideas. Put more succinctly, who will be the true God in our life, God or self?

In the Garden, God immediately gave clear instructions regarding the scope of authority and responsibility of his appointed representatives (Gen 2:16-17). There is no lack of clarity that God's will is for his creatures to choose abundance and life, and not autonomy and death. As Brevard Childs points out, "God has expressed his will from the beginning. . . . For the writer of Genesis 2, to be human consists in living in freedom, within a community, and under the divine imperative."[6] That's pretty clear. Live as sons and daughters of the Most High King; serve and protect the place God has given you; enjoy the Tree of Life and all the trees of the Garden (that's choice *a*). Do not try to be God and make your own rules (that's choice *b*). God is God. You are not God. Humility is required for living in peace with each other in the cosmos. If we choose to go against God and God's instructions for living in this world he gave us, we will experience relational and physical conflict and death. Biblically, choice *a* is good; choice *b* is evil. Choose *a*. God, being love, quite literally offers us the world. Love is other-directed. It does not grasp but gives the other, even a created other, the freedom to stay or to leave.

God Is Not an Abuser, and We Should Not Be Either

Back to our earlier question: *Why would a good God create a world in which we could make choices that lead to so much pain, suffering, and evil?* There are many responses to this problem. Most simply, however, God is not an abuser and never wanted us to be either.

According to my research, abuse can be defined as *patterns of behavior aimed at gaining power and control over another person.* The tools of this coercive control are mainly manipulation, intimidation, and domination.[7]

---

[6]Brevard S. Childs, *Old Testament Theology in a Canonical Context* (Philadelphia: Fortress, 1990), 51.
[7]My definition is derived especially from the National Domestic Violence Hotline, www .thehotline.org/is-this-abuse/abuse-defined/. See also Evan Stark, *Coercive Control: How Men Entrap Women in Personal Life* (Oxford: Oxford University Press, 2009), and Andrea Mathews, "When Is It Emotional Abuse? How to Differentiate Between What Is Emotionally Abusive, and What Isn't," *Psychology Today*, September 26, 2016, www.psychologytoday.com/us/blog /traversing-the-inner-terrain/201609/when-is-it-emotional-abuse.

Abusers restrict or deny the freedom of another person. The history of the world is largely the record of what humankind does with power.[8] The most common complaint against God in relation to the problem of evil is that an all-powerful God would allow evil and suffering in a world of humans he created with the freedom of choice. But as Heschel observes,

> Why were so few voices raised in the ancient world in protest against the ruthlessness of man? Why are human beings so obsequious, ready to kill and ready to die at the call of kings and chieftains? Perhaps it is because they worship might, venerate those who command might, and are convinced that it is by force that man prevails. The splendor and the pride of kings blind the people.[9]

And I ask, Why do so few voices in the modern world protest against human ruthlessness and oppression? Not only did the prophets raise this question, but the leaders of the civil rights movement were reading Abraham Heschel also, and his writings helped provide words for the injustice, racism, and antihumanism experienced by many in that era. Our capacity for goodness rivals our capacity to inflict harm. We see the depths of evil and suffering we impose on others by our freely made choices and yet, evil and suffering malignantly grow. As the lyrics of a song from Matthew West express, we sit back and shake our fists at heaven and ask, "Why don't you do something about this!"[10] Whereas God responds, "I did do something! I created you and gave you the capacity to recognize evil and the ability to take action to prevent it, heal the damage, and do good!" Evil persists primarily because "good" people look the other way when our assignment from the beginning is to square up to it and say, "Not on my watch!" Abuse and oppression are a violation of God's express will and character.

God will not use his power to manipulate us to love him or to choose to do good. God will not intimidate us to do his commands, not even the ones to enjoy and be thankful. God will not dominate, force, or coerce us to take responsibility and authority to bring peace and repair the world. God gives us the liberty every day to choose good or evil, life or death, blessing or curse.

---

[8]Abraham Joshua Heschel, *The Prophets*, vol. 1 (Peabody, MA: Hendrickson, 2017), 170.
[9]Heschel, *Prophets*, 170.
[10]This is the message of the song by Matthew West, "Do Something," www.youtube.com/watch?v=0IP4FWEJJmU.

But we tend toward doing what seems best in our own eyes to satisfy our personal needs and desires. The world now has billions of unyielding little gods. Therefore, chaos and evil proliferate.

Heiser put this succinctly: "Evil is the perversion of God's good gift of free will."[11] We often decide what we like based on impulse and take what we want without consideration of the impact of our actions on others. When we reject the call to be stewards of creation and our fellow human beings, dominion is replaced with domination, invitation with intimidation, and merciful patience with manipulation. I'm included in the "we," but we can choose differently.

The divisive state of the world during the pandemic demonstrated how quickly we're ready to throw the first stone and forfeit relationship for our right to be right. We easily gravitate toward being the judges and moral executioners of our neighbors, our family members, and anyone else who doesn't agree with our opinions or decisions. We assume our sources and opinions are right and those who disagree with us are wrong. But according to Genesis 1–2, every human being is family—kin with one another and with God. How quickly we become like Cain and Abel; verbally, emotionally, financially, spiritually, and sometimes literally attacking and killing our brothers and sisters. However, this is not what God wants. We shouldn't think that "whatever happens below reflects the will of God above."[12]

THE PATH TO RESTORE THE WORLD: OUR ROLE

Abraham Heschel notes,

> Above all, the prophets remind us of the moral state of a people: Few are guilty, but all are responsible. If we admit that the individual is in some measure conditioned or affected by the spirit of society, an individual's crime discloses society's corruption. In a community not indifferent to suffering, uncompromisingly impatient with cruelty and falsehood, continually concerned for God and every man, crime would be infrequent rather than common.[13]

---

[11]Heiser, *Unseen Realm*, 66.
[12]Heschel, *Prophets*, 214.
[13]Heschel, *Prophets*, 16.

God's intended place for humanity in the physical universe has been drasti-
cally underestimated in light of our God-given responsibility and authority.[14]

Human identity as the image of God provides the understanding that a
major reason there is evil in the world is that humanity abdicates our God-
appointed responsibility and God-given authority to bring about and
maintain goodness, order, harmony, and justice. Each person has a role to
play in response to the prayer Jesus taught us, "Your Kingdom come, your
will be done, here on earth as you have willed in heaven." We are God's
agents to bring divine goodness whatever our circumstance. As John Stuart
Mill stated, "Bad men need nothing more to compass their ends, than that
good men should look on and do nothing."[15]

Perhaps it is hardest to accept that God gives humanity the freedom to
be cruel, hateful, and heartless. As Karen Baker-Fletcher wrote, "Evil is a
result of the freedom inherent of all creation. God did not create evil, but
God created all creation in freedom."[16] These evils destroy innocence,
kindness, and harmony. We witness the lack of humanity in those who
commit atrocities; these horrors cry out from every corner of the world
throughout history, from wars to back alleys, from migrant fields to bed-
rooms in our own homes and neighborhoods. The very earth is repulsed and
bears witness to the brutalities perpetuated against God and his creation.

But every time someone brings light into the darkness, that person is
participating in creation. Every time she turns chaos into order, she is participating in creation. Every time he engages in the process of transforming
his life from self-centered willfulness into loving kindness, he partakes in
the kingdom of God. Every time they choose to trust in the goodness of God
above the weight of their circumstances or wrongs, they participate in ushering in the new creation.

This is the great hope and vision of the prophets since humanity left the
Garden sanctuary. We long for the new Eden, a sanctuary. Eve hoped Cain
would be the one provided by Yahweh to fulfill his promise that her seed

---

[14]Humanity created in the "image" of God, as cited in Gen 1:26-28, was not lost in the biblical
narrative after the opening two chapters. The "image" and expectation of humanity to maintain
conduct befitting the image of God continues, as evidenced by Gen 5:3; 9:6.

[15]John Stuart Mill, "Inaugural Address" (speech, St. Andrews University, Scotland, 1867).

[16]Karen Baker-Fletcher, *Dancing with God: The Trinity from a Womanist Perspective* (St. Louis:
Chalice, 2006), 79.

would crush the serpent's head (Gen 4:1-2; 3:15). Lamech hoped Noah would be the one to deliver humanity from our burdensome toil and bring us rest (Gen 5:28-29). Abraham was called to spread God's blessings to the nations so that all could enter into the peace offered by God's covenant (Gen 12:1-3). God's mission has always been for all people and nations to be gathered back to God in order to find salvation and wholeness (Is 49:5-6).

BEGINNING OF THE PATH TO RESTORE THE WORLD: GOD'S ROLE

Since God gave humanity the responsibility and authority to rule the world, the only way God can restore the world is through that same humanity to whom dominion had originally been given. But no human on their own could do that. It had to be a divine human. It had to be God himself clothed in human flesh. Christ came as the ultimate image of God to "show us the Father" (Jn 14:8-14). Through our faith in following Jesus Christ, we become transformed into his image from one degree of glory to another degree of glory, as we cooperate with the Holy Spirit to renew our minds and learn to think differently through God's Word (2 Cor 3:17-18, 4:4-8; Rom 12:1-2).

Jesus fulfilled the Law—all the requirements of righteousness of the Law—by living in complete faith and oneness with God his entire life. As Michael Heiser once tweeted, "Every day in the life of Jesus the Messiah was an assault against the powers of darkness."[17] In successfully doing so, Jesus earned the title of the Second Adam: the human being who paid the legal debt for our rebellion against God. Jesus was the first and only human legally qualified to reverse the judgments held against us, keeping us in bondage. He therefore stands in the presence of God as our representative. As the perfect and flawless one, he laid down his life in exchange for all of humanity—his life for our life. Death had no legal claim on him, no list of complaints. Jesus rose from death and ascended back to heaven, seated in the position of authority above every power and principality in this age and in the one to come (Eph 1:18-23). All who look to him can declare to the powers of retribution: This one paid the price for my self-centeredness and wrongs. By this one, I stand pure and holy, no longer subject to the legal claims held against

---

[17]Michael S. Heiser. I have not been able to find this quote or date that he tweeted it, but he is credited with the statement (or very similar) as I recall it.

me, free to enter before the throne of grace any time, with clean hands and head held high, because of Jesus the Lord and Messiah.

Jesus not only showed us God in person, but he took on himself the entire mess that we made. He bore in his own body every blow that humanity has struck against God through the harming of other human beings (including ourselves) and every part of creation. Every wound inflicted on self or another he took on himself. God himself, coming in the person of Jesus, absorbed into his own body the entire fallout of humanity's cruelty, and paid the just price for our wrongs against God and one another. By taking all the hurts and pain of the world on himself, God absolves anyone who accepts the pardon he paid. God in the person of Jesus is the provision for humanity's fresh start. Every person who receives this incomprehensible grace becomes a new human being, forgiven and wiped clean before our maker (see Col 1:13-23; Heb 1:3-4; 2:1–3:1).

God then begins the process of restoring his image in each person. He resides inside each one who receives him, through his Holy Spirit. Divine Spirit dwelling in human spirit, empowering each one (Rom 12:1-3). Peace with God is restored. Peace with one another is made possible. The image of God can take shape within each life. Humans can take up the charge to be stewards and co-heirs with Jesus in this world—establishing justice and righteousness, and restoring lives, homes, communities, and cultures to wholeness (2 Cor 5:16-21).

FROM MY STORY: A PROCESS OF CHANGE

Once I realized that I had unknowingly participated in allowing hardships and traumas to drag me through the mud and ruin my life, I got the will to begin the process of change. The first step was changing my mind about how I saw myself and the things that had happened. While I was innocent and vulnerable regarding many of the wrongs foisted on me, I recognized that I had made a covert contract with dark forces. I believed that the constant barrage of attacks would stop if I simply cowered under them. This lie conditioned my thinking process from early childhood so that I would be afraid, and so that I would accept physical and emotional blows as an expected part of my life. The lies promised to make the pain subside if I submitted to the attacks, and I agreed to accept the hopelessness of my life as I had come to see it. But things never got better. I began to see that there was a malevolent being at work that had been lying to me before I had the capacity for logic or discernment. Thankfully, he was exposed. The pain got worse, but when I finally rose up and began to take my stand against the darkness, I no longer saw myself as a victim. I learned to doubt the lies, to believe that God loved me, and to fight so that each debilitating situation would turn into something good for myself and others.

This new pattern of thinking helped me come to believe that there are malevolent spiritual forces at work to deface all image-bearers of God. But God had sent Jesus Christ to destroy the works of the devil and to take authority over all powers of wickedness, and he had given me authority to fight evil by the power vested in me through what he accomplished by his spotless life, death, resurrection, and ascension. "The reason the Son of God appeared was to destroy the devil's work" (1 Jn 3:8). Even the wrongs that I had knowingly participated in were covered by the work of Jesus. I was forgiven, free, and empowered. I came to believe these words of Scripture: "Our struggle is not against flesh and blood, but against the rulers, against the authorities, against the powers of this dark world and against the spiritual forces of evil in the heavenly realms. Therefore, put on the full armor of God, so that when the day of evil comes, you may be able to stand your ground, and after you have done everything, to stand" (Eph 6:12-13). My declaration became, "Devil, you're going to regret ever laying a hand on me and those I love."

This does not mean I go about looking for evil, for my daily mission is to seek ways to love, help, and better care for people. I look for beauty and laughter, and I'm motivated by joy. I'm simply aware that there are natural, human, and spiritual forces at work that seek to steal, kill, and destroy what is good, lovely, pure, and peaceable. Jesus came so that you and I might have life, abundantly (Jn 10:10).

Through the suffering and evil of this world, we see our own complacency and complicity—though many do much, most do little.

May this be our commitment: "As much as I am able, I will be a voice and a power to bring harmony, goodness, justice, and rightness into the circumstances in which I find myself. Every day has purpose, meaning, and direction. Whether I'm working, resting, or playing, may I take up my responsibility and authority in every place and situation each day to be God's image-bearer—a representative ushering in the power of goodness for the well-being of all around me."

Part Four

UNSEEN CAUSES

SPIRITUAL FORCES AT WORK

Whether the global north likes to acknowledge it or not,
the Bible and modern witnesses testify to the presence
of unseen agents, some of which are evil.

ESTHER ACOLATSE

THE THOUGHT OF DEMONS OR DARK FORCES that we cannot see is too frightening for some and too absurd for others. Nevertheless, most of history and most people in the modern era recognize that both benevolent and malevolent spiritual beings inhabit our world. While angels and guardian angels are far more pleasant to think about, to have a more complete account of the problem of evil requires we consider the culpability of spiritual beings for evil. As Esther Acolatse, professor of pastoral theology and intercultural studies asserts, "Without a thoroughgoing scriptural account of the powers and the Spirit, our explanations of evil in this world will lack the texture that adequately accounts for the collusion of individual sociopolitical structures and otherworldly evil spiritual forces—and thus forms a comprehensive account."[1]

---

[1]Esther E. Acolatse, *Powers, Principalities, and the Spirit: Biblical Realism in Africa and the West* (Grand Rapids, MI: Eerdmans, 2018), 8.

Before the modern philosophical and scientific era, people believed that gods or other spiritual entities ruled the world and were responsible for agricultural successes or failures, weather patterns, fertility, and their personal well-being. Agents in the unseen realm or karma inflicted illnesses, caused drought or rain, and determined war or peace. In the ancient Near East, outside of the God of the Bible, gods needed to be appeased or pleased in order to grant a person's desired outcomes. However, the God whose personal name is Yahweh could not be manipulated or coerced, and likewise does not manipulate or coerce those who choose to serve him. While many moderns deny the possibility of hierarchies of nonhuman spiritual beings, the Bible speaks of powers, principalities, rulers, and authorities that influence the physical realm, including nations and our personal lives, when given entrance.

Chapter Ten

MALEVOLENT FORCES AND THE RISE OF THE SATAN

The seventy-two returned with joy and said, "Lord, even the demons submit to us in your name." He replied, "I saw Satan fall like lightning from heaven. I have given you authority to trample on snakes and scorpions and to overcome all the power of the enemy; nothing will harm you."

Luke 10:17-19

For many Westerners, the idea of an unseen spiritual realm seems uneducated or ridiculous. However, throughout recorded history until the Enlightenment, people believed in an unseen realm that drove the physical realm, from exerting influence over personal and family domains to all systems of earthly governance and even over the forces of nature and the elemental world. It is modern arrogance, or perhaps ignorance, to consider belief in the spiritual realm as primitive or less informed than modern concepts of science and causation. We begin the exploration of unseen forces that intend to harm humans by first looking at the concept of "an accuser" and the development of Satan. The primary targets for these ill-intentioned spiritual entities are human beings, due to our created purpose to represent God's governance of goodness and order in the world. However, I understand that unless people have experienced power encounters, they may be unwilling to consider the possibility of unseen spiritual forces. Therefore, let me begin with such an encounter from my life and family. This story poignantly illustrates the actions of nonhuman actors with evil intent to destroy the good that God intended for me and my family.

STORY FROM MY FAMILY: WHEN AN EVIL SPIRIT ENTERS

Although I've had many power encounters myself, I begin with a story as told to me from Walter T. Faro Sr., my late husband. Before I begin, let me tell you a little about Walt. According to the many tales and pictures from his brothers and friends, he was an extroverted, fun-loving boy and teen. He lived in the same house, with the same parents, until he enlisted in the army. He described his life as stable, happy, and filled with local adventures. He was one of the funniest people I ever met, and deeply caring. He and his four brothers generally looked after each other in their early years.

At age nineteen he enlisted for military service in Vietnam with a group of his buddies. He had been told that the draft would begin soon and if they enlisted, they could pick their branch and assignment. He experienced no abuse and remembered no traumas prior to his service in Vietnam. But when his platoon walked into his first firefight he froze when a bullet grazed his eyebrow and took out the face and the life of his friend next to him. He described to me that in that moment of terror, he heard a voice say, "I'm Sergeant Rock. Let me in and I'll protect you."

For the next twenty years, Sergeant Rock directed his life and at times gave him superhuman abilities, such as seeing in the dark and increased strength in combat. He, and later his psychologist at the VA, reasoned that it was simply a superego, an enhancement of his own psyche and abilities under the stress of hostility and conflict. This is one explanation. But the explanation he later learned includes the spiritual dimension's impact on the psyche. After becoming a Christian, Walt's new insight into the influence of the demonic realm on his mind helped him gain freedom from its power over him.

During those twenty years after Vietnam, the need for a continual adrenaline rush along with the voice of Sergeant Rock in his head pressed him to seek training in Shotokan Karate, a traditional martial art. After the war, he went on to study in Japan for several months each year and to successfully compete internationally. And eventually, "job" opportunities opened up for him: first with underground organizations in the U. S., and quickly thereafter with foreign governments around the world. Although he also had a normal work résumé, he would leave those jobs for weeks ("on vacation") or for months (between jobs), first as an assassin and then as a mercenary hired for various assignments, including to protect whatever or whoever needed protection, to participate in arms deals, and to train paramilitary terrorist or ambush teams. He worked in Colombia, Haiti, Asia, Africa, and the Middle East.

Along with these jobs grew his desire to die. The more dangerous the job and the better chance he had of getting killed, the more likely he was to take it. He told me, "The one to fear the most is the one who is not afraid to die." Walt became highly successful, and the demand for his skills increased in the underground market. But when he came home after each job, this voice—this dark presence—left him, and he was alone and afraid. He described walking into empty churches between jobs and shaking his fist at God, yelling, "Why did you do this to me!" Because, in his church growing up, he had been taught that everything that happens is God's will.

Walt told me many tragic stories of outrageous brutalities and moral wrongs that afflicted his conscience his whole life. The atrocious acts the soldiers were expected to commit for the US government, which were meant to terrorize the Vietnamese, lit his rage and fueled his trauma.

He was instructed to dismember the Viet Cong to demoralize them; he was commanded to kill one of his fellow soldiers who snored in his sleep and gave away their position; he was given hallucinogenic drugs meant to stimulate more violence among the soldiers; he was sprayed with Agent Orange, which was meant to defoliate the forests and land, and had devastating DNA–altering effects on humans;[1] he crawled in underground dirt tunnels as a "tunnel rat" to kill the men and boy warriors hiding there; he was ordered to kill women and children in a

---

[1] Walter Faro, "Agential Orange: Immortal Performatives and Writing in Ashes," *Postmodern Culture* 28, no. 2 (2018): www.pomoculture.org/2020/10/20/agential-orangeimmortal-performatives-and-writing-with-ashes/. See also "Agent Orange," Military Wikia, https://military.wikia.org/wiki/Agent_Orange; Richter, *Stewards of Eden*, 82-83.

village. . . . The images and voices never left him and haunted his waking dreams. Recent reporting has documented that barbaric events like the My Lai massacre and Tiger Force "are only the tip of a vast submerged history of atrocities in Vietnam."[2] But, Walt kept on living, and grieving.

At age forty, we met when he was the general manager of a tool and die shop that was one of my insurance clients. After he seemingly randomly told me a couple of stories from his life, he was surprised that I was not afraid of him. I could see his pain. After a few conversations, I shared with him some of my story, including my traumas and the reality of Jesus' saving love in my life. At that point, he laughed and walked out of the room.

But he recounted to me that when he was alone in his apartment that night, he challenged God, angry that he had met a Christian. Since he had been taught in his church that everything that happens is God's will, he hated God and wanted to hate me for believing in God. That night, he and God argued for six hours, or, as he describes, he yelled at God, and God answered him calmly but with greater authority. Neighbors in his apartment building later told me they knocked on his door that night, yelling at "the two of them" to shut up. They described hearing Walt yelling and then hearing a second voice that was loud and deep but completely calm. Over the phone the next day, and later many times in person, Walt described to me that before the six hours were up, God had explained to him that he had not done all those horrors to him in Vietnam or afterward. Rather, it was human will that committed all the evils. At the end of the six hours, Walt encountered the love of God in a dramatic and life-transforming way. He surrendered his life to the most powerful being in the universe, forgave God, and received God's forgiveness.

---

[2]Nick Turse, "The Vietnam War Crimes You Never Heard Of," *George Washington University, History News Network* (blog), 2017, https://historynewsnetwork.org/article/1802. "Military records demonstrate that the 'Tiger Force' atrocities are only the tip of a vast submerged history of atrocities in Vietnam." See also History.com editors, "My Lai Massacre," History.com, April 17, 2020, www.history.com/topics/vietnam-war/my-lai-massacre-1#:~:text=The%20My%20Lai%20massacre%20was,Lai%20on%20March%2016%2C%201968; Cody J. Foster, "Did America Commit War Crimes in Vietnam," *New York Times*, December 1, 2017, www.nytimes.com/2017/12/01/opinion/did-america-commit-war-crimes-in-vietnam.html.

For the first time in a couple of decades, he slept peacefully and wanted to live.

Walt also came to understand and believe that Sergeant Rock was not his alter ego but a demonic spirit that had come to destroy him and harm others through him until his own life gave out. This powerful demonic presence had kept him alive to do as much damage as possible. It continued to harass him for a while after he began seeking to follow Jesus Christ. He described leaving his home without Sergeant Rock for the first time, completely terrified because he felt unprotected, so he rushed back home. All his old tools and skills that used to give him "strength" left him feeling vulnerable. God as protector was an entirely different presence: a presence of powerful goodness and love. But this was foreign to Walt. He was accustomed to terror and intimidation, and was trying to learn a new kingdom.

Walt began a path to be, as he called it, "a good man," to follow Jesus Christ. He said only Jesus could forgive all the horrific things he had done. However, he was never able to forgive himself for one act in particular: taking the life of two women and three children in a village in Vietnam, even though it was a direct order, and he would have had to pay with his own life if he had disobeyed.[3] Nevertheless, he began a path toward inner peace and sought to be a man that both he and God would be proud of.

Tragically, a few years into his faith, malpractice by a dentist followed by complications from compounded medical conditions along with treatment of PTSD ground him down. During his years of continual, increasing physical pain, Sergeant Rock sought reentry into our lives and the life of our son, Walter Jr. My personal encounters with this evil entity were not pleasant. Once when I came home, Walt was sitting on the edge of the sofa facing the door. As I walked through the door, he lowered his head, glared at me, and in a low voice that was not his own, he growled loudly, "You're not welcome here! Get out!" Recognizing that this was not my husband, I

---

[3]See previous footnote about atrocities such as the My Lai massacre in Vietnam.

immediately said to the dark spirit, "No! *You're* not welcome here! *You* get out now!" Walt shook his head, looked quizzically at me for a moment, and said in his own voice, "Hi, did you just get home? How was your day?" I didn't tell Walt until days later what had happened. I was not afraid of the encounter, but I was angry at this entity's relentless audacity to seek every opportunity to regain entrance into our home through my husband's illness.

This was just one example of what some call "power encounters." An important thing I learned through that long season is how vital it is for us to become as mentally healthy and stable as possible, because the point of entry for evil is through our minds—our thoughts. When we are mentally healthy there is no place for lies and deception to take a foothold and wreak havoc in our lives and in the lives of those around us. Evil has no power over us except what we concede by opening our minds to lies about ourselves or others. If we listen to lying, deceiving, diminishing, frightening, angry, abusive, or cruel words that worm their way into our heads, we become captive to those malevolent thoughts or traumatic memories and act on them to our harm.

IMAGE FROM GENESIS: THE SERPENT

The agency of malevolent forces is first brought forward in Genesis through the imagery of the serpent (*nakhash*, Gen 3:1). In addition to action-consequence and the forces of nature that can inflict harm without evil intent, the Bible speaks of dark spiritual powers that act with sinister scheming. These are nonhuman beings that have the freedom to rebel against God and live in enmity against his representatives—humans made in God's image.

In Genesis 3, the serpent is placed in contrast with all the other land animals, as one who "had been (and still was) more shrewd than every animal of the field" (Gen 3:1).[4] This creature is also set apart from other animal life in that he speaks. Ancient Near Eastern research shows that the serpent was most typically understood as a "chaos creature," or a "disruptive free

---

[4]Zevit, *What Really Happened*, 162.

agent"—a composite being belonging to the spiritual realm.[5] Therefore, this creature is presented as an "interposer" from a different jurisdiction, entering to disrupt the relationship between Yahweh God and his human representatives.[6] The serpent immediately enters the scene in an adversarial role as the antagonist against God, with its own plans for humanity and God's world. For ancient Israelites, this narrative contained the language and imagery of a cosmic battle that would affect their personal lives and history.[7] Evil is not the absence of good, but the twisting of God's words to go in a direction that is different from the divine intention. The biblical understanding sees evil as corrupted goodness.

As Ziony Zevit observes, the serpent "would talk of trees, but would think of death."[8] He pushes the woman to judge the veracity of what God has spoken by objectifying both God and his words, talking about them in the third person, distancing God as an outsider.[9] Although the woman could see the tree, the serpent presses the woman to see the forbidden tree *differently*, in a new way: not as bad and to be avoided but rather to be desired.[10] By objectifying the content of God's words, he separates the words from their relationship with the speaker of the words, making it easier to manipulate the meaning of God's command. Indeed, this is the serpent's tactic, and the woman, in her naked naiveté, takes the bite, choosing to believe the serpent above her Creator. "On the surface, this seems like a simple, even silly rule," Old Testament scholar Sandra Richter points out,

---

[5]For a thorough discussion of the identity and role of the serpent in the text and in ancient Near Eastern literature, see John H. Walton and N. T. Wright, *The Lost World of Adam and Eve: Genesis 2–3 and the Human Origins Debate* (Downers Grove, IL: IVP Academic, 2015), 132-36; Todd L. Patterson, "The Righteous and Survival of the Seed: The Role of Plot in the Exegesis and Theology of Genesis" (PhD diss., Trinity Evangelical Divinity School, 2012), 140-53; Brevard S. Childs, *Myth and Reality in the Old Testament* (London: SCM Press, 1962), 49; Richard E. Averbeck, "Ancient Near Eastern Mythography as It Relates to Historiography in the Hebrew Bible: Genesis 3 and the Cosmic Battle," in *The Future of Biblical Archaeology: Reassessing Methodologies and Assumptions*, ed. A. R. Millard and James Karl Hoffmeier (Grand Rapids, MI: Eerdmans, 2004), 343-53; R. W. L. Moberly, "Did the Serpent Get It Right?," *Journal of Theological Studies* 19, no. 1 (1988): 24.

[6]See Hugh C. White, "Direct and Third Person Discourse in the Narrative of the 'Fall,'" *Semeia* 18 (1980): 96-98.

[7]Averbeck, "Ancient Near Eastern Mythography," 344, 347, 352.

[8]Zevit, *What Really Happened*, 166.

[9]Zevit, *What Really Happened*, 166.

[10]Faro, *Evil in Genesis*, 111-14.

"But in reality, this one edict encompasses the singular law of Eden—God is God and we are not."[11]

The serpent tells the woman, "If you eat from [the forbidden tree] your eyes will be open and you will be like God" (Gen 3:4, 7). The phrase *opening the eyes* had a particular meaning in the rituals of idol making in ancient Egypt and Mesopotamia: "[It] is the moment at which the image becomes a god."[12] This provides us with the man and the woman's underlying motive. They didn't just want to try some new fruit or to be smarter or wiser than they already were. They wanted to be gods! They would be their own boss and no longer serve or obey someone else, or so they must have thought. What they didn't realize, however, was that in obeying the serpent they would become an underlord to a new master who was leading them to their own demise and the demise of the goodness of creation. Going against God's one prohibition would not bring them freedom, for "you are slaves of the one you obey" (Rom 6:16). They simply changed their loyalty from the LORD God to the lord of chaos and lies.

The choice to flatly disobey Yahweh God's command was legal and governmental. It was an act of treason that turned the earth into a conflict zone by establishing two kingdoms: the kingdom of God and the alternate kingdom against God. Nonhuman adversarial agents were at work to destroy the harmony and good that God intended. As Richter describes, "God's perfect plan (and humanity's perfect world) was a matter of choice. Did *'Ādām* want this world? Or one of their own making? The ones made in the image of God could not be forced or coerced, but instead were called upon to choose their sovereign. And choose they did."[13]

Malevolent forces introduced in the rest of the Old Testament are present, but, especially to the modern reader, they are lurking in the shadows of the Old Testament texts. The concept and identity of a "Satan" (as we will soon see) is developed throughout the Hebrew Bible, built during the Second Temple period, and comes into full exposure in the New Testament when the light of the world enters in the person of Jesus Christ. Christ as the Word

---

[11]Sandra L. Richter, *The Epic of Eden: A Christian Entry into the Old Testament* (Downers Grove, IL: IVP Academic, 2008), 92.

[12]Catherine L. McDowell, *The Image of God in the Garden of Eden: The Creation of Humankind in Genesis 2:5–3:24 in Light of the Mīs Pî, Pīt Pî, and Wpt-r Rituals of Mesopotamia*, Siphrut: Literature and Theology of the Hebrew Scriptures (Winona Lake, IN: Eisenbrauns, 2015), 7, 169.

[13]Richter, *Epic of Eden*, 106.

becomes fully visible, illuminating the conflict clearly, and vanquishes the ancient authorities and spiritual powers of darkness.[14]

Satan in the Old Testament?

Many scholars have said there is no Satan in the Old Testament, mainly because Satan is not used as a proper personal name in the Bible until the New Testament.[15] While other scholars argue that although a single villain with the personal name of Satan is not specified, the imagery, personifications, and use of language clearly point to a *satan*, the entity later referred to by the personal name *Satan*, or *the Devil* (in Greek) in Second Temple literature and in the New Testament. In a leading lexicon for the Hebrew Bible, *satan*, as "a" *satan* (without a definite article), or "the" *satan* (with the definite article), is used as a noun referring to an "adversary, opponent . . . in the military and political sphere 1S 29:4 1K 5:18 11:14, 23, 25 . . . in jurisprudence Ps 109:6 . . . accuser, or opposing party . . . (or) the one who hinders a purpose . . . Nu 22:22, 32."[16] As a verb, *satan* is defined as "to be at enmity with, be hostile towards, make an enemy of Ps 38:21; 109:4," referring to one who accuses, opposes, or executes judgment against someone, and can refer even to one who executes the defendant.[17] Someone who is a *satan* or who

---

[14]Sally Douglas, "A Decoding of Evil Angels: The Other Aetiology of Evil in the Biblical Text and Its Potential Implications in Our Church and World," *Colloquium* 45, no. 1 (2013): 43n3: "*NT* understandings of enslaving cosmic evil are evidenced in the various exorcism accounts in the gospels (Mk 5:1-20; Mt 8:28-9:1; Lk 4:31-37; 8:26-39; 9:37-43). This is also exemplified in stories such as binding the strong man and the parable of the grain (Mt 12:22-32; 12:43-45; 13:18-19; Mk 3:20-30; 4:14; Lk 11:14-26). In the epistles the reality of a framework of cosmic evil that exists in battle with the faithful appears in many places (see Gal 1:3-4; 4:8-10; Eph 6:10-18; Col 1:13-14; 2:15-20; 2 Thess 2:9-12; Jas 4:7; 1 Pet 5:7-10; 1 Jn 2:13-14; 3:8-10; Jude 8-9, 23; Rev 20:7-10; see also Rom 7:14-25)." See also Archie T. Wright, *The Origin of Evil Spirits: The Reception of Genesis 6:1-4 in Early Jewish Literature* (Minneapolis: Fortress, 2015), 1. As Wright argues, "By the turn of the Common Era there was in place a world-view within Judaism in which the activity of autonomous or semiautonomous evil spirits was regarded as a reality. This view is exemplified, for example, in the ministry of Jesus as described in the Synoptic Gospels of the NT. By contrast, there is little evidence in Jewish literature during the earlier biblical period for such evil spirits."

[15]Peggy L. Day, *An Adversary in Heaven: Satan in the Hebrew Bible* (Atlanta: Brill Academic, 1988); T. J. Wray and Gregory Mobley, *The Birth of Satan: Tracing the Devil's Biblical Roots* (New York: St. Martin's, 2005), 51-73.

[16]Ludwig Koehler et al., "שָׂטָן" (*śāṭān*), in *The Hebrew and Aramaic Lexicon of the Old Testament*, (Leiden: E.J. Brill, 1994–2000), 1317.

[17]Michael S. Heiser, *The Unseen Realm: Recovering the Supernatural Worldview of the Bible* (Bellingham, WA: Lexham, 2015), 57; for *Satan* as a denominative verb, see Koehler et al., *Hebrew and Aramaic Lexicon*, 1316, "Ps 38:21 [Heb] (38:20 [Eng]); 71:13; 109:4, 20, 29; Zech 3:1." In a semantic analysis of the Hebrew root glossed nominally as Satan, accuser, or adversary, Ryan

satans you is not out for your good. Here are some examples of how *satan* is used as a noun in the Old Testament:

Satan as an indefinite noun (satan)

- 1 Samuel 29:4: "He must not go with us into battle, or he will turn [*satan*, be an opposer, adversary] against us during the fighting."

- 1 Kings 5:4 [Hebrew 5:18]: "But now the LORD my God has given me rest on every side, there is no adversary [*satan*, an adversary] or disaster."

- 1 Kings 11:14: "Then the LORD raised up against Solomon an adversary [*satan*, an adversary], Hadad the Edomite."

- 1 Chronicles 21:1: "Satan [*satan*, an accuser] rose up against Israel and incited David to take a census of Israel."

- Psalm 109:6: "Appoint someone evil to oppose my enemy, and let an accuser [*satan*, an accuser, adversary] stand at his right hand."

Satan as a definite noun or as a proper name (Hasatan)

- Job 1:6-9, 12; 2:1-4, 6 (These two passages will be discussed in detail the next chapter.)

- Zechariah 3:1-2: "Then he showed me Joshua the high priest standing before the angel of the LORD, and Satan [*hasatan*, the accurser] standing at his right side to accuse [*satan* as a verb] him. The LORD said to Satan [*hasatan*, the accuser], 'The LORD rebuke you, Satan [*hasatan*, the accuser]! The LORD, who has chosen Jerusalem, rebuke you! Is not this man a burning stick snatched from the fire?'"

Like the serpent in the Garden, *satan* is not a friendly agent. Furthermore, there is thematic development of the use and concept of *satan* through the Old Testament.[18] Theologian Greg Boyd argues that the Old Testament uses of the common ancient chaos monsters of Leviathan, Yamm, and Behemoth "are the rough equivalents of the New Testament's view of Satan as the principality and power of the air as well as the ruler of this world."[19] Old Testament

---

Stokes finds that a *satan* is generally not simply one who accuses another, but rather, one who would take another's life by physical attack. Ryan E. Stokes, "Satan, Yhwh's Executioner," *Journal of Biblical Literature* 133, no. 2 (2014): 251-70.

[18]Robin Routledge, *Old Testament Theology: A Thematic Approach* (Downers Grove, IL: IVP Academic, 2012), 122.

[19]Gregory A. Boyd, *God at War: The Bible and Spiritual Conflict* (Downers Grove, IL: IVP Academic, 1997), 306n43.

scholars such as Richard Averbeck and Terence Fretheim demonstrate that modern scholars have not taken seriously enough the cosmic battle imagery and language that the ancient writers and readers conceptualized.[20]

Furthermore, many scholars read the two Old Testament texts of Isaiah 14:12-15 and Ezekiel 28:11-19 as descriptions of the rebellion of Satan or some other ruling spiritual entity, due to arrogance and pride in its own power and beauty, desired to be a god on par with or in rivalry against Yahweh God. While some scholars insist that the passage is simply continuing a description of a powerful earthly ruler, Isaiah begins with words about earthly oppressors and subduers of nations and then moves to the spiritual forces behind the earthly, speaking of this being as one "fallen from heaven, morning star, son of the dawn" (Is 14:12). Consistent with ancient Israelite and Near Eastern worldviews, each nation was allotted to ruling spiritual beings who directed the affairs of human rulers.[21] Likewise, in Ezekiel 28, the prophet begins the section speaking of the earthly ruler of Tyre but transitions to the celestial being behind his power. In fact, this one was, "in Eden, the garden of God. . . . You were anointed as a guardian cherub. . . . You were on the holy mount of God; you walked among the fiery stones. . . . Your heart became proud on account of your beauty. . . . So I threw you to the earth; I made a spectacle of you before kings" (Ezek 28:13-19).

It's not hard to see how or why the personification of this creature and those acting as a *satan* became the Satan in the Second Temple period, especially in "the books of Jubilees, Wisdom of Solomon, and Enoch. The Assumption of Moses (10:1) and the book of Jubilees (2:23-29) may be the earliest evidence for the term *satan* being employed as a proper name."[22] In this period between the close of the Hebrew Bible and the coming of Jesus, the fall of the "Day Star is interpreted as the fall of Satan and his angels (*Life of Adam and Eve* 12–15; see 2 Enoch 29:4-5). Angels were often compared to stars (Judg 5:20; Job 38:7; 1 Enoch 104:1; *Testament of*

---

[20] Averbeck, "Ancient Near Eastern Mythography," 355; Terence E. Fretheim, "Is Genesis 3 a Fall Story?," *Word and World* 14 (1994): 144-53.
[21] Heiser, *Unseen Realm*, 113-15; John Goldingay, *Daniel*, Word Biblical Commentary 30 (Grand Rapids, MI: Zondervan Academic, 2019), 291.
[22] David Seal, "Satan," in *The Lexham Bible Dictionary*, ed. John D. Barry et al. (Bellingham, WA: Lexham, 2016).

Moses 10:9). According to this tradition, Satan belonged to the first creatures
cast out of heaven by God."[23] This understanding, embraced by the first
century AD and the writers of the New Testament, is why Jesus calls Satan
"the devil," "a murderer," and "the father of lies" (Jn 8:44).[24]

SATAN IN THE NEW TESTAMENT

The New Testament is replete with passages regarding a particular adversary
of God and humanity. This adversary is called *Satan* (the Hebrew *satan* is
transliterated into Greek as *satan* or *satanas*) meaning accuser or adversary,
and the devil (*diabolos* in Greek), meaning "slanderous, gossip," or "mali-
cious talk."[25] The word *Satan* is used thirty-three times; the word *devil* is
used thirty-two times; *Beelzebul* is used seven times (from the Hebrew, a
Philistine god, literally "fly-lord"). The adversary is also referred to as *Belial*
(2 Cor 6:15, from the Hebrew, meaning "without value"), as the "ruler of this
world" (Jn 12:31; 14:30; 16:11), as the "god of this world" (2 Cor 4:4), as the
"prince of the power of the air" (Eph 2:2), and as a dragon (Rev 12:7).[26] The
diabolos is identified as an enemy actively working to destroy the lives of any
who follow God (1 Pet 5:8).[27]

Key to understanding the devil's method of bringing evil into our lives
and into the world is Jesus' description of him as "a murderer from the beginning . . . a liar and the father of lies." (Jn 8:44). The conflict on earth
becomes clearer when the identity of Satan as a murderer and a liar is
viewed in contrast to God as the giver and sustainer of life, whose character
is good and truthful. To see this further, let's look at the first recorded conflict between Jesus and the devil in Matthew 4 and Luke 4. These passages
give insight into what the Bible teaches us about Satan, Jesus, the implications for our own lives, and the importance of our response to the trials that
come to us.

Jesus' earthly ministry is initiated by his baptism, followed by his trip into
the wilderness. It's a one, two, three sequence. At Jesus' baptism, the Holy

---

[23]Seal, "Satan."

[24]Routledge, *Old Testament Theology*, 122-23.

[25]David M. Emanuel, "Satan," in *Lexham Theological Wordbook*, ed. Douglas Mangum, Lexham
   Bible Reference Series (Bellingham, WA: Lexham, 2014).

[26]Seal, *"Satan."*

[27]Emanuel, "Satan."

Spirit visibly descended on him and the voice of God announced from heaven, "You are my Son, . . . with you I am well pleased" (Lk 3:22; Mt 3:17). This declaration affirmed his divine identity and his appointment as the Messiah. He is the one that the Old Testament was searching for from Genesis 3:15 as the one who would crush the serpent's head—but his own heel would be crushed. He is the one who Noah's father hoped for who would deliver humanity from their toil and bring them rest, and onward through the kings and the prophets.

Immediately following this amazing moment of affirmation, the Spirit of God led Jesus into the wilderness to be "tempted by the devil" (Lk 4:1; Mt 4:1). After Jesus had fasted forty days, the very first words from the devil's mouth are "If you are the Son of God, tell these stones to become bread" (Mt 4:3). Two things are happening here. First, the devil is challenging Jesus' identity as the Son of God, the very affirmation that was just declared at his baptism through God's voice from heaven, "This is my beloved Son." You can hear an echo of the serpent's temptation in the Garden, "Did God really say?" (Gen 3:1). The devil is a liar and a murderer, but his only power is his words—if he can get God's image-bearers, God's appointed governors, to believe, speak, and act contrary to God's words and will, then the devil defies God's kingdom, empowered through us.

Through seeing the dynamic of how evil works to put God's words and character in question and challenge us to use our God-given power wrongfully, we can understand the potential corruption of power in the second half of the devil's first temptation of Christ. "If you are the Son of God, tell this stone to become bread." In other words, use the power God gave you to satisfy your own needs and desires.

Jesus' response to the temptation is taken right from Scripture. It ties together his earthly ministry with the Israelites' exodus from Egypt and also provides instructions for the people of God. "Jesus answered, 'It is written: "Man shall not live on bread alone"'" (Lk 4:4). Jesus and the devil, and the readers of the Gospels, knew the passage in Deuteronomy 8:1-3. God brought the Israelites through the "baptism" of crossing through the Sea of Reeds on dry ground and led them into the wilderness. The Israelites could have traveled from Egypt to the Promised Land in about two weeks. But since they chose to doubt what God promised them, they ended up wandering for forty years, dying in the wilderness, and only the next generation, who chose to believe God and received his promise.

Jesus had the choice to believe God's word or not. The quote that Jesus refers to is,

> Remember how the LORD your God led you all the way in the wilderness these forty years, to humble and test you in order to know what was in your heart, whether or not you would keep his commands. He humbled you, causing you to hunger and then feeding you with manna, which neither you nor your ancestors had known, to teach you that man does not live on bread alone but on every word that comes from the mouth of the LORD. (Deut 8:2-3)

The number forty in Hebrew is associated with testing. Jesus' successful emergence through the temptation scene reverses the betrayal in the Garden (Gen 3:1-6) and reverses the disobedience of the Israelites in their wilderness experience (Ex 15–Num 25).

The second temptation listed in Matthew 4 once again begins with the challenge to his identity and how he would use his power. But this time, the devil tempted Jesus to take a risk as a grand demonstration for others to see. The devil took him to the pinnacle of the temple and said, "If you are the Son of God, throw yourself down!" And then the devil quoted part of Psalm 91 to boost the strength of his temptation, where God promises that his angels will protect us (Ps 91:11-12). Jesus, however, refuses to abuse the power God gave him by putting on a show to prove to others that indeed he is anointed of God, and by trying to coerce or manipulate God into protecting his life. Jesus responds, quoting Scripture, "Do not put the LORD your God to the test" (Deut 6:16).

The Hebrew word in Deuteronomy 6:16 is *nasah*, to put someone to the test, to tempt. Although the word of God is tested in us to see whether we will trust God's goodness and character, the flip side is when we demand that God prove himself because we don't believe him. Many of us have done something rash or dangerous and said, "God if you bring me through this, I'll serve you." I recognize that we've probably all put God to the test. God is compassionate and understanding, especially as we're getting to know him and trying to figure out if we can really trust him. However, Jesus knew God perfectly. He had no need for God to prove himself, so Jesus had no need to put him to the test. As we get to know who God is and who we are, the need to want God to prove his care and his power diminishes.

The third temptation is also about the use of power. But here, the devil reveals who he is and where he gets his power. The devil took Jesus to a high mountain and "showed him all the kingdoms of the world and their splendor" (Mt 4:8). I quote the extended version from Luke, where the devil said to Jesus "I will give you all their authority and splendor; it has been given to me, and I can give it to anyone I want to. If you worship me, it will all be yours" (Lk 4:6-7). Let's look at this more closely. First, since this was an actual temptation, there had to be legitimacy in the devil's offer to Jesus. The devil legitimately had the power to give Jesus the authority and splendor of the kingdoms of this world—if Jesus worshiped him. From this statement, we understand why Jesus calls the devil the ruler of this world. His statement also reveals how he got this authority (*exousia*) and glory (*doxa*), because "it has been given to me."

Wait, you may say! Who gave the authority of the kingdoms of this world to the devil? A look at the word translated "has been given," reveals that it comes from the Greek word *paradidōmi*, which carries the sense of handing over something to someone. It can carry a positive or negative connotation, depending on the context. In taking this scene as a negative context, since this is something handed over to the devil, it can refer to a military or judicial surrender into custody (cf. Mt 4:12; 5:25; 10:19; Lk 21:16), or to betrayal (Mk 14:10; Lk 22:4, 6, 22; 1 Cor 11:23). In light of the authority God gave humanity as his corulers on the earth, the only scene that fits handing over authority to dark forces is Genesis 3, when humanity chose to believe the twisted words of the serpent rather than the words of God. Humanity betrayed God and handed over our authority to the father of lies. That's how the devil became the ruler of this world and all the children of *adam* his subjects, until and unless we turn our allegiance to God.

The evidence that the temptation of Jesus by the devil was about a power struggle over who will be the god of this world is evident in Jesus' response, "It is written, 'Worship the Lord your God and serve him only'" (Lk 4:8; Deut 6:13). Matthew's version includes, "Away from me, Satan!" (Mt 4:10). In Jesus' response, he is quoting a passage that follows the most important prayer in the Hebrew Bible: "Love Yahweh your God with all your heart and with all your soul and with all your strength" (Deut 6:4-5). Jesus clarifies that the clash is between the only two kingdoms on this earth: the kingdom of God and the kingdom of the devil.

Every source of power and every authority that is not aligned with God and his kingdom is aligned with the kingdom of the powers of the devil. Jesus stated this clearly: "Whoever is not with me is against me, and whoever does not gather with me scatters" (Mt 12:30; Lk 11:23), and the reverse, "Whoever is not against you is for you" (Lk 9:50). From a biblical perspective, the discernment of good and evil comes down to who you believe and who you serve, either God or anyone else.

As an aside, how can humanity both retain our authority as image-bearers and be subjugated to the devil? Think of it along the lines of hypnosis, where someone may yield their will to another through the power of suggestion and carry out (at least to some degree) the will of the other. Or, consider a bright, capable child growing up under the influence of an abusive person, or a narcissist, or some other personality disorder that thrives on controlling and manipulating others. The good in that child becomes twisted and distorted by the adult, who bends the child's will, who complies in efforts to secure some morsel of care, love, and identity. The abuser in this case takes advantage of the child's rightful need for love and protection but twists it for the abuser's own ends. Even when children of abuse become adults, if they don't receive healing from the lies and harm, no matter how strong, capable, and brilliant they are, they will continue to use their gifting and ability to please or appease an abuser, stripping their identity, their resourcefulness, and their potential for good.

What about the testing and temptations of Satan in *our* lives? Did you ever notice that the night before Jesus' crucifixion, Jesus said these words to Peter: "Simon, Simon, Satan has asked to sift all of you as wheat. But I have prayed for you, Simon, that your faith may not fail. And when you have turned back, strengthen your brothers" (Lk 22:31-32). Look at that again, Jesus said, "Satan has asked to sift all of you as wheat." The word *asked* in this sentence could be translated: "to ask for with emphasis and with implication of having a right to do so, *ask for, demand.*"[28] There was in Peter's life, and there may

---

[28]Fredrick W. Danker et al., *A Greek-English Lexicon of the New Testament and Other Early Christian Literature* (Chicago: University of Chicago Press, 2000), 344.

be in our lives, something that gives Satan legal ground to sift us like wheat. Do you know how wheat was sifted in those days?

First, wheat was threshed. It was spread out on either stone or tamped earth and beaten with a flail. Then, it was winnowed. The chaff was removed from the grain by throwing the grain up in the air outside, where the wind blew off the lighter chaff and the heavier grains fell back to the ground below where they were thrown up into the air again, and again. We're told that our lives might be sifted by Satan.

But then Jesus says, "But I have prayed for you, Simon, that your faith may not fail." Wait a minute. Certainly, Jesus could stop Satan from doing this. Surely, he had the power! What we miss is that Peter had a part to play in the flailing and the winnowing process. Peter had to not lose faith. And when he turned back, his assignment was to strengthen his fellow believers.

Peter demonstrates in his letter to the churches that Jesus' words did not just apply to him, but to all who follow Jesus. Peter opens his letter with the alert that "now for a little while you may have had to suffer grief in all kinds of trials. These have come so that the proven genuineness of your faith—of greater worth than gold, which perishes even though refined by fire—may result in praise, glory and honor when Jesus Christ is revealed" (1 Pet 1:6-7).

Peter, being familiar with the Hebrew Bible, would have known that the Hebrew word often used in Scripture for being tested or examined is *tsaraph*. This word also means to "refine" or "purify," as in the refining of gold or silver. Refining tests precious metals, proving their authenticity, and requires melting to expose and extract any impurities. Every word of God is tested and flawless (Prov 30:5; Ps 12:6 [Hebrew 12:7]; 18:30 [Hebrew 18:31]). The word of God is also tested in us to discover if we will rely on God or turn away and fulfill our own desires. As the psalmist states, "Test me, Lord, and try me, examine [*tsaraph*] my heart and my mind; for I have always been mindful of your unfailing love and have lived in reliance on your faithfulness" (Ps 26:2-3). Jesus did not yield to doubting God's goodness but trusted that the "not good" of hunger would be fulfilled at the right time and in the right way rather than by taking matters into his own hands independent of God. Peter clearly references this understanding of being tested and refined in our faith.

Peter continues in every chapter of his letter to talk about suffering evil and injustice. He concludes by urging us to humble ourselves under God's mighty hand but also reminds us that "your enemy the devil prowls around like a roaring lion looking for someone to devour. Resist him, standing firm in the faith, because you know that the family of believers throughout the world is undergoing the same kind of sufferings" (1 Pet 5:8-9). Flailing and winnowing applies to all of us in this life as a follower of Jesus.

The devil is described as a malevolent spiritual being with plans to bring us harm. The New Testament reminds us that Satan is trying to take advantage of us, to outwit us, and we should not be unaware or ignorant of his schemes (2 Cor 2:11). Therefore, Christians are instructed to "Finally, be strong in the Lord and in his mighty power. Put on the full armor of God, so that you can take your stand against the devil's schemes" (Eph 6:10-11). Many of us have been unaware of evil and ignorant of Satan's schemes. We have a part to play in this struggle against evil, like Peter did. As we engage in "the good fight of the faith" and remain steadfast in our faith, we can be confident that we will receive this promise: "After you have suffered a little while, [Christ] will himself restore you and make you strong, firm and steadfast" (1 Pet 5:10; 1 Tim 6:12).

Furthermore, our struggle with evil is not just against a devil or people, but occurs in multiple realms, "against the rulers, against the authorities, against the powers of this dark world and against the spiritual forces of evil in the heavenly realms" (Eph 6:12). In continuing our awareness of sources of evil as well as good in the spiritual dimension, it's helpful to examine more of the unseen realms in the Bible.

Chapter Eleven

DEMONS, ANGELS, AND OTHER SPIRITUAL ENTITIES

*For our struggle is not against flesh and blood, but against the
rulers, against the authorities, against the powers of this dark world
and against the spiritual forces of evil in the heavenly realms*

Ephesians 6:12

Many people love horror movies with strange occult, demonic, or other unnatural nonhuman creatures causing havoc, terror, and death. Most think the spiritual entities represented in horror movies are harmlessly entertaining. But they're not. I've been invited into the homes and lives of many people who prior to having supernatural experiences didn't believe in nonscientific explanations for unusual phenomena, and disregarded the seemingly bizarre world of the unnatural manifesting in common life. Recently, a good friend sent me an updated article in the *Indianapolis Star* titled "The Exorcisms of Latoya Ammons," which described events involving a woman and her three children in a small town not far from his home. The journalist reported the "systematic delusion or demonic possession" of this small family, which was graphically detailed in "nearly 800 pages of official records obtained by the *Indianapolis Star* and recounted in more than a dozen interviews with police, DCS personnel, psychologists, family members and a Catholic priest."[1] The "creepy occurrences" included an incident,

---

[1] Marisa Kwiatkowski, "The Exorcisms of Latoya Ammons," *IndyStar*, January 5, 2014, updated January 27, 2022, edition, www.indystar.com/story/news/2014/01/25/the-disposession-of-latoya -ammons/4892553/.

corroborated by a DCS worker and a nurse, in which "The 9-year-old had a 'weird grin' and walked backward up a wall to the ceiling. He then flipped over Campbell, landing on his feet."[2]

Although most Christians throughout history have believed in a cosmic conflict between God and opposing spiritual forces, this view has often been dismissed in the modern scientific era. I maintain that spiritual entities exist and that knowing about them helps us understand how evil functions in our world today. The cosmic conflict motif, as John Peckham puts it, "maintains that there is a conflict between the kingdom of God and the temporary domain of demonic agents (see, e.g., Acts 26:18; Col 1:13; Mt 12:24-29; Rev 12:7-10), which are celestial creatures that have rebelled against God's government (cf. 2 Pet 2:4; Col 1:16-17)."[3] While there are a multitude of academic works that discuss or refer to spiritual entities in Scripture, including a *Dictionary of Deities and Demons in the Bible,* many read these with a curiosity detached from past or current reality.[4] And then there are others who see a demon behind every bush and an angel in every tree. I seek to moderate the extremes.

This chapter delves into terminology and descriptions the Bible uses for spiritual beings, both benevolent and malevolent. The structure of this chapter differs from other chapters in that there is no image from Genesis or transition of a major theme from Old Testament to New Testament. Nevertheless, an examination of biblical terms is instructive for evaluating what the Bible has to say about God/gods (*Elohim/elohim*), about sons of God, about angels and heavenly hosts (armies), about cherubim and seraphim, and about powers, principalities, rulers, and demons. Furthermore, these descriptors are necessary for understanding the divine council and the hierarchies of power structures at work in the operation of good and evil in the cosmos. Recognition of

---

[2]Kwiatkowski, "Exorcisms." For an academic resource, see Betty Stafford, "The Growing Evidence for 'Demonic Possession': What Should Psychiatry's Response Be?," *Journal of Religion and Health* 44, no. 1 (2005): 13-20.

[3]John Peckham, *Theodicy of Love: Cosmic Conflict and the Problem of Evil* (Grand Rapids, MI: Baker Academic, 2018), 244. For more on the cosmic conflict motif, see Esther E. Acolatse, *Powers, Principalities, and the Spirit: Biblical Realism in Africa and the West* (Grand Rapids, MI: Eerdmans, 2018), 1-7; Clinton E. Arnold, *Powers of Darkness: Principalities and Powers in Paul's Letters* (Downers Grove, IL: IVP Academic, 1992); Tremper Longman III, Daniel G. Reid, and Willem A. VanGemeren, *God Is a Warrior* (Grand Rapids, MI: Zondervan Academic, 1995); Daniel I. Block and A. R. Millard, *The Gods of the Nations: A Study in Ancient Near Eastern National Theology* (Eugene, OR: Wipf & Stock, 2013).

[4]Karel van der Toorn, Bob Becking, and Pieter W. van der Horst, eds., *Dictionary of Deities and Demons in the Bible,* rev. 2nd ed. (Grand Rapids, MI: Eerdmans, 1999).

the language used in Scripture for various entities is also helpful in dispelling the ways some of these identifiers can be recklessly tossed around.

Recounting encounters with spiritual entities through a biblical framework can be difficult for many reasons. First, it is difficult because many people in the West do not consider the possibility that suffering in the physical realm could have a spiritual component or cause. Second, the physical realm and the spiritual realm are often intertwined in ways that are difficult to distinguish. And third, the one recounting their experience with the spiritual realm runs the risk of being diagnosed within the parameters of the American Psychiatric Association's Diagnostic and Statistical Manual of Mental Disorders (DSM). Nevertheless, here is one of my own encounters.

FROM MY STORY: POWER ENCOUNTERS

As a girl, I dabbled in the occult. My mother told me that some relatives on her side of the family were heavily into incantations and séances, so to some extent, perhaps, I inherited the inclination. My curiosity about the Ouija board at age eight grew when one friend and I took our hands off the planchette and it continued moving by itself, accurately spelling out words. By age twelve, my friends were trying séances and levitation. I was easily lifted to the ceiling of my friend's basement with just the index fingers of six young girls, who then screamed and dropped me! I decided not to try that again. But the sense of dark powers was intriguing to me, while I also continued to seek God and meaning in life as a young teenager.

In the year after I became a Christian at age sixteen, I experienced several unusual phenomena. On several nights I heard voices whispering nasty things in my ear as I was falling asleep. I would wake up and quote Bible verses that silenced them. On a couple of occasions, I saw black shadowy bodies crawling up my bed, trying to grab at my heart. They looked a lot like three-dimensional versions of the flat, black "demons" pictured in the movie *Ghost*, which came out some years later. One night as I opened the door to my bedroom to go to sleep, the coldness in my room was so startling that I immediately walked out and closed the door again. I told myself that this was silly because the windows were closed. I reentered and laid down on the floor to sleep (I had severe back pain at the time, so I could only sleep on the floor). As I was trying to fall asleep, it felt like a hand covered my mouth while another covered my eyes, and two more hands covered my ears. Then it felt like something paralyzed my body, and I was thrown up into the sky, spinning and seeing stars spin around me. Terrified, I tried to scream but couldn't move or make a sound. The only thing I knew to do was call out in my mind, *Jesus, Jesus, Jesus!*

Almost immediately, it felt like my body hit the floor, the hands came off my face, ears, and body, and I heard instead the silent, gentle voice of the one I could only imagine was the Lord, reassuring me, "I've got you. It's okay. You're safe. I've got you. You're safe. Don't be afraid." By then I had been reading in the Bible how Jesus always helped and healed all who came to him, and how he commanded dark spirits and demons to leave. And Jesus taught his followers to do the same. I was never again tormented by dark forces. I've encountered them in various ways many times since, but they are not a source of fear for me. After that incident, however, they crept into my life in much subtler ways. As the serpent in the Garden was crafty, so are these malevolent creatures. They hide and attack through people or circumstances to make you think that you're the problem, or that it's another person, or that it's the situation. These entities may hide their identity if their motives can be better accomplished in stealth mode.

Generally, very little instruction is available in the churches, seminaries, or Bible colleges about the terms used in the Bible for spiritual entities. This had led to much confusion in my own life and struggles with understanding the Bible and the workings of evil. Here is a guide, beginning with the most common and often misunderstood term.

ELOHIM AND ELOHIM (GOD AND GODS) IN THE OLD AND NEW TESTAMENTS

The Hebrew word *Elohim* or *elohim* is usually translated into English as God or gods.[5] This word is the plural form of the common Hebrew noun *el*, or

---

[5]Robin Routledge, *Old Testament Theology: A Thematic Approach* (Downers Grove, IL: IVP Academic, 2012), 82-83.

eloah. In the Hebrew Bible, not only God but other types of spiritual beings are called *elohim*, even as their attributes differ from one another.[6] One thing that *Elohim/elohim* have in common is that they inhabit the nonhuman realm, although their presence impacts the physical realm and can at times be seen and felt. Their rightful abode is in the spiritual world just as humanity's rightful domain is on the earth.[7]

For example, Exodus 12:12 speaks of "all the gods [*elohim*] of Egypt." *Elohim* occurs in the opening sentence of the Bible, "In the beginning, God [*Elohim*] created the heavens and the earth." Usually, when the Old Testament speaks of God it is using the Hebrew word *Elohim* (over two thousand times). Frequently, the names *Yahweh Elohim* are used together for emphasis and clarity to indicate the unique God whose personal, covenantal, and eternal name is known as Yahweh—the I AM of the Bible (e.g., Gen 2:4-5, 7-9; Ps 42:3). Most English Bibles render the name *Yahweh* as "LORD" in all capital letters out of respect for the Jewish custom of not spelling out or saying the divine name YHWH. This also distinguishes it from the Hebrew word *Adonai*, translated and written as *Lord*, which can also be used as a title for human lords or rulers. For example, Moses declared to Pharaoh, "There is no one like the LORD our God" (Ex 8:10).

After seeing what Yahweh had done, the Midianite Jethro observed, "Now I know that the LORD [Yahweh] is greater than all other gods [*elohim*]" (Ex 18:11). Moses declared, "For the LORD [Yahweh] your God [*Elohim*] is God [*Elohim*] of gods [*elohim*] and Lord [*Adonai*] of lords [*elohim*], the great God [*El*], mighty and awesome, who shows no partiality and accepts no bribes" (Deut 10:17). And Joshua, in his closing words to the Israelites before he died, declared to them, "But if serving the LORD (Yahweh) seems undesirable to you, then choose for yourselves this day whom you will serve, whether the gods [*elohim*] your ancestors served beyond the Euphrates, or the gods [*elohim*] of the Amorites, in whose land you are living. But as for me and my household, we will serve the LORD (Yahweh)" (Josh 24:15). Psalm 136:2 asserts, "Give thanks to the God [*Elohim*] of gods [*elohim*]. His loyal

---

[6]Karel van der Toorn, "God (1)," in *Dictionary of Deities and Demons in the Bible*, ed. Karel van der Toorn, Bob Becking, and Pieter W. van der Horst (Leiden: Brill, 1999), 362.

[7]Michael S. Heiser, "Divine Council," in *The Lexham Bible Dictionary*, ed. John D. Barry et al. (Bellingham, WA: Lexham, 2016). See also Jeffrey H. Tigay, *The JPS Torah Commentary: Deuteronomy* (Philadelphia: Jewish Publication Society, 2003), 514.

love endures forever." And the well-known first Commandment states, "I am the LORD [Yahweh] your God [*Elohim*]. . . . You shall have no other gods [*elohim*] before me" (Ex 20:1-2; Deut 5:6-7).

As shown, in the Bible, the word *gods* [*elohim*] sometimes refers to spiritual beings who are lesser than, different from, and lower in rank than Yahweh *Elohim* (1 Cor 8:6; 2 Cor 4:4).[8] Therefore, *elohim* does not imply coeternality with Yahweh God.[9] The Old Testament (Hebrew Bible) does not endorse or believe in polytheism. But it does describe spiritual entities that have generally been ignored by modern scholarship until recently. The Old Testament teaches that these gods and sons of God were created, and some will not live forever.

Here are some additional examples of the use of *elohim*. The personal name of the main god of Moab is Chemosh (Judg 11:24; 1 Kings 11:33); of the Canaanites is Baal (Judg 8:33; 2 Kings 1:2;18-21; Jer 11:13); of the Philistines is Dagon (Judg 16:23; 1 Sam 5:3-7); and a long list of the gods of other nations is given in 2 Kings 17:29-33. Idols are also called *elohim* (Deut 4:28; 2 Kings 19:18; Acts 19:26). In contrast to Yahweh, "Egyptian gods [*elohim*] are not eternal, not all-seeing and all-knowing, and not all-powerful . . . they have a beginning and an end, are born and eventually die."[10] However, they are "superior to humans, yet not infinitely superior." The Israelites are urged to forsake these deities: "Throw away the foreign gods [*elohim*] that are among you and yield your hearts to the LORD, the God [*Elohim*] of Israel" (Josh 24:23).

Michael Heiser summarizes the biblical uses of *Elohim/elohim* like this:

> The biblical writers refer to a half-dozen different entities with the word *elohim*. By any religious accounting, the attributes of those entities are *not* equal.
>
> Yahweh, the God of Israel (thousands of times—e.g., Gen 2:4-5; Deut 4:35)
>
> The members of Yahweh's council (Ps 82:1, 6)
>
> Gods and goddesses of other nations (Judg 11:24; 1 Kings 11:33)[11]

---

[8]Boyd, *God at War*, 11.
[9]See, for example, Deut 32:24-25; Ps 86:8; 96:4; 135:5; Is 6:2-8; 43:10-11, Jer 5:7, 23:18, 22.
[10]van der Toorn, "God (I)," 354.
[11]For reference of *elohim* to gods of other nations, also see, for example, Ex 12:12; 20:3; Josh 24:15; Ps 96:5; Jer 2:28; 11:13.

Demons (Hebrew: *shedim*—Deut 32:17)

The deceased Samuel (1 Sam 28:13)

Angels or the Angel of Yahweh (Gen 35:1-7)[12]

Although *Elohim/elohim* (spelled the same in Hebrew, which does not have capital letters) refers predominantly to the Creator God as well as various kinds of spiritual entities, this does not imply that the biblical writers thought gods of other nations, demons, or angels approached the preeminence or uniqueness of Yahweh or shared his attributes.[13] There is no pantheon of competing deities in the Bible, but there are spiritual beings that have differing degrees and realms of power and dominion. Yahweh *Elohim* is unique and incomparable to any other spiritual entity (Deut 6:4). To quote Heiser again, "The Old Testament writers understood that Yahweh was an *elohim*—but no other *elohim* was Yahweh. He was species-unique among all residents of the spiritual world."[14]

Additional identifiers in the Bible refer to spiritual beings actively engaged in either full cooperation with God or full rebellion against God. These additional terms include sons of God (*bene elohim/bene elim*), sons of the Most High (*bene elyon*), angels (*malakim*, meaning "messengers"), and others that will be addressed. The Hebrew Bible offers solid evidence for "a three-tiered council" in which "Yahweh was the supreme authority over a divine bureaucracy," with a "second tier of lesser . . . [*elohim*], also called the 'sons of God' or 'sons of the Most High' (*bene elyon*)," and a third tier of angels (*malakim*).[15] As G. B. Caird observes, "In Jewish belief the pagan gods were in reality angelic beings whom God had delegated some measure of his own authority, but whose character had become

---

[12]Michael S. Heiser, *The Unseen Realm: Recovering the Supernatural Worldview of the Bible* (Bellingham, WA: Lexham, 2015), 30, emphasis original; Marjo Christina Annette Korpel, *Rift in the Clouds: Ugaritic and Hebrew Descriptions of the Divine* (Münster: Ugarit-Verlag, 1990), 270-71. The singular form, *El*, a general term for a deity, is found in many ancient Semitic languages, but occurs less than one-tenth as often as *elohim* in the Hebrew Bible.

[13]Twice Moses is described as "a god," or like a god to Pharaoh, in Ex 4:16; 7:1.

[14]Heiser, *Unseen Realm*, 31-32. Yahweh is all-powerful (Jer 32:17, 27; Ps 72:18; 115:3), the sovereign King over all the other *elohim* (Ps 95:3; Dan 4:35; 1 Kings 22:19), the creator of the other members of his host-council (Ps 148:1-5; Neh 9:6; cf. Job 38:7; Deut 4:19-20; 17:3; 29:25-26; 32:17; Jas 1:17) and the lone *elohim* who deserves worship from the other *elohim* (Ps 29:1).

[15]Heiser, "Divine Council."

corrupted by an idolatrous worship, which exalted them to a divine and absolute status."[16]

Sons of God

In the beginning, before anything else existed, there was God. Somewhere in the space of eternity past, God created spiritual beings that he considered family, calling them "sons," or in modern parlance, "children." These "sons (or children) of God" (*bene elohim*) are also referred to metaphorically as "the morning stars," or the first celestial shining ones who reportedly "rejoiced together" and "shouted for joy" when God laid the foundations of the earth (Job 38:4-7). There are a few variants of the "sons of God" terminology used in the Hebrew that refer to divine or celestial beings—a heavenly host that is part of God's ruling household (see Gen 6:2, 4; Ps 29:1; 82:6; 89:7; Job 1:6; 2:1; 38:7; Deut 32:8; 1 Kings 22:19). Before the physical realm existed, there was the spiritual realm.

God is nonmaterial, as are the celestial sons of God. This does not mean they are without substance or invisible, except to most of us humans living in the physical realm who lack the ability to see into the realm of the spirit. God is able to manifest in the physical realm. He created everything, including all spiritual and human beings. But before God created the visible universe and the earth with its creatures, he created a spiritual family that he calls "sons" or "children" with many of his attributes: creativity, power, and intelligence.[17] These spiritual beings became capable of manifesting—in various ways—in the physical realm once God created it. This is the reason the Bible contains many instances of spiritual beings appearing in the physical world, and some human beings crossing over and engaging with the spiritual world, especially the prophets, like Moses, Isaiah, Jeremiah, Ezekiel, and Micaiah, who saw God's throne room and heavenly court.

The concept of *sons of God* is embedded in the ancient world of ruling families, which included a "dynastic bureaucracy" of tiers of authority, beginning with the king, followed by persons appointed to key positions—generally family members—and continuing down through various layers of

---

[16]G. B. Caird, *Principalities and Powers: A Study in Pauline Theology*, The Chancellor's Lectures for 1954 at Queen's University, Kingston Ontario (Eugene, OR: Wipf & Stock, 2003), 48-49.

[17]Note: in Hebrew the masculine plural ending is inclusive, used to refer to either a multiple of male or a mixed multiple of male and female.

familial and governmental responsibilities for the administration of the kingdom.[18] In the New Testament the concept of God's family is also found in the prayer to "the Father, from whom every family in heaven and on earth derives its name" (Eph 3:14-15). God invites the spiritual and earthly beings he created in his own image and likeness to participate in the administration of his kingdom as sons and daughters of the Most High King.

Important to sons of God terminology is family. Family is supposed to be a close unit looking after each other. All of God's children, celestial and human, were supposed to use our gifts, talents, and abilities to make life better for all of us, for the whole family as well as for each person. However, certain members of the spiritual and the earthly family decided to cut themselves off from their family relationships, foremost from their Father, the Creator God. They were unwilling to participate in the *goodness for all* plan that God intended from the beginning. The first recorded family rebellion on earth happened in the Garden when the serpent convinced the humans to join in the decision to forget about God's plan and instead take what they thought would be in their own best self-interest. This act fractured creation's harmony, bringing the cosmic conflict to the earthly realm.

The second rebellion against the rule of God is reported in Genesis 6:1-6, where spiritual and earthly beings crossed the line God had made for a harmonious creation and produced hybrid beings. The passage reads:

> When human beings began to increase in number on the earth and daughters were born to them, the sons of God saw that the daughters of humans were beautiful ["good"], and they married ["took"] any of them they chose. Then the LORD said, "My Spirit will not contend with humans forever, for they are mortal; their days will be a hundred and twenty years."
>
> The Nephilim were on the earth in those days—and also afterward—when the sons of God went to the daughters of humans and had children by them. They were the heroes of old, men of renown.
>
> The LORD saw how great the wickedness of the human race had become on the earth, and that every inclination of the thoughts of the human heart was only evil all the time. The LORD regretted that he had made human beings on the earth, and his heart was deeply troubled. (Gen 6:1-6)

---

[18]Heiser, *Unseen Realm*, 24-25.

This is a cryptic and disputed passage. However, the majority of current scholarship acknowledges that the term *sons of God* refers to spiritual beings who originally were a cooperative part of God's family (although many *sons of God* are still part of God's family). These "sons of God . . . took" the daughters of humanity (*adam*). The translation *marriage* is far too generous: *took* is accurate. The word used in Hebrew is the same one used in Genesis 3 when the woman *took* the fruit from the tree of the knowledge of good and evil at the serpent's prompting. The verb *to take* is also often used of a man taking a woman sexually. There's no ceremony and often no consent.

The children born of the unholy union between the "sons of God" and the "daughters of humanity" were *gibborim*, or mighty men (and women?) of old. Whether the *gibborim* were different creatures than the Nephilim is uncertain. Possibly, *Nephilim* is another term for the sons of God who departed and fell from their privileged position in the divine council.[19] The term *Nephilim* comes from the Hebrew word *naphal*, "to fall," and could be translated as "the fallen ones." The text seems to read that either hybrid beings called Nephilim were present on the earth at the time of the *gibborim* (the mighty ones) or the Nephilim were these *gibborim*, the progeny of the forbidden union. The Septuagint translates Nephilim into Greek as the *gigantes*, which in English is the "giants," and later texts in the Old Testament seem to associate these creatures with giant clans found in Canaan.

Although the flood was sent to wipe out the corruption and violence in the land, the flood did not seem to wipe out the Nephilim because they are referred to again when the Israelite spies, sent by Joshua to spy out the land of Canaan, return with the report that they saw Nephilim (Num 13:33), directly linking them to "the giant race of the Anakim, and by extension the Rephaim, Emim, and Zamzummim" (see Deut 2:10-11, 20).[20] Some surmise that the command to Joshua and the ancient Israelites to attack the Canaanites was separated into two different assignments: that they were only commanded to wipe out the relatives of the Nephilim, a.k.a., the giant offspring of the nonhuman sons of God that interbred with humans in Genesis 6:1-4; but

---

[19]Brian Neil Peterson, "Nephilim," in *The Lexham Bible Dictionary*, ed. John D. Barry et al. (Bellingham, WA: Lexham, 2016).
[20]Peterson, "Nephilim."

the humans living in Canaan they were to subjugate or displace.[21] The idea and the biblical-linguistic arguments are intriguing, and have the benefit of eliminating language of genocide. Strong notice should also be given to the opening chapters of Joshua (Josh 2–6), in which Rahab declares and exhibits her decision to become a Yahweh worshiper, and her whole family is spared. In the dialogue, she states that all the people had heard the incredible stories of how the God of the Israelites protected and guided them and they were afraid. The implication of her story, and how she becomes part of the lineage of David, is that any human who had turned to become a Yahweh follower could have been spared.

Returning to the Nephilim, a large body of Second Temple literature attests to the concern about the pollution of the human bloodline with fallen spirits, and the rebellion of spiritual or angelic beings that produced "semi-divine giants" who led rebellions on the earth.[22] Some of these texts include 1 Enoch 6–11 and Jubilees 7–10, which are expansive retellings of Genesis 6 and the flood narratives, including the divine secrets, skills, warfare, wickedness, and violence that these creatures taught humanity and their resulting punishment. Multiple Dead Sea Scrolls, drawing on the events depicted in Genesis 6:1-4, speak of demons arising from the sexual union of the sons of god with humans.[23] For example, the Dead Sea Scroll of the "Enochic Book of the Giants attests the Nephilim several times (4QEnGi[b] 3:8)."[24] Targum Pseudo-Jonathan "names the angels who fell from heaven (Shamhazai and Azael). In 1 Enoch, the parallel account to Gen. 6:1-4, 'the angels, the sons of heaven' saw and desired the daughters of men . . . two hundred of them, 'came down' (6:6) and acted promiscuously with earthly women (7:1), polluting the earth with their monstrous progeny, the Nephilim (9:9; 10:9)."[25] These beings, including the Watchers, Azazel, and others, "became the basis for the Jewish theology of the origin of demons in the Second Temple era."[26]

---

[21]Peter W. Coxon, "Nephilim," in *Dictionary of Deities and Demons in the Bible*, ed. Karel van der Toorn, Bob Becking, and Pieter W. van der Horst (Grand Rapids, MI: Eerdmans, 1999), 618; Heiser, *Unseen Realm*, 189-217.

[22]Coxon, "Nephilim," 619; for extensive bibliography see Coxon; Peterson, "Nephilim."

[23]See Heiser, *Unseen Realm*, 92-100, especially 99 and 99n16, 99n17.

[24]Coxon, "Nephilim," 619.

[25]Coxon, "Nephilim," 619.

[26]Michael S. Heiser, *Demons: What the Bible Really Says About the Powers of Darkness* (Bellingham, WA: Lexham, 2020), 12.

The New Testament picks up on the Second Temple literature and alludes to Genesis 6:1-4 in 2 Peter 2:4, referring to "the angels who sinned" and were imprisoned awaiting punishment. Likewise, Jude 6 describes the "angels who did not keep their positions of authority but abandoned their proper dwelling—these he has kept in darkness, bound with everlasting chains for judgment on the great Day."[27] And Jesus speaks of a place "prepared for the devil and his angels" (Mt 25:41), thereby connecting "the realm of death with supernatural rebels."[28]

Although the Hebrew never refers to the sons of God as "angels,"[29] the Septuagint regularly translates "sons of God" with the Greek word *angelos/ angeloi theou,* which is generally translated into English as "angels of God" or "messengers of God."[30] Let's look at what the Old and New Testaments tell us about angels and related celestial beings.

ANGELS, ARCHANGELS, AND HEAVENLY HOST (ARMIES)

Many people believe in angels, which may be thought of as "ethereal beings" with greater powers than human beings that are helpful to them in various ways.[31] Usually paintings, icons, memes, and media portray angels as having wings, and they generally are not gender specific. The Bible provides more specific information.

The Hebrew word for angel is *malak* (plural, *malakim*) and the Greek word is *angelos* (plural, *angeloi*). These describe a function, or job description, rather than a type of being (like *elohim*, demons, or cherubim).[32] An angel refers to someone sent on a mission to deliver a message or to carry out a task. Most commonly, angels refer to divine emissaries who are sent by or on behalf of Yahweh. In both the Hebrew and Greek, these envoys can

[27]J. A. McGuire-Moushon, "Divine Beings," in *Lexham Theological Wordbook,* ed. Douglas Mangum, Lexham Bible Reference Series (Bellingham, WA: Lexham, 2014); Heiser, *Demons,* 12n19.

[28]Heiser, *Demons,* 12n20.

[29]Heiser, "Divine Council"; Jan Willem van Henten, "Angel (II)," in van der Toorn, Becking, and van der Horst, *Dictionary of Deities and Demons,* 51.

[30]Van Henten, "Angel (II)," 51.

[31]CBS News, "Poll: Nearly 8 in 10 Americans Believe in Angels," CBS News, December 23, 2011, www.cbsnews.com/news/poll-nearly-8-in-10-americans-believe-in-angels/; Karl Albrecht, "Science Class Isn't Working," *Psychology Today,* September 29, 2017, www.psychologytoday .com/us/blog/brainsnacks/201709/science-class-isnt-working.

[32]McGuire-Moushon, "Divine Beings."

be human or supernatural. There is no mention in the Bible of angels having wings, except for cherubim and seraphim, which technically are not angels. J. A. McGuire-Moushon points out that "In ancient Near Eastern polytheistic contexts, divine emissaries were lower-ranking gods serving the more powerful deities."[33]

Angels are also associated with God's mighty heroes (the good *gibborim*) and his heavenly host, or divine warriors (*tsaba*, or plural, *tsebaot*, a.k.a. *sabaoth*) involved in making sure his word and his will are carried out. Consider, for example, Psalm 103: "Praise the LORD, you his angels [*malakim*], you mighty ones [*gibborim*] who do his bidding, who obey his word. Praise the LORD, all his heavenly hosts [*tsebaot*], you his servants who do his will" (Ps 103:20-21).

However, angels sometimes are distinct from, and sometimes are synonymous with the "heavenly armies," or "hosts," in the Septuagint and in the New Testament.[34] For example, right after the birth of Jesus an angel (*angelos*) appeared to the shepherds in Bethlehem: "The glory of the Lord shone around them." Suddenly, a throng or multitude of heavenly host (*stratia*, army or soldiers) or the celestial army appeared with the angel, giving praise to God and saying, "Glory to God in the highest heaven, and on earth peace to those on whom his favor rests" (Lk 2:9, 14).

The letter to the Hebrews makes clear that God's angels, or messengers, are sent on assignment to serve and assist humans who are likewise in God's service: "He makes his angels spirits, and his servants flames of fire. . . . Are not all angels ministering spirits sent to serve those who will inherit salvation?" (Heb 1:7, 14; Ps 104:4).

As well as delivering messages from God, these powerful spiritual beings can be sent to guide, provide, and protect humans from danger: such as leading Abraham's servant on a long and uncertain journey to seek a wife for Isaac (Gen 24:7, 40); leading the Israelites during their wilderness travels after the exodus (Ex 14:19; 23:20-23; 32:34; 33:2); bringing food and water to Elijah after he fled from Jezebel (1 Kings 19:5-6); protecting Daniel from

---

[33]McGuire-Moushon, "Divine Beings."
[34]For example, see 1 Kings 22:19; Ps 148:2; Jer 33:22; Dan 4:35; Neh 9:6. See also Michael S. Heiser, *Angels: What the Bible Really Says About God's Heavenly Host* (Bellingham, WA: Lexham, 2018), 17-23.

the lions when thrown into their den (Dan 6:21-22); and assisting Jesus after his forty-day fast in the wilderness and the subsequent temptations by the devil (Mt 4:11).[35] Psalm 91 speaks of angelic protection: "For he [Yahweh] will command his angels concerning you to guard you in all your ways; they will lift you up in their hands, so that you will not strike your foot against a stone" (Ps 91:11-12).

Other examples in the New Testament include the angel of the Lord who appeared to Zecharias, standing to the right of the altar of incense in the temple that was in Jerusalem. He spoke to Zecharias, Mary, and to Joseph (Lk 1:11, 19, 26; Mt 1:20; 2:13). Angels are also "involved in the judgment . . . especially in the second coming of Christ (e.g., Matt 13:39-49; Mark 13:27; Acts 12:23; 2 Thess 1:7)" and throughout the book of Revelation.[36]

Occasionally a human being who delivers a message on behalf of another person is also called a messenger, using the same Hebrew word *malak/malakim*, or from the Greek *angelos/angeloi*. For example, Jacob sent messengers (*malakim*) ahead to his brother Esau to make peace with him (Gen 32:3, 6 [32:4, 7 Hebrew]), and Moses sent messengers (*malakim*) to the king of Edom to request passage through their land (Num 20:14).[37] The New Testament uses the word *angelos* to refer to human messengers only a few times. When John the Baptist was imprisoned by Herod, he sent messengers (*angelos/angeloi*) to ask Jesus if he was the Messiah (Lk 7:24); and Jesus sent messengers (*angeloi*) to go ahead of him to prepare the village for his arrival (Lk 9:52).

In a few instances, the New Testament also speaks of nonhuman angels who sinned (2 Pet 2:4; Jude 6) and who rebelled against God to join forces with Satan, or the devil (Mt 25:41; Rev 12:7-9).[38] But most of the time, *malak* and *angelos* refer to spiritual messengers or a "supernatural emissary" working on the behalf of God and humans. Furthermore, there are *a lot* of angels in the heavenly realm: "Then I looked and heard the voice

---

[35]S. A. Meier, "Angel (I)," in van der Toorn, Becking, and van der Horst, *Dictionary of Deities and Demons in the Bible*, 47. See also Mt 2:13-20; Lk 1:11-38; Acts 12:7-11.

[36]McGuire-Moushon, "Divine Beings."

[37]Other examples of human messengers (*malakhim*) occur in Deut 2:26; Josh 6:17, 25; 1 Sam 11:7; 2 Sam 11:19; Is 18:2, Ezek 23:40; 30:9; Neh 6:3; Jas 2:25.

[38]McGuire-Moushon, "Divine Beings."

of many angels, numbering thousands upon thousands, and ten thousand times ten thousand. They encircled the throne and the living creatures and the elders" (Rev 5:11).

There's also a special category of angel that is mentioned only twice in the Bible and only in the New Testament: an archangel. The Greek word is *archangelos*, a combination of the word *ruler* (*archē*) and *angel* (*angelos*). When speaking about the return of Jesus Christ, Paul writes, "The Lord himself will come down from heaven, with a loud command, with the voice of the archangel and with the trumpet call of God, and the dead in Christ will rise first" (1 Thess 4:16). The other mention is in Jude 9, when Michael is referred to as an "archangel" who disputed with Satan about the body of Moses. Michael is also mentioned in Revelation 12:7; he leads a military attack with "his angels" (*hoi angeloi autou*) against "the dragon and his angels." After which, "That ancient serpent called the devil, or Satan, who leads the whole world astray," is, "hurled to the earth, and his angels with him" (Rev 12:9). In the Old Testament, the term *archangel* is not used. However, in Daniel 10:13 and 10:21, the angel Michael is called "one of the chief princes" (*sar*), and in Daniel 12:1 he is called "the great prince" (*Hasar Hagadol*), who protects God's people.[39] Second Temple Jewish literature has extensive language pertaining to archangels, especially in 1 Enoch and 2 Enoch, the *Testament of Abraham* (1:4 and 14:10), and 3 Baruch 11:8.[40] But there are some heavenly creatures commonly mistaken as angels.

CHERUBIM AND SERAPHIM

Cherubim and Seraphim are winged, divine "hybrid figures."[41] Their form, or appearance, combines both human and animal attributes in a spiritual body. They are mostly located around Yahweh God's heavenly throne. They are protectors of the presence and holiness of God, guarding sacred space. Cherubim, the plural of cherub, are not the chubby little winged babies depicted in medieval paintings and Christmas cards.

---

[39]Heiser, *Angels*, 121-22, 121n14; McGuire-Moushon, "Divine Beings."
[40]Michael S. Heiser, "New Testament Terms for Unseen Divine Beings," in *Faithlife Study Bible* (Bellingham, WA: Lexham, 2016).
[41]Heiser, *Angels*, 25.

Their primary function is to guard the Tree of Life and the throne room of God.[42]

Cherubim are mentioned more than ninety times in the Old Testament and once in the New Testament.[43] They first appear in Genesis 3:24, where an unknown number of cherubim are stationed with flaming swords, flashing back and forth to keep humans safely away from the Tree of Life. Ezekiel speaks of an "anointed guardian cherub" appointed to the Holy Mountain of God, who was in Eden, the Garden of God, who became proud and rebelled against God and was therefore thrust out and thrown to the earth (Ezek 28:11-19). Although this passage begins by speaking of the King of Tyre, it transitions to the ruling spiritual power over the earthly king and is no longer speaking of mere earthly realms. Most traditions associate this cherub with the rebellion of the serpent, and later with the being called Satan and the devil in Second Temple Jewish and subsequent literature.[44]

Cherubim made of gold symbolically covered and protected the ark of the covenant in the Holy of Holies in the tabernacle and later in the temple (e.g., Ex 24:18-22; 37:7-9). God is described as "enthroned" between the cherubim or above the cherubim (1 Sam 4:4; 2 Sam 6:2; 2 Kings 19:14; Is 37:16; Ps 80:2; 91:1). Images of cherubim were also woven into the curtains inside the tabernacle and temple (Ex 26:1; Ezek 41:18). Inside Solomon's temple they also placed two approximately fifteen-foot-tall (ten cubits) golden cherubim. They stood behind the ark of the covenant with outstretched wings touching each other in the middle and touching the walls of the Holy of Holies (1 Kings 6:23-29; 2 Chronicles 3:10-13, 5:7).

In Ezekiel's vision, cherubim have four faces: the face of a cherub (not explained or described), a man, a lion, and an eagle. Under their wings they had the form of a human hand (Ezek 10:7). Their whole body—their backs, hands, wings, and "the wheels" beside them—was full of eyes and whirling (Ezek 10:6-14). The cherubim carved into the walls of the temple displayed only two faces, one human and one lion (Ezek 41:18). When the

---

[42]T. N. D. Mettinger, "Cherubim," in van der Toorn, Becking, and van der Horst, *Dictionary of Deities and Demons in the Bible*, 190.

[43]Stacy Knuth and Douglas Mangum, "Cherubim," in *The Lexham Bible Dictionary* (Bellingham, WA: Lexham, 2016).

[44]Heiser, *Unseen Realm*, 81-91.

glory of Yahweh departed from the temple, the cherubim also departed (Ezek 10:18-19).

Seraphim are only specifically referred to in Isaiah's vision (Is 6:1-7).[45] Like cherubim, they guard the throne room of God. They are described as having three pairs of wings—two that cover their face, two that cover their feet, and two for flight—and they have hands. Thus, they are hybrids with human and animal characteristics. Their name seems to come from the word for "burning one," or a fiery, threatening serpent. Also like the cherubim, they would be viewed as protection "by those welcome in the sacred space they guarded, but as a terror to those unwelcome."[46]

These celestial creatures protect sacred space. The rebellion of one such high-ranking cherub due to pride is catastrophic (Ezek 28:11-19).

DEMONS, RULERS, PRINCIPALITIES, AND POWERS

Descriptions of malevolent spiritual forces and demons are rooted in the Hebrew Bible and expanded greatly during the Second Temple period, especially in the books of Enoch, Jubilees, and other texts found in Qumran. Further, depictions of these spiritual entities emerged robustly in the New Testament.[47]

In Hebrew or related Semitic languages there is no word equivalent to the Greek term *demon* (*daimōn* or *daimonion*).[48] The closest Hebrew word to *demon* is *shedim*, which likely came into the Hebrew from the ancient Mesopotamian language of Akkadian. This word occurs in the Hebrew Bible twice, in Deuteronomy 32:17 and Psalm 106:37 (Ps 105:37 LXX), where the Septuagint (written between the mid-third to second century BC) translates *shedim* with the Greek *daimonia* (the plural of *daimonion*). In both verses, the Israelites abandoned their God and wrongfully sacrificed to these

---

[45]However, the word "*seraphim* appears seven times in the Hebrew Bible (Numbers 21:6, 8; Deuteronomy 8:15; Isaiah 6:2, 6; 14:29; 30:6." See Abigail Stocker and John D. Barry, "Seraphim," in *The Lexham Bible Dictionary*, ed. John D. Barry et al. (Bellingham, WA: Lexham, 2016).

[46]Heiser, *Angels*, 25.

[47]See Heiser, *Unseen Realm*, 11-37, and the plethora of supporting footnotes and resources he provides.

[48]Heiser, *Demons*, 5; John H. Walton, "Demons in Mesopotamia and Israel: Exploring the Category of Non-Divine but Supernatural Enemies," in *Windows to the Ancient World of the Hebrew Bible: Essays in Honor of Samuel Greengus*, ed. Bill T. Arnold, Nancy L. Erickson, and John H. Walton (Winona Lake, IN: Eisenbrauns, 2014), 229.

demons or "false gods," sacrificing their sons and daughters to these lowly creatures (Ps 106:37-38).

As to the origin of demons, multiple Dead Sea Scrolls speak of demons called "bastard spirits" arising from the Gen 6:1-4 passage that came from divine-human cohabitation (4Q510).[49] Jewish traditions held a supernatural view of Genesis 6:1-4.[50] In classical Greek literature, the original meaning of *daimōn* "from the time of Homer onward was 'divinity,' denoting either an individual god or goddess."[51] The Greco-Roman use of *daimōn* and *daimonion* was supernatural but neither good nor evil.[52]

In the New Testament, the words *daimonion* and *daimōn* always refer to evil spirits, translated into English as *demon* (e.g., Matt 11:18; Mk 1:34, 39; 3:14; 16:9; Lk 4:33; 7:33; 8:27, 30; Jn 7:20; 8:48, 52; and Rev 18:2). These creatures are also called "unclean" or an "impure" spirits (e.g., Mt 10:1; 12:43; Mk 1:23, 26; Lk 4:33; Acts 5:16; 8:7; Rev 16:13), and they are responsible for many illnesses and physical and mental afflictions (Mk 5:2-8, 15).

These generally unseen beings are part of an assemblage of dark spiritual forces that wrongfully inhabit and impact the physical realm and world systems of power. Christians are admonished to face up to the cosmic conflict:

> Finally, be strong in the Lord and in his mighty power. Put on the full armor of God, so that you can take your stand against the devil's schemes. For our struggle is not against flesh and blood, but against the rulers [*archē*], against the authorities [*exousia*], against the powers [*kosmokrator*] of this dark [*skotos*] world and against the spiritual forces of evil [spiritual evil/wickedness] in the heavenly realms. Therefore put on the full armor of God, so that when the day of evil comes, you may be able to stand your ground, and after you have done everything, to stand. (Eph 6:10-13)

Before the time of Jesus, belief in spiritual powers and authorities is evident from reading the Septuagint and Second Temple literature, where terms in the Hebrew for the heavenly hosts and other spiritual beings are translated into the Greek using the language of powers (*dynameis*), authorities (*exousiai*),

---

[49]See Heiser, *Unseen Realm*, 92-100, especially 99 and 99n16, 99n17.

[50]G. B. Caird, *Principalities and Powers: A Study in Pauline Theology*, The Chancellor's Lectures for 1954 at Queen's University, Kingston, Ontario (Eugene, OR: Wipf & Stock, 1956), 13.

[51]G. J. Riley, "Demon," in van der Toorn, Becking, and van der Hoorst, *Dictionary of Deities and Demons in the Bible*, 235.

[52]McGuire-Moushon, "Divine Beings."

principalities (*archai*), and rulers (*archontes*), attributing different spiritual beings with ranks and functions. For example, in Psalm 103:21 and 148:2, *hosts* is translated from the Hebrew into Greek as *powers* (*dynameis*). And we see the following description in Daniel 7:27: "The sovereignty (or kingdom, *basileia*), power (*exousia*) and greatness of all the kingdoms under heaven will be handed over to the holy people of the Most High."[53]

In fact, where "the Hebrew speaks of God's hosts," Caird demonstrates that the Septuagint uses the language of powers (*dynameis*), authorities (*exousiai*), principalities (*archai*), and rulers (*archontes*) when speaking of angelic beings.[54] The use of these terms fits into the Hebrew concept of tiers of authority in both God's kingdom and the kingdom set up in opposition to God, which is then expanded throughout the New Testament. Here's a small selection of examples.

The New Testament uses the Greek word *archē* and *archōn*, translated into English as *ruler, prince,* or *authority* to refer to a person of high or highest rank (e.g., commander or high priest).[55] It is also used "of angelic or transcendent powers, since they were thought of as having a political organization,"[56] as in Romans 8:38, in 1 Corinthians 15:24, in Ephesians 1:21; 3:10; 6:12, and in Colossians 1:16; 2:10, 15. The term *archōn* is used by the Septuagint to translate the Hebrew word *sar,* or *prince,* for the angelic beings in charge of nations in Daniel 10:13, 21; 12:1.

Another word for a high-ranking position is simply *throne* (*thronos*). While this term is applied to human rulership, it is used for God's throne as the highest seat of governing authority and the position of authority held by the apostles and the twenty-four elders around God's throne. Frequently, however, *thronos* refers to malevolent spiritual beings and their "sphere of authority and the ability to rule that sphere," which is "conceptually linked to the worldview articulated in Deut 32:8-9."[57] *Thronos* often appears in conjunction with *lordships* or *dominions* (*kyriotēs*), *authorities* (*exousia, exousiai*), and *powers* (*dynamis, dynameis*).

---

[53]Caird, *Principalities and Powers*, 11-12.

[54]Caird, *Principalities and Powers*, 11-12.

[55]McGuire-Moushon, "Divine Beings"; Fredrick W. Danker et al., *A Greek-English Lexicon of the New Testament and Other Early Christian Literature* (Chicago: University of Chicago Press, 2000), 138.

[56]Danker et al., *Greek-English Lexicon*, 138.

[57]Heiser, "New Testament Terms for Unseen Divine Beings."

The term *kyriotēs* (*lordships* or *dominions*) has a wide range of use, but Paul applies it to demons and "to entities that pagans perceived to have power and to which they rendered sacrifice" (1 Cor 8:5; 10:20).[58] Heiser asserts that Paul would have in mind "the demons of Deuteronomy 32:17," called *elohim*, whom he considered "to be real, having genuine powerful authority in certain places of the earth."[59]

The word *exousia* refers to positions of human authority as well as dark supernatural authorities. It is "the term most frequently used in the NT for the right to use power bestowed by an office."[60] It is used to refer to the "power of Satan" (Acts 26:18) and also to "supernatural beings, which Christ has overcome and against which Christians must struggle."[61] Often used with *exousia* (the right to use power because of one's office) is the word *dynamis*, which "denotes power (i.e., force, capability, potency)" without specifying rank or position.[62] Greek literature sometimes used this word to refer to armies.[63]

In sum, this chapter has displayed a range of spiritual beings that inhabit the invisible and the visible realm, representing benevolent and sinister powers that influence the thoughts and actions of humans to bend either toward God's will or to any and every other will in opposition to God's good purposes. Recognizing the complexity of the spiritual as well as the earthly realm lends appreciation for the fact that people often have difficulty trying to figure out what hit them when evil slaps them in the face. It also expands our appreciation for the magnitude of the universe that God is administering. And it clarifies the magnificence of Christ, who between the resurrection and his return is bringing every principality, power, and authority into captivity through the Church: "For he must reign until he has put all his enemies under his feet. The last enemy to be destroyed is death" (1 Cor 15:25-26). Evil and all that oppose God will come to an end, for "at the name of Jesus every knee should bow, in heaven and on earth and under

---

[58]Heiser, "New Testament Terms for Unseen Divine Beings."

[59]Heiser, "New Testament Terms for Unseen Divine Beings."

[60]Heiser, "New Testament Terms for Unseen Divine Beings." See 1 Cor 15:24; Eph 1:21; 3:10; 6:12; Col 1:16; 2:10.

[61]McGuire-Moushon, "Divine Beings." See 1 Cor 15:24; Eph 1:21; 6:12; Col 2:15; 1 Pet 3:22.

[62]Heiser, "New Testament Terms for Unseen Divine Beings."; see Rom 8:38 and Eph 1:21.

[63]Heiser, "New Testament Terms for Unseen Divine Beings."

the earth, and every tongue acknowledge that Jesus Christ is Lord, to the glory of God the Father" (Phil 2:10-11; Rom 14:11-12; Is 43:23).

Our awareness of the cosmic conflict prompts us to retune our thoughts more accurately to hearing God's word and to attune our actions more precisely with God's purposes. Recognition of the vast spiritual network of benevolent and malevolent forces and gaining some understanding of how they operate should enhance our appreciation for the complexities of entities and forces at work in the cosmos. This awareness should also compel us to humility before God and compassion toward ourselves and one another for the scope of entities operating in the cosmos and beyond.

Chapter Twelve

THE DIVINE COUNCIL AND THE "RULES OF ENGAGEMENT"

God has taken his place in the divine council;
in the midst of the gods he holds judgment.

Psalm 82:1 (NRSV)[1]

If you were to design a universe as the most powerful, loving, and just being in it, what would be your master plan? How would you use your power to set up a system and delegate responsibilities to the created entities in alignment with the core attributes of benevolence, mercy, and grace? This chapter seeks to explore how and why God set up the earthly and spiritual realms to operate through a divine council, based on an understanding of the ways the Bible describes it. The reason God chose to rule this way has more to do with his character than his power. We begin with another clip from my story, move on to an image from Genesis that exemplifies the concept of a divine council, explore the biblical language and textual evidence of a divine court, and move to a conversation about the significance of this to the operation of evil in our world and why God designed "rules of engagement" as part of his method of running the universe.[1]

The Old Testament speaks of God governing the cosmos through an assembly of tiered spiritual beings, frequently called gods (*elohim*) or sons of

---

[1]The first to use this military term to refer to God's actions in spiritual conflict is John Peckham, "Rules of Engagement: God's Permission of Evil in Light of Selected Cases of Scripture," *Bulletin for Biblical Research* 30, no. 2 (2020): 243-60; Peckham, *Theodicy of Love: Cosmic Conflict and the Problem of Evil* (Grand Rapids, MI: Baker Academic, 2018).

God (*bene elohim*) that join Yahweh in making decisions about what should go on in the earthly realms and in implementing those decisions.[2] Yahweh God presides over a divine council, or "Yahweh's Council," which is an assembly of celestial (and occasionally human) beings where something is being decided or someone is being judged.[3]

Part of God's master plan was to delegate and share his power through a divine council as well as to work with and through his human image-bearers in order to bring his divine will in heaven to earth. Without our cooperation it's not likely to happen. Looking through history, we recognize that a great deal of life has to do with the use of power. Abraham Heschel writes, "History is first of all what man does with power."[4] He further observes that in the Bible:

> The prophets never taught that God and history are one, or that whatever happens below reflects the will of God above. Their vision is of man defying God, and God seeking man to reconcile with Him. History is where God is defied, where justice suffers defeat. . . . There was a moment when God looked at the universe made by Him and said: "It is good." But there was no moment in which God could have looked at history made by man and said: "It is good."[5]

History is also what malevolent spiritual rulers do with power through earthly people and governments. All spiritual entities, like human beings, were created by God in God's image and likeness as powerful, imaginative, and juridical beings with the freedom to make decisions independently from their Creator. God designed "His intelligent creations to participate with Him in how things are done."[6] A requisite of love and relationship is giving another the freedom to stay or to leave. God, in love and for the sake of relationship, gave that freedom to those made in his image. Some of the

---

[2]Peckham, "Rules of Engagement," 246-47; John Goldingay, *Old Testament Theology*, vol. 2, *Israel's Faith* (Downers Grove, IL: IVP Academic, 2016), 45; John E. Hartley, *The Book of Job* (Grand Rapids, MI: Eerdmans, 1988), 71.

[3]Extrapolated in part from Ellen White, *Yahweh's Council: Its Structure and Membership* (Tübingen: Coronet Books, 2014), 173; E. T. Mullen Jr., "Divine Assembly," in *Anchor Bible Dictionary*, ed. David Noel Freedman (New Haven, CT: Yale University Press, 1992), 2:214.

[4]Heschel, *Prophets*, 170.

[5]Heschel, *Prophets*, 168.

[6]Michael S. Heiser, "The Divine Council in the Pentateuch: A Conference Paper," Evangelical Theological Society Annual Meeting (San Antonio, TX, 2017).

spiritual beings chose the domain of God while others chose to build their own dominions.

Behind all human conflict is the cosmic conflict caused by rebelling spiritual forces, which is an "incredibly pervasive and significant biblical theme," as Tremper Longman points out.[7] Both Old and New Testaments describe spiritual entities that have authority over nations and people to influence their thinking, and, thus, the ways they use power. All will be held accountable for the choices they make and the actions they take, especially in regard to their use or abuse of their power. For God's kingdom is not about power, but about love, about family. Building trusting relationships can never occur through force or dominance. God gives us freedom with the hope that we will find him worthy of our love and trust. This story from my life is one of the ways I learned this.

FROM MY STORY: FAMILY LESSONS IN THE USE OF POWER

One night, while I was wondering if I was ever going to see my son alive again, I locked myself in my bathroom and prepared to do something that I thought might bring down a lightning bolt to strike me. After the death of Walter Jr.'s dad six years earlier, which was followed by additional losses, Walter Jr. became hard and cold. At thirteen he dropped out of high school and began his departure from civil society. At sixteen he left home, making money any way he could. I tried everything I knew to reel him in, to get him back on track and just to stay alive.

That night, locked in my bathroom, I raised my fist at God and started yelling, "You're a terrible father! A terrible father! You could be helping me out here! You could be doing something to help my son! But you're not doing anything! I'm all alone here! You know what I'm thinking anyway, so there, I said it!" and I went to bed.

Early the next morning, I heard a gentle silent voice that I had not heard in a very long time speaking inside me, "What does my Word say about who I am?" For me, *Word* refers to the Bible. At the time, I

---

[7]Tremper Longman III, *Daniel*, NIV Application Commentary (Grand Rapids, MI: Zondervan, 1999), 254.

was working on my PhD in theology and immediately a passage in Isaiah 54:13 came to mind, which says, "All your children will be taught by the LORD, and great will be their peace." I pondered this throughout the day. Every morning for the next two weeks, I was awakened with a new verse about the character of God as a loving parent.

After two weeks, I was awakened with a request from this gentle silent voice, "Ingrid, I want you to believe in your son." My immediate response was to shrug my shoulders, put up my hands, and blurt out, "But there's nothing to believe in!" Every morning for the next two weeks this request came to me: "Ingrid, I want you to believe in your son." I continued the practice of thinking of Bible passages that spoke of God's faithfulness and care. These began to work a peace and a calmness in me. I became assured that God was working in ways I couldn't see, speaking to my son in ways he could understand, whether or not I could see or hear anything to confirm it. I became certain that Walter would live, that we would come through all our hardships. Then, at the end of two weeks, he stopped home, for food.

While he was in the kitchen he asked, "Mom, do you believe in me?" In a flash, I knew God had prepared me for this moment. I knew what I would have said just two weeks earlier. But instead, I was able to say with full assurance, "Yes, I believe in you! And I know that everything we've been through, every loss we've had, will be turned around and life will be good! You'll see. Life will be good!" As he turned to look at me, I saw that his eyes were wet with tears. He had not cried since his dad died nearly seven years earlier. He said softly, "Thank you, mom. Because if you don't believe in me, how can I believe in myself? You know me better than anyone." That encounter cracked the door open for his gradual return to life, to love, to God, and to a future with hope.

In the months that followed, God also showed me the ways I had tried to manipulate my son when he wouldn't listen to me, or do what I asked him to do. I'd say things that I had learned from my mom, such as, "You're breaking your mother's heart!" and other accusatory words, trying to make him feel guilty about his behavior. Sometimes he would comply but with an attitude. Mostly, he would get angry and walk out. I simply wanted him to do what I said because, after all, I reasoned, I was the parent and I knew what was best for him! If he just did what I said, things would go better for him!

One day, after a round of my pushing and his retreating, that same silent voice spoke within me, "Have I ever manipulated you? When you've run from me, ignored me, done wrong or hurtful things, how have I treated you?" I realized that God had never manipulated me. Rather, he waited for me to come to him. And when I asked, he would tell me what I needed to know, encourage me, or embrace me, but he never used his almighty power to guilt, coerce, or intimidate me. If I persisted in rejecting his words or presence, he eventually stepped back and allowed me to make decisions on my own. Especially when I was younger, my changes in behavior usually came by bearing the consequence of my choices, which would help me learn to make healthier choices. But no matter how deep the pile of mess I made, when I turned and asked for wisdom and help again, God always showed up, but never with a wagging finger or condemnation. That was a stunner for me!

The next day I asked Walter to forgive me for being manipulative, and I invited him to call me out any time he felt like I was. I remember the first time he called me out. When I started playing mind games with him, he turned and said to me, "Mom, I never noticed how passive-aggressive you could be." Thankfully, I withheld the first words that popped into my head, caught my breath, realizing that he was right! And I apologized.

Since that time, Walter steadily turned his life around. He has a powerful story of his own to tell. While I'll always be his mom, we've become close friends, and he's become an incredibly wise man that I can trust and confide in.

This template of parenthood helped me understand the way God has set up his family in heaven and on earth. God by his sheer omnipotent power could subdue anyone into submission to his will. However, God is not a tyrant, and he is not an abuser. He will not manipulate, intimidate, or dominate to get his way. While a demonstration of God's might may elicit cowering into submission, it will never win or change hearts.[8] As God taught me, the goal in raising my son and my daughter couldn't only be compliance with my adult power, but to help them grow to be wise and responsible human beings while having healthy, trusting relationships.

Power can never forge a bond of loving care and commitment. This concept guides the conversation into the divine council and sharply contrasts with the abusive tactics. The divine council concept is not just about developing a judicial system, it relates to the establishment of faithful family functioning.[9]

IMAGE FROM GENESIS: INTRODUCING THE DIVINE COUNCIL

The first hint in the Bible of nonearthly beings called on as God's divine council occurs in Genesis 1:26, with God speaking to an unnamed "us": "And God [*Elohim*] said, 'Let us make humankind in our image.'"[10] In this verse, since *Elohim* is referring to the God of creation, who is the "us" that he is addressing? Scholars have interpreted this passage in four ways:[11] (1) God is addressing the earthly elements involved in the creation process (i.e., "heaven and earth to witness"), although there is no similar precedent for this in the Bible; (2) "us" is being used as the "plural of majesty" or "plural of deliberation" like a grand or editorial "we," although the arguments for this view fall short; (3) "us" is used as a "plural of fullness," referring to the plurality of the godhead, the Trinity, although it is unlikely that this is the original intention of the author or the understanding of the ancient Israelite listeners and readers; or, (4) God is addressing the heavenly court, the divine council of spiritual beings as in Psalm 82:1-3; 89:7; Isaiah 6; Ezekiel 1; Job 1:6; 2:1. This last option, the divine council, is best supported in the Hebrew Bible. As Randall Garr summarizes in his extensive work on the subject, when God "reveals his intention to make the human race," he is

---

[8]Peckham, "Rules of Engagement," 88.
[9]Michael S. Heiser, *The Unseen Realm: Recovering the Supernatural Worldview of the Bible* (Bellingham, WA: Lexham, 2015), 25.
[10]LEB (Lexham English Bible) translation.
[11]For a succinct summary see John Wenham, *Genesis 1–15*, Word Biblical Commentary 1 (Grand Rapids, MI: Zondervan Academic, 2014), 27-28. See also Robin Routledge, *Old Testament Theology: A Thematic Approach* (Downers Grove, IL: IVP Academic, 2012), 82.

situated "in his divine community" of heavenly beings who are fully in unity and "support of their leader."[12]

There are two other times after the first chapter of Genesis when God speaks to "us." These are when God said, "The man [humankind] has now become like one of us, knowing good and evil" (Gen 3:22); and God said, "Come, let us go down and confuse their language so they will not understand each other" (Gen 11:7). In detailed exegesis of these three passages (Gen 1:26; 3:22; 11:7), Garr "shows the inadequacies of considering the plurality language as presumed instances of the plural of solidarity, self-deliberation, self-exhortation, and the plural of majesty."[13] Garr (rightly) regards these options as "interpretive sleight of hand."[14] Two more narratives in Genesis further support this view: one in which Abraham and Sarah are visited by three people, one is identified as Yahweh (Gen 18:1-2, we'll look at this in more detail later); and another in which Jacob sees the "angels of God" ascending and descending on the stairway (*sullam*) where heaven meets earth (Gen 28:12).[15] These heavenly hosts are actively at work moving between the visible and invisible realms, generally unseen to us.

These passages point to the presence of a heavenly council of celestial beings with whom God engages in dialogue and action prior to and after the creation of humans. Humanity was made by God in consultation with a council of spiritual beings. Elsewhere in the Bible, the divine council is referred to as sons of *Elohim* and the heavenly host, with God being the LORD (Yahweh) of hosts (*tsebaot*). God chose to administer his creation and adjudicate his almighty power through relationship with his image-bearers.

THE DIVINE COUNCIL OUTSIDE GENESIS AND SPIRITUAL RULERS OF NATIONS

The Old Testament gives many examples of a divine council and realms of authority held by spiritual entities actively at work in the world. Old Testament

---

[12]Garr, *In His Own Image and Likeness*, 201.

[13]Heiser, "Divine Council in the Pentateuch." See Garr, *In His Own Image and Likeness*, 18, 19-20.

[14]Heiser, "Divine Council in the Pentateuch," 85-88.

[15]Heiser, "Divine Council in the Pentateuch," states, "Viewing it (the *sullam*) as the place where the business of the unseen world intersects with the human world might be more appropriate. The latter instance of מַלְאֲכֵי אֱלֹהִים [*angels of* God] has Jacob meeting 'angels of God' and considering the location the 'camp of God.' The sense is consistent."

scholar John Goldingay states that the *elohim* who oppose God's kingdom hold "supernatural centers of power" and can "deliberately oppose Yahweh's purpose."[16] Heiser points out, "The notion that different nations were allotted to different gods or heavenly beings was widespread in the ancient world."[17] Ultimately, however, God will judge them.[18] We'll look at the relationship between these celestial beings (*elohim*) and the nations before we move on to understanding the rules of engagement in determining earthly matters.

THE DEUTERONOMY 32 WORLDVIEW AND NATIONAL DEITIES

In ancient times, people believed that specific deities held control of territories and nations, and as a secondary matter, over the inhabitants of those regions. The evidence for this belief is convincingly provided through a significant corpus of ancient Mesopotamian literature cited by Old Testament scholars Daniel Block in *The Gods of the Nations*.[19] Block documents various *elohim* as both the ruling gods over a particular nation and also frequently serving in the pantheons of other nations to provide different administrative functions to their ruling deity.[20] Like human rulers, their primary interests lay in staking out and protecting their property and territorial claims, which overrode their interest in the people.[21] The needs of the people were of secondary importance, at best, and people were there to serve their needs and their purposes for power.

New Testament scholar G. B. Caird explains that each nation had its own *elohim* and "guardian, except Israel, which comes under the direct sovereignty of God," that is, Yahweh.[22] In other words, while the gods of other nations were territorial, the God of Israel was personal. Yahweh was different from all the other *elohim* in that he called *a people* to himself and gave them a land. Furthermore, Yahweh self-identifies as the supreme *Elohim* over all

---

[16]Goldingay, *Old Testament Theology*, 2:43; Peckham, *Theodicy of Love*, 69.
[17]John J. Collins et al., "Prince," in *Dictionary of Deities and Demons in the Bible*, ed. Karel van der Toorn, Bob Becking, and Pieter W. van der Horst (Grand Rapids, MI: Eerdmans, 1999), 663.
[18]Goldingay, *Old Testament Theology*, 2:43; Peckham, *Theodicy of Love*, 69.
[19]Daniel I. Block and A. R. Millard, *The Gods of the Nations: A Study in Ancient Near Eastern National Theology* (Eugene, OR: Wipf & Stock, 2013).
[20]Block, *Gods of the Nations*, 22-23.
[21]Block, *Gods of the Nations*, 164.
[22]G. B. Caird, *Principalities and Powers: A Study in Pauline Theology*. The Chancellor's Lectures for 1954 at Queen's University, Kingston, Ontario (Eugene, OR: Wipf & Stock, 1956), 5, 7, 15.

elohim and nations and holds them accountable to him while still acknowledging the presence of regional deities.[23]

In the Song of Moses in Deuteronomy 32, the greatness and faithfulness of
Yahweh God is proclaimed, along with a brief history of his interaction with
the nations and with his people Israel, of their rebellions against God, and of
the judgments that would follow. Tucked in Deuteronomy 32:8-9 we find
what some have come to call a "Deuteronomy 32 worldview," or more broadly,
the recognition of celestial rulers of the nations and of this world.[24] Deuteronomy 32:8-18 presents a cosmic worldview of supernatural forces (*elohim*)
given earthly jurisdictions over the governance of nations, which is also seen
in Psalm 2:1-12; 82:1-8; 1 Kings 22; 2 Kings 17:24-26; Acts 14:16-17; 17:26-30.[25]
The passage in Deuteronomy 32:8-9 requires some explanation. Verse 8 reads:

> When the Most High apportioned the nations,
>   when he divided humankind,
> he fixed the boundaries of the peoples
>   According to the number of the gods. (NRSV)

The last line of the passage of the Masoretic Text of the Hebrew Bible (compiled between the sixth and tenth centuries AD) and many English translations read, "according to the sons of Israel." However, scholars agree that the
oldest wording found of the Hebrew text of Deuteronomy 32:8 from the
Dead Sea Scrolls (4QDeut) is "sons of God" (*bene Elohim*) and therefore is
most likely the original. This is further supported by the Septuagint text in
Greek "the angels of God [*Elohim*]." Both of these readings are from around
the third century BC.[26] The Masoretic Text of the Hebrew compiled from
the sixth to the tenth centuries AD reads "sons of Israel." The older versions
support the understanding of a divine council. Deuteronomy 32:17 also uses

---

[23]Block, *Gods of the Nations*, 164-65, 168.

[24]Heiser, *Unseen Realm*, 113-14, 159n7, 176, 280-81, 295, 328-32; Peckham, *Theodicy of Love*, 58,
68-73; Marvin Tate, *Psalms 51–100*, Word Biblical Commentary 20 (Grand Rapids, MI: Zondervan Academic, 2015), 340.

[25]Heiser, *Unseen Realm*, 113-22; Peckham, *Theodicy of Love*, 70-71; Caird, *Principalities and Powers*,
4-8; see also White, *Yahweh's Council*, 34-42.

[26]Tigay, *Deuteronomy*, 302. White, *Yahweh's Council*, 35-39; Michael S. Heiser, "Deuteronomy 32:8
and the Sons of God," *Bibliotheca Sacra* 158 (January-March 2001): 52-74; Collins et al. state, "The
MT reads 'sons of Israel,' but the LXX reading *angelon Theou* is now supported by a Hebrew
fragment from Qumran Cave 4 [4QDeut¹] which reads *beney elohim*; Dietrich & Loretz
1992:153-157)" ("Prince," 663).

language known to describe demonic-type entities: "They sacrificed to false gods [in the Hebrew *sheddim*, demons, in the Greek *daimonia*], which are not God—gods [*elohim*] they had not known, gods that recently appeared, gods your ancestors did not fear."[27]

The biblical texts assert that God will judge the rebellion of the *elohim* who perverted themselves and subverted humanity to overthrow God's rule.[28] This is also strikingly seen in Psalm 82. Old Testament scholar Beth Tanner points out that this psalm "gives us a window on the assembly of the gods, a place where the gods are gathered to make decisions about the world."[29] The passage describes God's judgment of these corrupted *elohim*, once part of God's ruling elite, who are sentenced to eventually die like humans.[30]

> God [*Elohim*] stands in the divine assembly [or, assembly of God, *El*];
>   in midst of the gods [*elohim*] he [*Elohim*] passes judgment.

The members of this assembly of spiritual entities (gods) were accused of perverting justice by showing partiality toward the wicked and dealing unjustly toward the helpless (poor, weak) and the orphans. In Psalm 82:6-7, God further states:[31]

> I, Myself, have said, "You [plural] are gods [*elohim*],
>   and sons of the Most High [*bene elyon*], all of you [plural].
>
> [Note: "sons of the Most High" is equivalent to "sons of God/*Elohim*"]
>
> However, like humans [*adam*], you will die [plural],
>   and like one of the rulers [*sarim*, princes] you will fall [plural].
> Rise up, O God [*Elohim*]! Judge the earth!
>   For you, yourself, will inherit [or, take possession of] all the nations.

The uniqueness of Yahweh *Elohim* (the LORD God) among the other beings called *elohim* is also explicit in Psalm 89, which clarifies that these

---

[27]Caird, *Principalities and Powers*, 57. Heiser points out in *Unseen Realm*, 325-26, that in the New Testament, the Greek word *daimonion*, generally translated "demon(s)," occurs over sixty times, which might indicate their significance.

[28]For a thorough exposition on the two themes of divine council and spiritual rulership over the earthly systems of governance, see Heiser, *Unseen Realm*, 110-25, 163-80.

[29]Beth LaNeel Tanner, "Book Three of the Psalter: Psalms 73–89," in *The Book of Psalms*, ed. Nancy L. deClaisse-Walford, Rolf A. Jacobson, and Beth LaNeel Tanner, New International Commentary on the Old Testament (Grand Rapids, MI: Eerdmans, 2014), 641.

[30]My translation from the Hebrew.

[31]For more in-depth analysis, see Heiser, *Unseen Realm*, 26-27; Peckham, *Theodicy of Love*, 71-72.

elohim are divine entities but not humans, for their abode is in the heavens, the spiritual realm. It reads:

> The heavens praise your wonders, LORD,
>> your faithfulness too, in the assembly of the holy ones.
> For who in the skies above can compare with the LORD?
>> Who is like the LORD among the heavenly beings? [*bene elim*—alternate
>> form of *bene Elohim*]
> In the council of the holy ones God is greatly feared;
>> he is more awesome than all who surround him.
> Who is like you, LORD God Almighty? [Yahweh *Elohim* of
>> Armies {*Sabaoth*}]
> You, LORD, are mighty, and your faithfulness surrounds you.
>> (Psalm 89:5-8 [Hebrew 89:6-9])

In this Psalm, Yahweh is set apart above all the "sons of God" and the "holy ones." God in his faithfulness is surrounded by his council. *Elohim* is also the God of Armies (or hosts, *tsebaot*). These "gods" or "sons of God" are not worshiped and clearly not on par with Yahweh but serve in his heavenly assembly, or divine council. Similar expression is found in Exodus 15:11, "Who is like you among the gods, Yahweh? Who is like you—glorious in holiness, awesome *in* praiseworthy actions, doing wonders?"[32]

In the Septuagint and Second Temple literature, *sabaoth* (or *tsebaot*, hosts, or armies) and *elohim* are referred to as principalities (*archai, exousiai*) and powers (*dynameis*) who rule over the nations of the world and participate in the divine council either cooperatively with God and humanity or antagonistically.[33]

It is not surprising that the Old Testament does not have more to say directly about evil forces, demons, or a celestial figure named Satan, since humanity handed over their authority to serve the powers of a kingdom in opposition to Yahweh God in Genesis 3, 6, and 11. Through betrayal of their allegiance to God, humanity yielded their authority to serve the serpent and other *elohim* in rebellion against God.[34]

---

[32]LEB translation.
[33]Caird, *Principalities and Powers*, 11-15.
[34]See Lk 4:5-7: "The devil led him up to a high place and showed him in an instant all the kingdoms of the world. And he said to him, 'I will give you all their authority and splendor; it has been given to me, and I can give it to anyone I want to. If you worship me, it will all be yours.'"

However, when Jesus Christ came as the Second Adam, a "Son of Adam," he took back legal authority over all spiritual powers in league against God through living a perfect life of obedience to God the Father. The opposing forces had no legal claim on Jesus. He canceled our debt we owed due to the decrees against us, nailing our debts to the cross. Jesus thereby "disarmed the rulers and authorities" and triumphed over them through his death, resurrection, and ascension to the right hand of the Father—since they had no legal basis to hold his body in death. Jesus then handed his authority to his disciples, and to all who believe in his name. Jesus lawfully took back humanity's right to wield authority over the spiritual powers of darkness and restored to us our God-given authority (Mt 10:1-8; Mk 16:15-18; Jn 17:20-21; Eph 1:15-23). Why then does evil still pervade?

"RULES OF ENGAGEMENT" IN THE COSMIC CONFLICT OF GOOD AND EVIL

One of life's biggest questions is how a God who is wholly loving and just can allow evil. The "rules of engagement" theory, as presented by John Peckham, provides a significant response.[35] As he points out, "The very way one conceives of God and God's providential involvement in this world bears significantly not only on how suffering and evil are understood, but also on how they are felt and processed."[36] Peckham defines rules of engagement as "jointly recognized parameters within which an accuser may make a case."[37]

The Bible makes frequent references to a heavenly courtroom scene, where accusations against humans or nations or spiritual entities are brought before God as judge. Sometimes accusations are made against God, challenging his character or his justice, as we will see in an analysis of Job. God is depicted as sitting amid "the gods," or divine beings, so that God makes decisions along with his heavenly court. Occasionally a human is present in the council (Is 6:1-13; Ezek 1; Zech 3:6-10).

---

[35]I have taken the term "Rules of Engagement" from John C. Peckham's work in *Theodicy of Love: Cosmic Conflict and the Problem of Evil* (Grand Rapids, MI: Baker Academic, 2018); Peckham, "Rules of Engagement: God's Permission of Evil in Light of Selected Cases of Scripture," *Bulletin for Biblical Research* 30, no. 2 (2020): 243-60.

[36]Peckham, *Theodicy of Love*, viii.

[37]Peckham, "Rules of Engagement," 250.

Peckham writes that love requires the "freedom to trust or distrust God," so that in God's "response to demonic allegations against his character, then, God could not immediately bring about a state of affairs wherein everyone freely recognizes his perfect goodness and love."[38] In this framework, God allows the devil and other complicit forces "a specified jurisdiction, including agreed on parameters within which to work," which he calls "covenantal rules of engagement" as "part of a bilateral agreement between parties that effectively limits the action of both and that neither party can unilaterally change."[39]

Genesis 1 informs us that God created all things good. There was no conflict or animosity. There were no wars or hidden motives. Life, as God intended, was given order and abundance. An all-powerful, all-creative God could have decided to make a cosmos in which there were no other intelligent, free-thinking beings: a simple autocracy with creatures lacking the ability to rebel or make independent decisions. Beautiful but sterile. Living but lifeless in terms of relationship. Conflict free but without any creative force aside from God alone.

This reminds me of some sci-fi movies, such as *Blade Runner* and its sequel *Blade Runner 2049*, in which humans make or marry robots that they program to always give the right answer and always do the right thing, according to the human. Other similar stories include a world in which robots take over to eliminate the untidiness of human feelings, errors, or ideas that had not been preprogrammed for the optimal survival of the robots. Can compassion, care, or concern for beings other than oneself or a designated despot survive in a world without some range of freedom of thought, expression—and error? Indeed, it's the errors, weaknesses, frailties, failings, and hurts that require compassion, care, and concern. Let's consider this conundrum through the lens of the divine council and heavenly courtroom scene as the character of God and humans are subjected to cosmic prosecution.

Victor Hamilton points out that in Genesis 3, the heart of the serpent's challenge to Eve and Adam is its slander of God's character. The serpent forces the question whether they will believe that God is trustworthy and wants their best, or that God is a liar who is withholding goodness from

---

[38]Peckham, *Theodicy of Love*, 104.
[39]Peckham, *Theodicy of Love*, 104.

them so that they should desert their allegiance and trust the serpent instead.[40] Peckham shows that in the opening chapters of the Bible, "The character of God is front and center. . . . From Genesis to Revelation, questions regarding God's character and government are raised in heaven and on earth. . . . A conflict over character cannot be settled by sheer power."[41] The questions remain: "Is God just? Does God love perfectly? Is evil God's fault?"[42]

Richard Davidson states, "Before God executes judgment (either positively or negatively) toward an individual or a people, He first conducts legal proceedings, not for Him to know the facts, but to reveal in open court, as it were, that He is just and faithful in all His dealings."[43] Scripture carries a "covenant lawsuit motif," as theologian Kevin Vanhoozer observes: the "great theater of the world turns out to be a courtroom" in which, "What is being tried is covenant faithfulness: the righteousness of God."[44]

In each of the following examples from Scripture, judgments are made before a divine council over which God presides. But the council includes "the open demonstration of God's government before celestial beings, countering the cosmic allegations against God's character."[45] In other words, allegations can be brought against God himself and those who serve God. Paul in the New Testament seems to express his sufferings in light of this understanding, as he writes to the church in Corinth: "God has exhibited us apostles last of all, as men condemned to death; because we have become a spectacle to the world [*kosmos*], both to angels and to men" (1 Cor 4:9; cf. 6:2-3). As Peckham states, "This concept of cosmic trial proceedings might suggest a broader framework for the repeated New Testament calls for Christians to be witnesses and testify, alongside other frequent imagery of legal court proceedings."[46]

---

[40]Victor P. Hamilton, *The Book of Genesis: Chapters 1–17*, New International Commentary on the Old Testament (Grand Rapids, MI: Eerdmans, 1990), 188-89.
[41]Peckham, *Theodicy of Love*, 89, 91.
[42]Peckham, *Theodicy of Love*, 91.
[43]Richard M. Davidson, "The Divine Covenant Lawsuit Motif in Canonical Perspective," *Journal of the Adventist Theological Society* 21, no. 1–2 (2010): 83; Peckham, *Theodicy of Love*, 92.
[44]Kevin J. Vanhoozer, *Faith Speaking Understanding: Performing the Drama of Doctrine* (Louisville: Westminster John Knox, 2014), 104-5, 107.
[45]Peckham, *Theodicy of Love*, 96.
[46]Peckham, *Theodicy of Love*, 96.

Although God is omnipotent, his power is self-limiting because of his moral character. God never breaks his promises or his covenants; the agreements God makes are binding on his actions, by his own decree. Scripture provides many examples where "it appears there are 'rules' that might prevent God from doing or preventing what he otherwise would choose to do or prevent."[47] Peckham summarizes:

> Put briefly, in any instance where God does not intervene to prevent some horrendous evil, to do so might have (1) been against the rules, (2) impinged on creaturely free will in a way that would undercut the love relationship, or (3) resulted in greater evil or less flourishing of love. . . . Since the cosmic war is not one of sheer force but one of character—a challenge to God's moral government and thus a battle for hearts and minds—there must be known limits or rules within which the enemy can operate. (cf. Job 1–2; Dan 10)[48]

It is important to note that humanity's rebellion against God opened the door for malevolent spiritual beings to gain access to use the power that had been given to humans within the physical realm. Humanity's complicity with spiritual forces opposed to God also gave those forces the right to challenge God in the physical realm, as well as access to use the power that had been allotted solely to humans. Tragically, every time humans fail to trust in God, we abdicate our dominion over creation and relinquish our authority to evil entities.

God did not initiate the process of evil: we did, and we do. As Peckham writes, "Creatures have departed from God's ideal will, thereby actualizing evil."[49] He continues, "Any conflict between an omnipotent God and others could not be one of sheer power but . . . a dispute over God's moral character and government," and allegations "raised before the heavenly council, claiming that God is not wholly good, loving, or just . . . cannot be won by the mere exercise of power but . . . by an extended demonstration of character in a cosmic courtroom."[50] Here are a few examples.

The Divine Council, Rules of Engagement, and Job. The book of Job provides an example in which horrific things happen to good people. In

---

[47]Peckham, *Theodicy of Love*, 108.
[48]Peckham, *Theodicy of Love*, 109.
[49]Peckham, *Theodicy of Love*, 110.
[50]Peckham, "Rules of Engagement," 88.

reading it we discover that our knowledge of the ways of God and the ways of the cosmic legal system is severely limited.

The opening two chapters of Job are heavily contested regarding the role that God and the *satan* play in causing Job's calamities. Gaining a perspective on the divine council and the rules of engagement sheds light on these issues. The opening verse of the book informs us that Job was not an Israelite and that he was "blameless, upright, fearing God and turning away from evil" (Job 1:1). The introduction continues to describe the abundance of his family, prosperity, influence, and piety. By the sixth verse of the first chapter, and again at the beginning of the second chapter, the reader is given privileged information that the human participants in the story are not given: that the sons of God (*bene Ha-elohim*) "came to present themselves" before Yahweh, and also that the accuser (the *satan*) came into the midst of Yahweh's council (Job 1:6; 2:1).[51] Here, the accuser enters Yahweh's council as an intruder—or a court prosecutor—and demonstrates an adversarial role against God and Job. Scholar Carol Newsom describes the dialogue between Yahweh and the *satan* as having "a formal, almost ritual" quality.[52]

In both scenes, when the accuser enters the divine council Yahweh asks him, "Where have you come from? . . . Have you considered ["set your heart on"] my servant Job? There is no one on earth like him; he is blameless and upright, a man who fears God and shuns evil" (Job 1:7-8). Newsom finds that God is not asking for information, but "Yahweh's challenging question suggests an ongoing rivalry with the *satan*."[53] The accuser puts forth the case before the council that the only reason Job fears God is because God protects and prospers him and gives him everything he could want. Therefore, the *satan* contends, that if God removed his hedge of protection and Job lost what is valuable to him, Job would curse God. As Peckham points out, the *satan* is not only accusing Job of duplicity in his motives, but he is also accusing God of being unjust, and a liar who has not rightly discerned the character of Job: "In Frances Andersen's view, 'God's character and Job's are both slighted.' Lindsay Wilson adds, this 'is a questioning not just of Job's

---

[51]White, *Yahweh's Council*, 23, 65-66.
[52]Carol A. Newsom, "Job," in *New Interpreter's Bible* (Nashville: Abingdon, 1996), 4:348.
[53]Newsom, "Job," 349.

motives but also of God's rule.' Victor Hamilton comments, further, this is 'patently slanderous.'"[54] To this legal challenge to God's character (and Job's), Yahweh responds, "Look, all that belongs to him is in your power ["hand"]. Only do not stretch out your hand against him" (Job 1:12 LEB).

Let's consider the legal basis for Yahweh's response. In Part three, I explained that evil entered the world when humanity's rebellion against God forfeited our creational authority over the earth to malevolent spiritual forces (Gen 1:26-28; 2:15; 3:1-7). This betrayal gave dominion over the earth to the alien powers of darkness and put humans in subjection to them. It is likewise in the New Testament. For example, in the temptation of Jesus in the wilderness, "The devil led him [Jesus] up to a high place and showed him in an instant all the kingdoms of the world. And he said to him, 'I will give you all their authority and splendor; *it has been given to me*, and I can give it to anyone I want to'" (Lk 4:5-6; Mt 4:8-9, emphasis mine). This was a real temptation. The devil is stating that a legal transaction took place between him and humanity in which we handed over, or betrayed, our power to the adversary of God. Although Job was blameless and feared God, he was human and not perfect; therefore, the *satan* had a legal right to bring his accusation, but Yahweh still set the parameters. As Peckham states, in Job, "The *satan* possesses power to work evil in this world as its temporary ruler, but only within limits that are openly negotiated and modified before the heavenly council."[55]

The accuser's first massive attack against Job wiped out his children and his wealth. Yet, Job remained faithful and did not curse God. The second scene with the *satan* entering the divine council begins like the first. Yahweh affirms Job's integrity and the accusations had been proven false. However, the *satan* ramps up his charges against God and Job, asserting that if Job's health was threatened, he would curse God. Yahweh responds like he did to the first accusation, acknowledging that the power was in the hands of the accuser to afflict, but that he set the limits, forbidding the *satan* to take Job's life. Once again, "In all this, Job did not sin with his lips" by cursing God for

---

[54]Peckham, "Rules of Engagement," 248; Francis L. Anderson, *Job* (Nottingham, UK: Inter-Varsity, 1976), 89; Lindsay Wilson, *Job* (Grand Rapids, MI: Eerdmans, 2015), 34; Victor P. Hamilton and David Noel Freedman, "Satan," in *Anchor Bible Dictionary* (New York: Doubleday, 1996), 5:985.

[55]Peckham, *Theodicy of Love*, 95.

his calamities. The book of Job then continues with over thirty chapters of arguments between Job and his "friends," with Job asserting his innocence and his friends insisting that Job must have sinned for these disasters to have fallen on him.

Although Yahweh answers Job, he does not provide direct answers to the questions he and his friends had been asking about why the calamities fell so hard on an upright and blameless person. Rather, Yahweh begins by responding to Job's first lament that it would have been better that he was never born than to see such devastation and sorrow (Job 3:1-26). Yahweh speaks of giving birth to the earth as a mother gives birth to a child: with the world bursting forth from the womb, God wrapping it in clouds like swaddling while all the sons of God shout for joy (Job 38:1-11)! Yahweh reminds Job that he first was a father and a mother to creation. God gave life to the dawn and all that lives with wisdom and in community with the heavenly host. Birthing language is used again in Job 38:28-29, "Does the rain have a father? Who fathers the drops of dew? From whose womb comes the ice? Who gives birth to the frost from the heavens?" God created all and oversees all. Each creature is cared for and has a purpose beyond the capacity for Job to fully comprehend (Job 38–39).

In the next section, Job 40–41, Yahweh again answers Job and speaks of his judgments and justice. Yahweh proclaims that the earthly powers and pride that terrorize humanity and wreak havoc will eventually be put in place and brought low. Within both answers is the invitation for Job to trust the Lord's goodness, decisions, and justice. In the closing chapter, Job responds positively, retracts his complaints, and declares, "My ears had heard of you but now my eyes have seen you" (Job 42:5). Job has encountered the living God and is at peace. Yahweh justly restores Job as best as possible with the losses he experienced. While Yahweh takes accountability for Job's hardships (Job 42:11), within his heavenly courtroom scene it is acknowledged that the accuser, the *satan*, who had access as prosecutor and the power to inflict pain, had legally incited Yahweh to allow the evils (Job 2:3). And "The LORD blessed the latter part of Job's life more than the former part" (Job 42:12).

Although still challenging, Peckham's rules of engagement provide an insightful lens to understanding the workings of evil in Job. The courtroom scene is a legal means through which the *satan* can challenge God and Job's character. "Ultimately, God limits evil, and out of God's love for us and our freedom, God allows limited power to the *satan* in order that the consistency of God's character might be demonstrated. Evil, then, is not caused by God, but by antagonistic powers that can exist within the space of God's self-limit."[56] Let's look at another example with a different outcome.

The Divine Council, Rules of Engagement, and Ahab. In this account, King Ahab of the northern kingdom of Israel set out in his heart to attack the Arameans to take back the land of Ramoth-Gilead, which he claimed belonged to him and not the Arameans (1 Kings 22; 2 Chron 18). Ahab sought his then friend King Jehoshaphat of the southern kingdom of Judah to join with him in this land-grab attempt against the king of Aram. King Ahab consistently demonstrated his antagonism against Yahweh and his allegiance to the gods of Baal of the Canaanites. He had already made a small land grab by having his neighbor Naboth killed so he could steal his vineyard and property after Naboth refused to sell it to the king. He and his wife, Jezebel, daughter of King Ethbaal of Tyre and Sidon in Phoenicia, tried to kill the prophet Elijah. The biblical record states that Ahab "did more to arouse the anger of the LORD, the God of Israel, than did all the kings of Israel before him" (1 Kings 16:33). In Ahab's latest offense, he relied on his prophets of Baal for advice and rejected the admonition of Micaiah, a remaining prophet of Yahweh. Micaiah describes his vision of the heavenly council scene and declares it to Ahab and Ahab's consort of false prophets saying,

> Therefore, hear the word of the LORD: I saw the LORD sitting on his throne with all the multitudes of heaven ["the host/army of the heavens"] standing around him on his right and on his left. And the LORD said, "Who will entice Ahab into attacking Ramoth Gilead and going to his death there?"
>
> One suggested this, and another that. Finally, a spirit came forward, stood before the LORD and said, "I will entice him."
>
> "By what means?" the LORD asked.
>
> "I will go out and be a deceiving spirit in the mouths of all his prophets," he said.

---

[56]Thank you to Rachel Hastings for this wording. See also Peckham, "Rules of Engagement," 251.

"You will succeed in enticing him," said the LORD. "Go and do it."

"So now the LORD has put a deceiving spirit in the mouths of all these prophets of yours. The LORD has decreed disaster [evil, calamity] for you." (1 Kings 22:19-23; cf. 2 Chron 18:21-23)

This courtroom judgment scene is set up to fulfill the words spoken earlier by Elijah when he prophesied to Ahab of his coming death, which was justly due after he had wrongfully murdered his neighbor Naboth, adding to his expansive acts of wickedness. Elijah states, "You have sold yourself to do evil in the eyes of the LORD. He says, 'I am going to bring disaster [evil, calamity] on you.' . . . There was never anyone like Ahab, who sold himself to do evil in the eyes of the LORD, urged on by Jezebel his wife" (1 Kings 21:20-25).

Yahweh, in consultation with the divine council, determines the means of bringing justice to Ahab, who refused to do good but persisted in bringing disaster on others, receiving his just reward of disaster on himself after many warnings and opportunities to change his ways. In this way, evil was justly handled through the participation and cooperation of the heavenly courtroom.

The Divine Council, Rules of Engagement, and Sodom. In Genesis 18–19, we find what could be considered an enactment of the divine council proceedings. The scene is introduced by stating that Yahweh appeared to Abraham. Then the narrator describes three "men" approaching the camps of Abraham and Sarah. Abraham seems to immediately perceive a divine encounter and rushes to have food and footwashing (a polite protocol in the desert) provided for his heavenly visitors. The narrative assures one final time that the couple would have a baby even though Sarah was well past her childbearing years. Yahweh says to her, "Is anything too hard for the LORD?"

From there, the two men later identified as angels, or messengers (Gen 19:1) accompany Yahweh's personal appearance to Abraham and Sarah, and then proceed to Sodom and Gomorrah to personally look into the outcry that had come to Yahweh due to the great oppression and sin of the people there. But first, Yahweh stops to engage in conversation with Abraham, to let him know of the pending plans to destroy Sodom and Gomorrah due to their destructive culture. This conversation takes place because of

Yahweh's confidence in Abraham to do what is right and just (Gen 18:19). Abraham's questioning and challenge to Yahweh is welcomed as he asks,

> Will you sweep away the righteous with the wicked? What if there are fifty righteous people in the city? Will you really sweep it away and not spare the place for the sake of the fifty righteous people in it? Far be it from you to do such a thing—to kill the righteous with the wicked, treating the righteous and the wicked alike. Far be it from you! Will not the Judge of all the earth do right [justice]?" (Gen 18:23-25)

The challenge and conversation continue until Abraham is down to ten righteous in the city, which is where Yahweh sets his parameter for sparing the city. The next chapter continues with the two men/angels/messengers of God visiting the city to see the level of atrocities and to determine the just judgment for the cities and the people. Here we see the enactment of the decision of the divine council and the rules of engagement for allowing evil, or destruction to come in equal proportion to the evil, or destruction, committed. The prophet Jeremiah describes the crimes of the people of Sodom in this way: "They strengthen the hands of evildoers, so that not one of them turns from their wickedness" (Jer 23:14). Ezekiel describes them as "arrogant, overfed and unconcerned," adding these words from the LORD: "They did not help the poor and needy. They were haughty and did detestable things before me. Therefore I did away with them as you have seen" (Ezek 16:49-50). And as Isaiah declares, "They have brought disaster upon themselves. . . . They will enjoy the fruit of their deeds. Woe to the wicked! Disaster is upon them! They will be paid back for what their hands have done" (Is 3:9-11).

Abraham's declaration is a foundational affirmation held firm in biblical belief about God and the rules of engagement made by the divine council: The Judge of all the earth will do justice (Gen 18:25), toward the righteous and toward the wicked.

The Divine Council, Rules of Engagement, and Daniel. The divine council and rules of engagement are also seen in Daniel 7:9-27, where Daniel saw multiple thrones set up around the throne of the "Ancient of Days" with "thousands of thousands" attending him and "ten thousand times ten thousand" standing before him. "The court was seated, and the books were opened" and judgment pronounced against "the beast" and "the rest of the beasts" (Dan 7:10-12). The judgment was to slay "the beast" and remove the dominion of "the rest of the beasts" with an extension of life granted to them. The legal decision was made in the heavenly courtroom setting by the heavenly council.

Later in that same chapter, Daniel sees beasts, identified as kings and kingdoms, arising and waging war with God's people, overpowering them and wearing them down. But once again, "the court will sit" and the power and dominion of this final beast "will be taken away and completely destroyed forever" (Dan 7:26). Then, all the kingdoms and their dominions will be given to the people of "the Most High" (Dan 7:27), which seems to be a continuation of the decisions and actions of the heavenly courtroom. The divine council plays a role in determining the time and means of the end of the age, when God's kingdom prevails over human and spiritual conflict and evil once and for all.

The Divine Council and Rules of Engagement in the New Testament. Consistently in the New Testament, malevolent spiritual entities called the devil, demons, and unclean spirits are identified as enemies of God and humanity. As Brian Gregg points out, "The conflict between God and Satan is clearly a central feature of Jesus' teaching and ministry" and is significantly more pronounced in the New Testament than in the Old Testament.[57] As C. S. Lewis states, Christianity "does not think this is a war between independent powers. It thinks it is a civil war, a rebellion, and that we are living in a part of the universe occupied by the rebel."[58] Although some theologians of the last decades dismiss these powers, they do so to our harm.

Rules of engagement are demonstrated when Jesus says to Peter, "Simon, Simon, Satan has asked to sift all of you as wheat" (Lk 22:31, see chapter 10, under "Satan in the New Testament"). The word translated Satan has "asked" is *exaiteō*, means "to ask for with emphasis and with the implication of having a right to do so, *ask for, demand.*"[59] Although the text does not explain what right Satan had, Jesus surprisingly does not stop Satan's attack, but tells Peter instead that he is praying for him that his faith would not fail.

---

[57]Brian Han Gregg, *What Does the Bible Say About Suffering?* (Downers Grove, IL: IVP Academic, 2016), 66.

[58]C. S. Lewis, *Mere Christianity* (San Francisco: HarperOne, 2015), 45.

[59]Danker et al., *A Greek-English Lexicon of the New Testament and Other Early Christian Literature* (Chicago: University of Chicago Press, 2000), 344.

He concludes by saying, "When you have turned back, strengthen your brothers" (Lk 22:32). This has a somewhat eerie echo of Job 1:1-6. Jesus, who saw Satan fall like lightning from heaven, who healed all who came to him, who cast out every demon and legion of unclean spirits, who stilled the wind and the waves, let Peter know that Satan seemed to have some legal right to thresh and winnow, to flail and throw into the wind the lives of not only him, but "all of you."

Whether Jesus was referring to the twelve disciples or all Christians is not specified. However, in Peter's letter to the churches, he assures the believers at least five times that they will go through trials, hardships, injustices, and suffering (1 Pet 1:6-10; 2:18-20, 21-26; 3:17-18; 4:12-19; 5:6-11). Although Peter does not speak of a divine council, he recognizes that our faith is on trial (1 Pet 1:6), that there will be a judgment (1 Pet 4:17), and that "the devil prowls around like a roaring lion, seeking someone to devour" (1 Pet 5:8).

The antagonistic works of Satan are expressed by Paul when he writes that he and his companions tried to visit the believers in Thessalonica, "but Satan blocked" their way (1 Thess 2:18). Jesus' beloved disciple John states, "that the whole world is under the control of the evil one" (1 Jn 5:19). Paul recognizes this and expects the readers to understand that we are at war. Satan is identified as the "god of this age" that "has blinded the minds of unbelievers, so that they cannot see the light of the gospel that displays the glory of Christ, who is the image of God" (2 Cor 4:4). This is the "great dragon . . . that ancient serpent called the devil, or Satan, who leads the whole world astray" (Rev 12:9). The adversary works on the minds of people. If evil spiritual beings can get us to think and speak like them, we will do their evil work for them against God. No matter how good or noble a person's work may appear, if it is contrary to God's good plans, biblically, it is evil.

Similarly, the apostle Paul urges his brothers and sisters in the faith in Rome, "Do not conform to the pattern of this world, but be transformed by the renewing of your mind. Then you will be able to test and approve what God's will is—his good, pleasing and perfect will" (Rom 12:2).

Furthermore, the New Testament affirms that human beings who have chosen allegiance to the Lord will one day judge the earth and the divine realm as well: "Do you not know that the Lord's people will judge the world? And if you are to judge the world, are you not competent to judge trivial cases? Do you not know that we will judge angels? How much more the things of this life!" (1 Cor 6:2-3). The book of Revelation also points to a divine council. God is seen on the throne surrounded by twenty-four thrones and elders who are making judgments about the earth (Rev 4–5). In Revelation 20, the courtroom scene reappears with thrones and judgments being made about the end of times of the present earth and the end of the reign of Satan, the dragon, and the opening of the book of life.

This chapter began with the question, If you were to design a universe as the most powerful, loving, and just being in it, what would be your master plan? God used his power to set up an equitable system that delegates responsibility to a divine council in alignment with his core attributes of justice, mercy, and grace. God participates with his created beings and allows his character to be tested, put on trial, and judged. Therefore, he is not unjust when one day each of us will stand before this heavenly courtroom, the divine council. However, those who have already submitted their sin and character flaws to judgment and received forgiveness through Jesus Christ's atoning blood will stand forgiven, cleansed, free of guilt and shame, and pass securely into the joy of God's kingdom, both in this life where evil still attacks and in that to come when evil is no more.

Part Five

GOD AT WORK

Do not be overcome by evil, but overcome evil with good.

Romans 12:21

In the journey through this book, we have explored ways that evil and suffering enter our lives through many paths and sources: through the consequences of our actions and the actions of others; through nature that has been corrupted through millennia of ignorance and greed; through human needs and desires, pride and insecurity, and misused authority; and through malevolent forces bent on destruction through chaos, corruption, and death. Now we dig deeper into the question, Where is God in all this, and how do we cooperate in order to overcome evil with good?

I begin with Jesus' words when he was questioned by Pontius Pilate, accused of sacrilege and sedition by the religious elite who sought to have him killed because he threatened their religious power and political comfort. He said, "My kingdom is not of this world. . . . My kingdom is from another place" (Jn 18:36). As philosopher Dallas Willard states, when we pray "Thy kingdom come," we are participating in God's plan for his heavenly, non-earthly system of operation "to take over at all points in the personal, social, and political order where it is now excluded: 'On earth as it is in heaven.' With this prayer we are invoking it, as in faith we are acting it, into the real world of our daily existence."[1] We need to understand the authority and responsibility that God gave to humanity in creation. When self-centeredness usurps God-centeredness, creation is thrown into chaos and the door is opened for evil to twist God's intended goodness in the world. How do we practically bring a kingdom operating from above into this kingdom operating below?

---

[1]Dallas Willard, *The Divine Conspiracy: Rediscovering Our Hidden Life in God* (San Francisco: Harper, 1998), 56.

Chapter Thirteen

THE POWER OF MERCY AND GRACE

In some sense, God has chosen to be dependent on human (and nonhuman) agents in moving toward the divine objectives.

TERRANCE E. FRETHEIM

WELL-KNOWN NEW TESTAMENT SCHOLAR turned agnostic Bart Ehrman left his faith in God because of the problem of suffering.[1] He quotes Ivan's words from *The Brothers Karamazov*: "It's not God that I do not accept, you understand, it is this world of God's, created by God, that I do not accept and cannot agree to accept."[2] I understand this perspective. Jürgen Moltmann calls this *protest atheism*.[3] We hurt. We see immeasurable suffering around us, and it is natural to blame God, the creator of this world. However, *we have corrupted the world*.[4] When we see the suffering around us, we're looking at the work of our own hands, not the hands of God. Yet, God enters into our suffering with us.[5] He is Immanuel: God with us. He grieves with us, mourns with us, weeps with us, died for us, calls us to bear his image on earth, and invites us to rise victorious with him.

---

[1]Bart D. Ehrman, *God's Problem: How the Bible Fails to Answer Our Most Important Question—Why We Suffer* (New York: HarperOne, 2009), 3.

[2]Fyodor Dostoevsky, *The Brothers Karamazov (Bicentennial Edition): A Novel in Four Parts with Epilogue*, trans. Richard Pevear and Larissa Volokhonsky (New York: Picador, 2021), 235; Ehrman, *God's Problem*, 266.

[3]Jürgen Moltmann, *The Crucified God: 40th Anniversary Edition* (Minneapolis: Fortress, 2015), 344. See pages 343-91 for the full discussion.

[4]For example, see Paul Copan, *Is God a Moral Monster? Making Sense of the Old Testament God* (Grand Rapids, MI: Baker Books, 2011), 28.

[5]Claude F. Mariottini, *Divine Violence and the Character of God* (Eugene, OR: Wipf & Stock, 2022), 58-60; Moltmann, *Crucified God*, 347.

There is no evil-causing suffering in this world that could not have been stopped by the action of a single individual, a group of people, or by the accumulated actions of countless individuals who looked the other way, who betrayed goodness and rightness. This world operates largely under the auspices of malevolent beings working through cooperative humans. God calls, warns, and when repeatedly rebuffed, allows the consequences of collective humanity's freely made choices. The prophet Isaiah expresses God's grief when he declares, "All day long I have held out my hands to an obstinate people, who walk in ways not good, pursuing their own imaginations" (Is 65:2; see also Is 59; Rom 1:18-32). "Woe to those who call evil good and good evil. . . . Woe to those who are wise in their own eyes and clever in their own sight" (Is 5:20-21).

Jesus expresses similar grief in his seven "Woe to you" declarations to the religious leaders of his day. He then prophesies the coming destruction,

> Jerusalem, Jerusalem, you who kill the prophets and stone those sent to you, how often I have longed to gather your children together, as a hen gathers her chicks under her wings, and you were not willing. Look, your house is left to you desolate. For I tell you, you will not see me again until you say, "Blessed is he who comes in the name of the Lord." (Mt 23:37-39)

God calls us to wisdom. He calls us to goodness. But he does not force our hand. Life in this earth is intended as a coregency between the divine parent with the divine children. As humans, we are both dust and divinity, flesh and spirit. There are no ordinary humans. We all bear the divine image. Each of us has great importance.

But we have considered ourselves *less than human*. We often act like beasts. No, worse. Too often, we become deformed into depraved humans who see only dust, only flesh and earthly elements with earthly desires. Blinded to the sublime and transcendent, we suffocate the divine breath so that we no longer feel the consequence of cutting off our connection with God and our own spiritually beautiful selves. Blindfolded to the light and the glory, we revel in darkness and roll in the dirt, as if our earthly bodies were not created as vessels for the divine spark of life and empowered to do what is right and good.

As corrupted selves, we love sensuality without sense. We crave feeling good without care for goodness. We point to evil and shake our fists at God but refuse to raise a hand to stop degradation and oppression. We make ourselves small and submit to malevolent spiritual and earthly powers of wickedness as if God did not promise to be with us. God placed the scepter in our hands, but we let our hands drop and give away God's authority to lesser beings, and then turn and blame God for the suffering in the world.

Among Ehrman's many examples of horrific suffering, he speaks of one of the Ethiopian famines in which "one million people, starved to death, in a world that has far more than enough food to feed all its inhabitants, a world in which American farmers are paid to destroy their crops and most Americans ingest far more calories than our bodies need or want."[6] At the end of one of his lists of "silent suffering," which includes the senselessness of sickness, divorce, broken families, and lost jobs, he asks, "And where is God?"[7] But I ask, and God asks, "Where are you?" Who is breaking down all the broken links in the supply chains of greed that withhold from the poor and give instead to economic and political suppressors? We complain about the world. We complain about God. We complain about our lives. We accuse God of causing the suffering and blame God for not fixing the problems. Systemic greed and injustice seem overwhelming at times. Many people risk their lives to make changes. Yet, as a good friend who's been working in the Middle East for fourteen years helping dislocated immigrants from multiple countries writes:

> God is good. We are evil and the world is broken because of that. Instead of doing away with the world, God is personally redeeming it. That is the biblical worldview in a few sentences. If that is true, then one of the most foundational aspects of reality is that God works good in the midst of evil. He brings redemption into the midst of suffering. In our violent and broken world, God brings life. In big and small ways, our 14 years here have constantly testified to this truth. The more we are willing to enter into the brokenness, the more we have opportunity to see God at work.[8]

Although we hear, see, and experience great tragedies, there are countless beautiful stories of transformed lives. Here's a story from a good friend of mine, Dr. Manuel (Manny) Scott.

---

[6]Ehrman, *God's Problem*, 10–11.
[7]Ehrman, *God's Problem*, 6.
[8]Anonymous, for the protection of my friend. In personal communication on March 18, 2021.

FROM MANNY SCOTT'S STORY

I met Manny when we were both master's students in a small preaching class. I could tell from his speaking and preaching that he had processed a lot of hardship in his life and had a powerful story to share with the world, but I didn't yet know anything about him.[9] At the time he was the assistant pastor at the Second Baptist Church in Evanston, Illinois. I wanted to hear more of what he had to say and for my son, Walter, to hear him preach.

Publicly, some of Manny's story is told in the 2007 hit movie *Freedom Writers*, starring Hilary Swank. The role of Marcus is based in part on Manny's early life. Growing up, he lived in twenty-six places around Los Angeles before he turned sixteen. He had skipped sixty to ninety days of school every year from fourth to ninth grade. His best friend was brutally murdered when he was in middle school. He dropped out of high school as a freshman (as my own son had) and didn't expect to live past eighteen. Life was meaningless and hopeless. But two people stepped into his world. First, one day, a homeless man came and sat next to him on a park bench. This man asked him if he knew where he would go after he died. Because Manny had felt that his own death was near, the question got his attention. That man told Manny about the good news of Jesus and let him know how much God loved him. He also told him that Jesus could change his life if he would only repent of his sins, place his faith in Christ, and commit to follow him. That conversation led Manny to become a follower of Jesus. He started going to church and decided that he needed to go back to school.

In his first English class at Woodrow Wilson High School, he encountered first-year teacher Erin Gruwell. With her fair skin, proper dress, and string of pearls necklace, she was out of place. But she came with aspirations to make a difference and got to know every student, pouring herself into caring about each one, learning their world and their stories. She helped Manny and his classmates improve their attitudes and grades.

[9]See www.MannyScott.com and https://premierespeakers.com/manuel-scott for more about his story and speaking.

Manny got accepted to the University of California at Berkeley, where he met and married Alice. His passion to pay it forward has opened the door for him to speak to over two million students, educators, and leaders around the world, spreading hope, teaching tools to teachers about how to make a difference in the lives of their students, and inspiring hundreds of thousands of students to have hope, to not give up, to give up addictions, and to not take their lives. Some of his books include *Turning the Page: A Memoir*, *Even on Your Worst Day, You Can Be a Student's Best Hope*, and *Teacher Secrets Every Educator Must Know to Empower Students in a Diverse, Digital World*.

In a bold video titled, "A Complicated Truth about School Shooters" released after the massacre in Uvalde, Texas, he speaks to how kids like this are created, which speaks to the larger picture of the proliferation of evil. Manny states, "There's a hopelessness among so many kids in this country . . . who need hope and help." He describes how evil is conceived in a young mind and can fester into murder. From his own story, he shares about the abuse, bullying, and neglect he experienced growing up: "I started hating myself. I started hating others. . . . Eventually, my hope just died . . . and when that died in me, an anger was born, and that anger was creating in me a bitterness that made me want to ruin people's lives. . . . When I saw happy people, I wanted to do something to get that smile off their face. . . . I wanted other people to experience the rage and the bitterness and the sadness that I was living with."[10]

Neither he nor I excuse the horrific actions made by those who choose to become abusers or murderers. Nevertheless, we call into action those of us who can care enough to recognize someone who has turned inward, becoming isolated and enraged, brewing revengeful and murderous thoughts. Each and every one of us can be helped if we are willing. Each and every one of us can help others if we put forth the effort.

We won't know who or how many lives we can impact for good simply by taking an interest in a hurting person's life, listening to their

---

[10]Manny Scott, "A Complicated Truth About School Shooters," May 2022, YouTube video, www.youtube.com/watch?v=3MIwGbylYsk.

story, and demonstrating that we care. Every day, every time you start your day, we have choices to make, to look for opportunities to participate in bringing goodness into the lives of people we meet, or to ignore others and focus on ourselves, our problems, and our needs. Increasing numbers of young people, especially, are depressed, anxious, murderous, or suicidal. If this is you, you're not alone. There are good people who can help. Move away from harmful, hateful, and angry people. Even if that describes you now, it does not need to define you or your future. Life can be full and meaningful. Look for beauty and ponder it. If you're hurting, look for kindness, and don't stop until you find it. And while you're looking, give kindness to someone else who's hurting, just once a week or once a day to start. No matter how poor or deprived you are, you can bring support and kindness into someone else's life, which will enrich your own. No matter how horrific your life has been—no matter how abused—your past does not have to define your future. Changing your present will reshape your past and transform your future.

Manny gives hope to millions of people around the world, especially students and teachers. The hardships and tragedies of his life became the fuel to empower his compassion and his work to see countless more lives empowered to turn around and live well. No matter how entrenched violence and conflict is in a person's family history or context, the decision to extend forgiveness, mercy, and grace instead of judgment and retribution can give a person the opportunity for another chance to experience goodness in life. God set the example in Jesus.

IMAGE FROM GENESIS: A COVERING OF MERCY

The biblical imagery of God's response to betrayal with mercy and grace comes from Genesis, through his provision of a covering called in Hebrew a *kuttonet*, a tunic or garment. The passage reads, "The LORD God made garments of skin for Adam and his wife and clothed them" (Gen 3:21). The specific term used here for garment refers to the covering of animal skin that Yahweh made for the man and the woman after they broke off their relationship with him. In the aftermath of human treachery, God did not give the man and the woman what they deserved for turning their back on his boundless goodness in creation. God showed mercy and grace even though they chose separation from God.

Although there are many biblical Hebrew words for garment, clothing, coat, loin cloth, and so on, the word used here, *kuttonet*, occurs in only one other passage in Genesis. *Kuttonet* refers to the special tunic, "the coat of many colors," that Jacob made for his favored son, Joseph (Gen 37:3, 23, 31-33). This is a garment indicating favored status. Elsewhere in the Pentateuch, the term *kuttonet* is used only to refer to the priestly tunic worn for serving in the tabernacle, and in Ezra-Nehemiah, for the priestly tunic for serving in the temple. The tabernacle and the temple are the place where the ruptured relationships between people, and between people and God are restored. In the Book of Sirach 45:8 (written by Jewish scribe Ben Sira ca. 200–175 BC) the *kuttonet* is the clothing worn by the priests as a symbol of authority.

In the Garden, the man and the woman, not realizing the havoc their betrayal would inflict on their relationship with each other, their offspring, and ultimately the entire earth, committed treason against God. They didn't realize the extent to which their betrayal would shatter their relationship with each other and the earth and bring conflict among their offspring. Nevertheless, God knew, and provided a covering that required the death of an animal in place of the death sentence they legally deserved. God covered them with divine mercy. Even though they expressed no remorse or sorrow for defying him, God extended his hand of grace. God acted first, knowing that in time, humanity would be redeemed and restored once again.

The importance of mercy is seen next in the tabernacle, and then the temple, where the centerpiece of worship in the Holy of Holies is the Mercy Seat, the name given to the place God manifested himself. Jesus is called the Mercy Seat (*hilastērion*, Rom 3:25).[11]

MERCY OVER JUDGMENT

Goodness is an essential attribute of God, established in Genesis 1, where God's assessment of his creation, "it is good," is repeated seven times. Mercy and grace are tangible expressions of goodness. From Genesis 3 through the

---

[11]Daniel P. Bailey, "Jesus as the Mercy Seat: The Semantics and Theology of Paul's Use of Hilasterion in Romans 3:25" (PhD diss., University of Cambridge, 1999).

rest of Scripture, the operation of God's mercy and grace are foundational to the expression of his character through his will to reconcile humanity and to heal their conflict with creation. God so values his image-bearers that he holds mercy as a higher value than judgment, even for the most heinous violations, unless they reject his mercy.[12]

Mercy and compassion, in Hebrew, often come from the word for womb, *rhm*, carrying the connotation of the protection and tenderness that a pregnant woman normally feels for her developing child. This is the first descriptor Yahweh God gave to Moses in the prominent scene where Moses asked God to show him his glory. But Yahweh responds that he would show him his goodness, and declares his name: "The LORD, the LORD, the compassionate (*rahum*) and gracious (*hannun*) God, slow to anger, abounding in love (*hesed*) and faithfulness (*emet*), maintaining love to thousands, and forgiving wickedness, rebellion and sin" (Ex 34:6-7). Another Hebrew word sometimes translated as *grace* or *mercy* is *hesed*, which is also translated as *lovingkindness, believing loyalty, faithfulness,* and *steadfast love.*

In the Greek, the main word usually translated mercy or compassion is *eleos,* which "often means to have pity or show compassion to someone in difficult circumstances. Paul uses the term to indicate God showing him mercy (Rom 11:30, 31, 32; 1 Cor 7:25; 2 Cor 4:1; 1 Tim 1:13, 16)."[13] The main Greek word for grace is *charis,* or *charitos.* It has to do with favor, an expression or act of kindness without obligation. It is also associated with the Hebrew word *hesed.*

Conceptually, it is possible to have justice without mercy. But it is not possible to have mercy without justice. In a system of pure justice, the guilty would always be punished and the innocent would always be rewarded. But what if there is no one in the system without guilt? The end would be only endless trial and punishment. However, in a system where only God is all-loving and without fault, mercy is required for all. Mercy is powerfully able to transform one who has done wrong into a beloved one, a living vessel of mercy and love. Ethan Coke expresses this well,

---

[12]John Frederick, "Mercy and Compassion," in *Lexham Theological Wordbook*, ed. Douglas Mangum et al., Lexham Bible Reference Series (Bellingham, WA: Lexham, 2014).
[13]Frederick, "Mercy and Compassion."

Often the justice of the Lord is pitted against his mercy—as though, by exercising mercy, he is no longer just or, by righteously judging the world, he is no longer mercifully loving. . . . This (the justice of the Lord) is not a terrifying reality to scare us into submission, but it's a hopeful reality. It reminds us that God is the Lord of creation, holding it to a standard of goodness that is perfectly just, while working on bringing that creation into freedom and glory. (Rom 8:18-21)[14]

Mercy and grace become meaningless if they are unhinged from justice and righteousness. Justice is only as good as the moral character of the one who is judging. The first agency of action-consequence is rooted in the laws of nature and justice. But the greater agency of mercy and grace is at work, which intervenes and overrules the first when the appropriate conditions apply.

God extends mercy and grace when a governing law has not yet been given or communicated. As the New Testament states, "To be sure, sin was in the world before the law was given, but sin is not charged against anyone's account where there is no law" (Rom 5:13). But when someone knowingly transgresses boundaries, the Lord intervenes in human lives on behalf of those who call on him and believe his word. God extends mercy to the repentant, and grace to the faithful.

The biblical term for doing wrong is sin, which carries a requirement of repayment to make it right again. Old Testament scholar Mark Boda summarizes the way God enters in to remedy our brokenness: "A basic pattern for the divine-human interplay in relation to sin runs the breadth of the Old Testament from Genesis to Chronicles. The normative form of this pattern begins with *human sin*, which prompts *divine discipline*. This discipline leads to a *human response* expressed as a cry to God . . . which then results in *divine grace*."[15] Divine discipline allows the consequences of one's actions to happen, with the hope of getting our attention and changing our desire so that we will turn away from the sin and back to God's love and mercy. We're

---

[14]Ethan Coke, "Judges" (essay written for OT 308 Historical Books and the Prophets, Northern Seminary, Lisle, IL, January 29, 2022).

[15]See also Boda, *Severe Mercy*, 519; cf. 354. This idea is also shown in Judg 2–3, with God's ultimate goal of "divine transformation" of the sinner through which God transforms the human creature through his divine grace, as seen especially in the eschatological writings of Jeremiah and Ezekiel (519, 364).

all tempted to do wrong. But, "When tempted, no one should say, 'God is tempting me.' For God cannot be tempted by evil, nor does he tempt anyone; but each person is tempted when they are dragged away by their own evil desire and enticed. Then, after desire has conceived, it gives birth to sin; and sin, when it is full-grown, gives birth to death" (Jas 1:13-15). The process of evil growing from self-centered desire is straightforward, which is why the Bible uses the term *sin*, not to scare us but to be realistic about how easily we harm others and ourselves.

Far from portraying God as an arbitrary mafia boss or cosmic bully, the Bible speaks with clarity of God's mercy and grace alongside his justice. He intervenes and redeems even the most-evil intentions of those who repent, and beautifully restores the lives of the faithful, even when they are marred by pain and the evil done against them. This pattern is portrayed throughout Scripture. Beginning in the Joseph narrative, through the Judges, continuing through David and the Prophets, and finally into the New Testament, we see his mercy displayed and his grace extended to all who will receive.

GOD'S OUTSTRETCHED HAND OF MERCY

God continually extends his hand in relationship far more than I can imagine having the patience to do so. Sometimes I wonder why people who repeatedly do cruel things are not struck down and why they seem to get away with so much damage. Despite God's grace, the prophet Isaiah observes: "But when grace is shown to the wicked, they do not learn righteousness; even in a land of uprightness they go on doing evil and do not regard the majesty of the LORD" (Is 26:10). God patiently and graciously sends people and circumstances into our lives to reveal where we are hardened, frozen, blinded, or not yet free. Our response is our choice, which is rarely an easy one due to the firm control we want to maintain on our own lives and the lives of others. But our choice will either bring us into freedom in the present or keep us chained to our self and to those we won't release. If we persist in our grip on resentment and disregard for God's mercy, our choices will eventually destroy us, or others.

Often people mimic relationship with God through outward religious practices. It's like a marriage relationship in which one spouse acts and says all the right things in public or social media, but there is no personal communication, no affection, no genuine caring about the thoughts, feelings, or life of the other—it's all a show to look good and get approval from people outside the home. This type of sin is pseudo-goodness or religiosity, when we say and do all the "right" things as an act for others, but our heart is not there. This external show does not result in true goodness, because it comes from a bitter seed. The words and actions may sound and look good, but when they are self-motivated to promote one's own agenda, they contain evil. Likewise, religious words and practices can never replace the daily building of a close, personal relationship with God. Jesus speaks of this when he refers to people who do many mighty works in his name but do not know God or do God's will. Jesus declares to them, "I never knew you. Away from me, you evildoers!" (Mt 7:23).

Religious behavior is like a son who takes his father or mother's money, credit, or good name to buy and do what he wants with it without asking his parents. Such behavior nullifies relationship. Jesus describes this in his parable about the prodigal sons. One son asked for his inheritance in advance and squandered it all. The father gave both of his sons the liberty to take what he had given them and manage their lives as they desired. When the son who had squandered his inheritance and renounced his family name returned to his home, his father ran to greet him, welcomed him back as a son, and integrated him back into the father's house. However, the real rogue was the other son who stayed home. For, outwardly he was doing all the right things, but inwardly he was resentful and bitter toward his father and his brother and lacked love and mercy. The brother who stayed home was the true prodigal. The son who left and returned laid down his guilt and shame to receive his father's mercy and grace, rebuilding relationship and love. The one who stayed behind did what was expected, but his heart was cold.

GUILT AND SHAME DESTROY—MERCY AND GRACE RESTORE

In Jesus' earthly ministry, he exemplified love by extending mercy and grace to all who came to him for help and healing. He instructed his disciples to be like him: "Heal the sick, raise the dead, cleanse those who have leprosy, drive out demons. Freely you have received; freely give" (Mt 10:8). Notice the last part of his sentence—freely you have received; freely give. We are only capable of freely giving to others what we have first freely received ourselves. In God's kingdom, goodness, mercy, grace, and love come from the Lord. Holding onto our guilt, shame, anger, bitterness, or resentment crowds out our ability to receive mercy, grace, forgiveness, and healing. Those who are judgmental and unable to give mercy and grace may have never freely received the goodness of God.

I remember a very close friend of mine who died after a long battle with cancer. She was one of the kindest people I've ever known and spent many of her final months visiting, helping, and comforting others with cancer. Once she told me that everyone with cancer she had the opportunity to speak with closely felt guilt over something in their life. Then she told me the guilt she carried for her resentment toward her father, who had also died of cancer. This was just her observation, and I haven't sought to find out if any studies or statistics back it up. However, I do wonder how many people live with a deep sense of guilt or shame that eats away at them and may impact their body's ability to heal or fight off disease, How many are driven by guilt or shame to run from people or from God, to dull painful memories through addictions, or to work themselves to exhaustion? Guilt and shame are thieves that steal our capacity for joy. But God draws us with his kindness (Rom 2:4).

When Jesus was asked, "What must we do to do the works God requires?" he answered, "The work of God is this: to believe in the one he has sent" (Jn 6:28-29). Believing in Jesus means following him, loving him, and doing his work. For each of us, this begins when we receive his love, goodness, mercy, grace, and forgiveness for the sin of going our own way. As we freely receive, we have the capacity to freely give to others from the fullness we have received.

How can we respond to the quote from *The Brothers Karamazov*, "It's not that I don't accept God, you must understand, it's the world created by Him I don't and cannot accept"?[16] The power dynamics that we live in have distorted God's creation and corrupted the way things are supposed to be in

---

[16]Fyodor Dostoyevsky, *The Brothers Karamazov by Fyodor Dostoyevsky*, Parts Edition (Hastings, East Sussex: Delphi Classics), 387.

this world. As Genesis 1:26 tells us, humans were created to exercise God's dominion and rule over the earth.[17]

When humanity chose to reject God's rule, the consequences did not just affect us but all of creation. In fact, all of creation is groaning, and waiting for us to step up into our God-given role as image-bearers. God never withdrew our responsibility, and through Jesus Christ he has handed back our legal authority over the powers of darkness. And although one day all the forces of evil will be judged, we continue to live in a time of mercy and grace. Peter describes it like this: "The Lord is not slow in keeping his promise, as some understand slowness. Instead he is patient with you, not wanting anyone to perish, but everyone to come to repentance" (2 Pet 3:9). We are living between two worlds. God's mercy toward us is vast.

Knowing that this present world is filled with evils, good people long for a life that we all somehow know is not here. But our role in cooperating with God is vital as we pray, "Your kingdom come, your will be done, here on earth, in my situation, as you will in heaven." Lord, help us know your ways, hear your word, and bring about your purposes each day in our lives.

---

[17]Christopher J. H. Wright, *Old Testament Ethics for the People of God* (Downers Grove, IL: IVP Academic, 2004), 119.

Chapter Fourteen

THE COSTLY WORK OF FORGIVENESS

Be kind and compassionate to one another, forgiving
each other, just as in Christ God forgave you.

Ephesians 4:32

MERCY AND GRACE are most fully expressed by the words and actions of forgiveness. When Jesus taught his disciples how to pray, his teaching focused attention on forgiveness: "And forgive us our debts, as we also have forgiven our debtors. . . . For if you forgive other people when they sin against you, your heavenly Father will also forgive you. But if you do not forgive others their sins, your Father will not forgive your sins" (Mt 6:12, 14-15).

This is a tough message. So tough, that the only time Jesus' apostles ever asked him, "Increase our faith!" was after he told them to forgive others. "If your brother or sister sins against you, rebuke them; and if they repent, forgive them. Even if they sin against you seven times in a day and seven times come back to you saying, 'I repent,' you must forgive them" (Lk 17:3-5). Forgiveness is the hardest thing we can do. Lord, increase our faith!

However, the context of and instructions on forgiveness are important. Jesus begins the conversation with his disciples about forgiveness with these words: "Things that cause people to stumble are bound to come, but woe to anyone through whom they come. It would be better for them to be thrown into the sea with a millstone tied around their neck than to cause one of these little ones to stumble. So watch yourselves" (Lk 17:1-3). Jesus' warning and teaching on forgiveness is rooted in his famous saying, *Love your neighbor as yourself*. That passage begins with the admonition that "You shall not hate your fellow countryman in your heart; you may surely reprove your neighbor, but shall not incur sin because of him. You shall not take vengeance, nor bear any grudge against the sons of your people, but you shall love your neighbor as yourself; I am the LORD" (Lev 19:17-18 NASB).

Tied in with forgiveness and loving others are three challenges. The first challenge is to tell someone when they have wronged you. Now, I recognize that when there are power dynamics in play, especially considering systemic injustices, going to someone who has wronged you can be extremely difficult to the point of needing the help of an advocate to find a way to speak out. But silence in the face of violation is not a solution.

The second challenge involves our heart and our attitude, and this is also costly. When Jesus says, "watch yourselves," he's first speaking with the awareness that there are ill-intentioned people who seek to damage you. But in the same breath, Jesus lets us know that one way or another, at some time or another, there will be consequences for evil actions. Therefore, also watch yourself in terms of your response to the evil they've done. Jesus' statement of "Woe" to the one who brings harm is an echo from Deuteronomy 32:35, which states that the responsibility to avenge evil belongs to God, and that he will repay (Rom 12:19-21). This does not mean we don't bring charges against the offender. By no means. However, "watch yourself" also refers to paying attention to the condition of our own heart. If we harbor hatred, bear resentment, or visualize ways to take revenge, we carry our offenders' sins like rotting meat in our soul, and our own heart becomes darkened.

Meditating on vengeance impregnates our mind with evil that grows into a monster we can't contain. Yielding to God our right for the kind of justice we want does not mean there will not be justice, or that we can do nothing about the wrong. Yielding to God simply acknowledges that, first of all, God loves you and wants you healed and set free. A polluted, blighted heart cannot make its way out of trauma into healing and life. Yielding to God also gives God space to work in the offender's heart and life, because God still loves that person and longs for reconciliation and restoration of all involved. The goal for the offender is repentance. Repentance means *to turn around and go a different direction.* God wants to turn around the life of the evildoer and thereby turn the evil around. He wants to bring goodness out of it.

The third challenge combines the words *forgive* and *love*. Unforgiveness is an iron chain that tethers our life to the one who offended us. Forgiveness is costly because it may require the offended party to yield their right to enact justice on their perpetrators. Unforgiveness holds us in bondage, while the offender might not be bothered in the least by the harm inflicted. However, both *forgive* and *love* are often tossed around as if either is easy to do. When we dismiss someone's anguish by flippantly saying "just forgive the person," we make light of the difficulty and the high cost of forgiveness and love. God paid the highest price to forgive us of our offenses and sin— God came to earth in Jesus to be like us, to be tempted in all things like us, to suffer like us, to fight against the powers of Satan and death, and to lay down his life for us. Jesus took on himself the debt of every transgression and sin ever committed by humanity. God so highly valued and so greatly esteemed the cosmos that he sent his one and only Son, Jesus Christ, to die so that we and all of his creation could be restored in the culmination of all things.

When Jesus asks us to forgive those who have violated us or owe us a debt of any kind, he is not asking lightly. Jesus knew the cost he would pay to forgive us. Jesus also asks us to forgive, because he knows that unforgiveness will turn inward like an abscess to corrupt our own hearts. It will turn people against each other so that we eat and devour one another until we are consumed (Gal 5:15). Forgiveness requires facing the evil done to us by the other. Forgiveness also requires facing the evil within our own self that seeks to retaliate or to recoil into oblivion. As Forbes contributor Amy Rees Anderson wrote, "Resentment Is Like Taking Poison And Waiting For The Other Person To Die."[1] Harboring unforgiveness kills our own heart and soul.

In the movie *Fiddler on the Roof*, which is about the Russian pogroms on the Jewish people, Tevye is told, "We should defend ourselves. An eye for an eye, a tooth for a tooth!" He responds, "Very good. And that way, the whole world will be blind and toothless."[2] There is no end to revenge when

---

[1]Amy Rees Anderson, "'Resentment Is Like Taking Poison and Waiting for the Other Person to Die,'" Forbes, April 7, 2015.

[2]"An eye for an eye leaves the whole world blind" is frequently attributed to M. K. Gandhi. The Gandhi Institute for Nonviolence states that the Gandhi family believes it is an authentic Gandhi

it is taken into our own hands. Peace begins when we relinquish our offender to the only just judge who can also forgive us our trespasses and restore us to wholeness.

FROM CAYSIE'S STORY OF FORGIVENESS

Caysie is one of my oldest and dearest friends. She has also experienced some of the worst abuses of anyone I personally know. We became friends shortly after she came to Christ in her thirties and we have walked some long roads together: talking, praying, and also, importantly, laughing. Recently when her father died, I thought she would be relieved that this man could never again say or do cruel things to her or her grandchildren. But to my surprise, she forgave him. I asked Caysie to tell me about the process she went through to forgive a man who never deserved the title of father. In Caysie's own words:

"I can't say it was a process. It didn't have a beginning, a middle, and an end. It was like the immediate sense of knowing I need to take my hand off a hot flame. The resentment and the anger that I felt over years of physical and emotional abuse had burned into my soul. It made me feel hate in my heart that I wouldn't even let God penetrate. But when my father was dying, I knew I needed to release the hatred. And the words that God kept telling me were, *I will forgive your trespasses as you forgive others who have trespassed against you.*

"I waited and I waited for my father to reach out to me and tell me he was sorry for what he had done, to ask me to forgive him, to tell me just once, once in my life, that he loved me and that he was proud of the woman I had become. I realized that I was putting a price on offering my forgiveness. I was putting a price tag on my willingness to forgive him, saying, "I will forgive you, but you must do these things first." That's the enemy telling you to hang on to your anger and make them walk through fire first before you forgive them. My father was surrounded by those who were already dividing up the spoils of his

---

quotation, but no example of its use by the Indian leader has ever been discovered. For possible sources, see https://quoteinvestigator.com/2010/12/27/eye-for-eye-blind/.

remaining assets and the few pieces of property he had left. I could not get to my father, and he didn't ask me to come.

"When I realized that I must forgive him even without him asking me for forgiveness, that if I don't forgive him, he's not going to get into heaven. Suddenly, the need for him to go to heaven became important to me because I knew that when he got there, God would set him straight. God would heal things that I can't. So I forgave him. I forgave him out loud in front of God. I forgave him for everything, for everything he had done to me, and even for what he did to my mother who also was an abuser in her own right.

"I yielded my right to hold on to my anger and hatred. When I forgave him, all the weight of a lifetime of pain and suffering was lifted from me in that moment. I credit this to God our Father in heaven. And I knew that if I forgave him, God would honor his commitments and forgive him too. Jesus said that "If you forgive anyone's sins, their sins are forgiven; if you do not forgive them, they are not forgiven" (Jn 20:23). I knew he was forgiven.

"When I got the phone call that my father had just taken his last breath and passed away, at the very moment I knew that God welcomed him into heaven with open arms. It wasn't that I had the power to say who was going to live in eternity with God and who wasn't. But God promised that he could cast our sins as far as the east is from the west (Ps 103:12). I believe he's in heaven now. I believe he is whole. I believe he is healed. I believe the spirit of this man that existed before alcohol destroyed all that was good is now dancing in the meadows of glory. And I pray that when my time comes, that God will also forgive me for anything that I have done or thought that is displeasing to him and harmed others. Then I will be dancing with my father in heaven. There will be no more trace of evil. We will be the people we were always meant to be, healed, enveloped in light and goodness. That's my story."

The peace that now flows from Caysie and into her life is remarkable. She no longer has any problem setting boundaries between herself and those who are cruel. She prays for them, speaks what's true, and walks safely away, feeling no need to change them or cater to them when they choose to remain selfish or stupid. She has also outlived by seven years the prognosis of six months that top doctors gave her, and she's getting healthier. I learned important perspectives on forgiveness from my friend Caysie.

You might have theological questions about her dad going to heaven. My first father-in-law made a deathbed confession of Jesus Christ that I got to hear. I've heard of many others. Thankfully, as she says herself, who gets into heaven is God's decision, so I'll also continue to trust God to be the judge of people's hearts and lives. Furthermore, the fruit of forgiveness in Caysie's life is abundant and keeps producing more life and joy. So, I'll look at the fruit of her forgiveness with thankfulness and awe.

IMAGE FROM GENESIS: JOSEPH AND JUDAH'S STORY

The story of Joseph and his family is the longest narrative in Genesis and also bookends a reversal of what went wrong in the Garden. The narrative in Genesis 37:2 opens by telling us three things about Joseph in one sentence: he was seventeen years old, he was "tending the flocks with his brothers," and he brought a "bad report" about his brothers to his father, Jacob.

There are two interesting subtleties in this sentence that give us a foreshadowing of Joseph's young personality and of the troubles that were just about to occur. The first subtlety is in the phrase that he was "tending the flocks with his brothers." In the other places in the Hebrew Bible, when someone is tending, or shepherding, flocks the sentence has a different structure, or ordering, of the words. The structure of this phrase in Genesis 37:2 hints that "Joseph was shepherding his brothers among the flocks."[3]

The second subtlety in this verse is a curious wordplay between "shepherding/tending" (*rh, roeh*) and "evil/bad" (*ra, raah*). These two very different words are spelled in Hebrew with the same three consonants, but only the vowels are different (and the vowels were not written in ancient Hebrew). This suggests that the "story's plot is constituted by conflict-resolution in which the dynamics of good and evil are central."[4]

---

[3]For exegesis of this passage, see Faro, *Evil in Genesis*, 177-78.
[4]Mignon R. Jacobs, "The Conceptual Dynamics of Good and Evil in the Joseph Story: An Exegetical and Hermeneutical Inquiry," *Journal for the Study of the Old Testament* 27 (2003): 312.

The third subtlety ties these two observations together. Joseph's shepherding of his brothers is part of the reason he brought a negative (*raah*) report to his father. The narrative continues to describe the dysfunctionality of Jacob's family. Jacob loved Joseph more than his other sons and demonstrated it by giving him a special tunic, a *kuttonet*. Jacob's love for Joseph is contrasted with Joseph's brothers who "hated him." Then when he told them his first and second dream, they "hated him more," resulting in a threefold hate-fest in six verses (Gen 37:3-8). Their hatred culminates in the brothers, led by Judah, taking the opportunity to sell Joseph to merchants heading to Egypt. They told their father, Jacob, that Joseph was killed by wild animals. Showing Joseph's *kuttonet* drenched in the blood of a goat, they asked Jacob, "Do you recognize this?" (Gen 37:32). The scene ends with Jacob mourning and refusing to be comforted, while Joseph is sold into slavery.

The next scene switches to Judah living with the Canaanites. The narrative moves quickly at first, as he "takes" an unnamed wife and has three sons. He takes a wife, named Tamar, for his first son, but the biblical text says Er (*er*) was *evil* (*ra*) in the sight of Yahweh, so Yahweh put him to death. The name of Judah's next son, Onan (*onan*), is a wordplay on the Hebrew for *disaster*, *false*, or *idolatrous* (*awen*). Onan sexually exploited his sister-in-law, Tamar, rather than upholding his legal and cultural responsibility toward her and his dead brother. Onan's actions were evil in the sight of Yahweh, who took his life also (Gen 38:10).

After years of waiting, Tamar boldly took action to receive the justice she had been denied. When Judah tried to have her put to death, she brought forward his staff, ring, and cord, and asked, "Do you recognize this?" using the same language spoken to Jacob when he was shown Joseph's blood soaked tunic. These words struck home to Judah as he faced his complicity in denying Tamar protection and threatening her life, as he also had done to his younger brother Joseph. This moment began the transformation of Judah into a godly leader. Judah declared that Tamar was more righteous than he, and returned with her to his home, to Jacob, so that the twins could be born and raised under Jacob's household. Thereafter, Judah is an advocate for his family and places his own life at risk for them, including Benjamin, Joseph's only full brother.

Joseph's integrity and faith resonate throughout the chapters that describe his thirteen years as a slave and a prisoner. He was despised and sold into slavery and expected to die by his older brothers. When he resisted sexual exploitation from his master's wife in Egypt, he was sent to prison. When he helped the Pharaoh's cupbearer and baker by interpreting their dreams in prison, he was forgotten. When he endured all these evils and hardships, he never called them good and he never planned to stay a slave or a prisoner. Joseph did not forget the dreams God gave him as a seventeen-year-old. Even though there was no one to encourage him and no Bible to read, he did not lose his faith. We can see this through what happens next in his story.

When the Pharaoh has two dreams of his own, neither his magicians nor his wise men are able to interpret them. Then the cupbearer speaks up and tells Pharaoh about Joseph. Now, after all these years, Joseph is in the Egyptian prison and probably had not bathed or changed his clothes in years. Suddenly, Pharaoh's men "hurriedly" grabbed him, threw him in water, shaved him (probably roughly, as he was a Hebrew slave of no value to them). They put clean clothes on him and thrust him before the highest human power in the known world, who was decked in gold, sitting on a throne, and surrounded by massive pillars and scores of attendants. Most likely no one had told him why he was there. Perhaps as a sacrifice to their gods? Anyone could have been intimidated into fear or silence in this situation. Immediately Pharaoh tells Joseph that he had had a dream (actually two) that no one could interpret, but he had heard that Joseph interprets dreams. Joseph has the presence of mind to immediately reply, "It is not in my power; God will answer *concerning* the well-being of Pharaoh" (Gen 41:16 LEB). And after hearing Pharaoh's dreams, Joseph gives the interpretation and has the confidence to give the Pharaoh advice as well. It's hard, almost impossible, to imagine how Joseph could have responded like this, unshaken by years of degradation and trauma.

However, Psalm 105 provides commentary on how Joseph came through. Here's the key passage that gives us insight to understand:

> They bruised his feet with shackles,
>   his neck was put in irons,
> till what he foretold came to pass,
>   till the word of the LORD proved him true. (Ps 105:18-19)

While Joseph endured the shackles of slavery, he never forgot the two dreams he received from God. The "word of Yahweh tested him" (*tsera-fathehu*). The Hebrew verb we've seen before, *tsaraph*, means tested, refined as by fire. What God had told Joseph through his dreams burned within him during his years of oppression, false accusations, neglect, abuse, and imprisonment. Day after day and night after night, he had the choice to decide whether or not what God showed him through his dreams were true. Joseph chose to hold onto God's word and believe God's word to him despite all the outward circumstances to the contrary. He did not lose faith. After enduring humiliating and harsh circumstances, in one day, he was lifted from prison to second in charge after Pharaoh.

However, his dream had not yet been fully fulfilled. He tried to forget his father's house, as we see in the naming of his first son, Manasseh, saying, "God has made me forget all my trouble and all my father's household" (Gen 41:51). But after seven years of abundance and the beginning of the severe famine, the rest of his dream began to come true: his brothers came and bowed down to him as a ruler in Egypt, not knowing he was their brother. As he had been tested and put through the fire, he tested his brothers. Could he trust them? What had become of their character? Judah's transformation emerges clearly when he speaks up in a lengthy address to Joseph. Judah seeks to protect his brothers and admits to the sin they had committed against their father and their brother Joseph, not realizing it was Joseph that he was addressing (Gen 44:18-34). When their promise to bring Benjamin to Egypt comes through, we see Joseph break down and weep, and finally reveal his identity to his brothers.

Although the reconciliation is beautiful in this story, we find that the brothers still have a hard time believing Joseph could actually forgive them for their cruelty when he was young. After Jacob's death, they fear reprisal and beg him to forgive them. Joseph responds by saying, "Do not be afraid, for am I in God's place? As for you, you meant evil against me, *but* God meant it for good in order to bring about this present result, to preserve many people alive" (Gen 50:19-20 NASB).

Joseph's response to them embodies the remedy against evil and the hope for good. Joseph had yielded in trust to God. He had seen the ways God turned around evil with all its damage. Through the hardships, Joseph remained faithful to God and believed that he would see the goodness and the promises of God in his life. Therefore, after some testing, he was able to forgive his brothers. And since they had confessed their wrongs and had transformed their lives, the brothers could be reconciled, even if not perfectly. Joseph's faithfulness and Judah's transformation brought about the reversal of evil, untwisting its stranglehold that could have killed them all and ended the lineage of Abraham and the Messiah, but instead preserved their lives and the lives of countless others.

Joseph's story powerfully portrays the costliness of forgiveness. Forgiveness does not guarantee reconciliation but places the burden of the offense on God. By lifting the resentment and anger off our shoulders and placing them onto God's shoulders, our hearts become open to the possibility of taking steps toward reconciliation. The story of Joseph illustrates that even if the other never repents, we can be set free from the chain tethering us to those who caused our suffering.

Chapter Fifteen

FOR THOSE WHO MOURN
TURNING ASHES INTO BEAUTY

WHEN JESUS INAUGURATED HIS MINISTRY, he read from the scroll of Isaiah 61:1-2. This is his mission statement, the purpose for which God sent him.[1] The passage in Luke reads,

> The Spirit of the Lord is on me,
>> because he has anointed me
>> to proclaim good news to the poor.
> He has sent me to proclaim freedom for the prisoners
>> and recovery of sight for the blind,
> to set the oppressed free,
>> to proclaim the year of the Lord's favor. (Lk 4:17-21)

As a young Christian, I turned to the text in Isaiah and read the verses that follow:

> To comfort all who mourn,
> To grant those who mourn *in* Zion,
> Giving them a garland instead of ashes,
> The oil of gladness instead of mourning,
> The mantle of praise instead of a spirit of fainting.
> So they will be called oaks of righteousness,
> The planting of the LORD, that He may be glorified. (Is 61:2-3 NASB)

I looked up the words for *garland* and *ashes* in a concordance that I bought to help in my personal Bible studies. Although I did not know any

---

[1] See also Ingrid Faro, "God's Comfort for Human Brokenness," in *Divine Suffering*, ed. Andrew J. Schmutzer (Eugene, OR: Pickwick, 2023), 222-50.

Hebrew, I noticed that in Isaiah 61:3, the word *garland*, or *beauty* in my translation at the time (*peer*) and the word *ashes* (*eper*) were the same three letters in Hebrew, but the first two letters were turned around. This spoke to me as I realized that's what God wants to do with our grief: turn it around. Over two decades later, while studying biblical Hebrew in seminary, I learned that what I had discovered so many years earlier was accurate regarding the way biblical Hebrew uses wordplay to create emphasis and to make a point.[2]

Embedded in the symbolism of the reversal of the two letters in these two words lies the story of redemption, God's good news. Ashes are what Job sat in after losing everything. Ashes are the substance that mourners scooped up and placed on their heads as the ultimate act of grief. Tamar, King David's daughter, put ashes on her head after she was raped and humiliated by her stepbrother (2 Sam 13:19). Ashes are all that's left when everything has been consumed.

The Hebrew word for a *crown of beauty, garland*, or *turban* (*peer*) is also placed on the head, but as a signifier of joy. This word, found in Isaiah 61:3, recurs in Isaiah 61:10, referring to the turban (*peer*) that a bridegroom wears during his marriage ceremony. It is used to describe the *beautiful headdresses* worn by Jerusalem's upper-class women (Is 3:20), and the special *turbans* worn by priests in the tabernacle and the temple (Ex 39:28; Ezek 44:18).[3]

The good news is that when we place the ashes of our greatest losses and darkest shame into God's hands, he takes the very substance of our grief and turns it into a crown of beauty. Furthermore, the end of Isaiah 61:3 contains the same three-letter root again—"that He may be *glorified*" (a form of the verb *peer*).[4] God longs for us to give him our sorrows and griefs so that he can enter into our suffering and transform the evils that devastated us into our greatest joy and honor, because he is a redeemer and *this* displays his glory (*peer*). God longs to take the ashes from our head and transform them into a magnificent headdress, because this reveals his heart for us.[5] Salvation

---

[2] For the definitive study on the biblical Hebrew use of metathesis, see Isaac Kalimi, *Metathesis in the Hebrew Bible: Wordplay as a Literary and Exegetical Device* (Peabody, MA: Hendrickson Academic, 2018), 1, 7, 72, 132, 160.

[3] Ludwig Koehler et al., *The Hebrew and Aramaic Lexicon of the Old Testament*, (Leiden: E.J. Brill, 1994–2000), 909.

[4] NASB translation.

[5] See also Faro, "God's Comfort for Human Brokenness," 231-36.

not only brings forgiveness but is not complete until the evils have been turned into goodness. This is comfort for the brokenhearted. This is good news for all who mourn.

FROM MY STORY: LOVE

Love, that one thing in life that is supposed to bring us to the greatest heights of joy and intimacy, can instead bring us to the greatest depths of grief and isolation. My life is rich with the love of family and close friends, but along with most of us, I also long for the love of personal intimacy. All too often, the experience of the unique trusted relationship we long for does not happen. Sorrows surrounding disappointed love may bring about the hardest suffering of all. There are many causes for a broken bond or the inability to bond: unhealed trauma, misunderstanding, distance, unfaithfulness, or the death or sickness of a loved one.

A broken relationship is a kind of death. When my desire for love was not reciprocated as I had hoped, I felt crushing disappointment. In struggling to accept this reality, I thought, *I have to love less.* I wanted to freeze my heart. I did not want to care anymore. I wanted to walk away. But then, from within, a gentle voice spoke softly to my heart, "No my child, now you have to love *more*." At that moment I realized that to be free from the bondage of resentment or regret, I needed to love without the demand to meet my expectations. For this person never did evil to me; never raised his voice or was unkind. He was always truthful, seeking my good, and added immeasurably to my life and my joy. However, the evils this one experienced left trauma and brokenness along with an unwillingness or inability to bond. Yet, in realizing how much I treasure this person and our friendship, I do not want to lose what we have. I could love for love's sake, not for the benefits I wanted from the relationship. The longings for intimacy haven't left. But I will trust God to fully meet all my needs and desires in the ways that only God knows will satisfy.

Loving more meant desiring the other's wholeness and good more than my desire for love returned the way *I wanted it* from this person.

> In that moment, love took wings. I felt a new freedom. Peace settled
> in my soul. Love grew rather than diminished. My desire shifted from
> satisfying my wants to wanting the flourishing of the other. In this
> process, I did need to set some new boundaries for my heart and my
> own well-being. But in releasing my expectations and
> disappointments, my heart expanded. Instead of withholding, I chose
> to receive the beauty this person brings to my life, and to give love
> without a price tag.

All of us are broken and have parts that are not healed. God comes alongside us, and longs for us to receive his comfort, healing, wisdom, and strength. Jesus invites us to carry out his mission and to come alongside those we meet along our journey with tangible good news. We are not the healers, but our presence and our prayers bring God's presence and healing through our voice and our actions. We must not be overcome with the troubles in the world—pandemics, mass chaos, ethnic atrocities, wars, divisions, and divisive speech continue to tear apart families, friends, communities, and nations. We must not be swept away by tidal waves of terror, fear, and evil. Rather, we can be part of a larger tidal wave bringing wholeness, unity without conformity, care, and provision from a place of inner and outer peace.

In Edith Eger's *The Gift*, she perceives that "While suffering is inevitable and universal, we can always choose how we respond," and "It's not what happens to us that matters most, it's what we do with our experiences."[6] She continues, "In my experience, victims ask, 'Why me?' Survivors ask, 'What now?'"[7] Abraham Heschel provides the insight that what is even more excruciating than suffering is the agony of sensing that there is no meaning to it.[8] In the face of suffering, it is incumbent on us to make meaning of it by turning it around and reversing the impact of evil into good, for ourselves and for all those affected through the ripples of our life. In this way, we each choose life or death in response to evil and suffering.

The words of G. B. Caird struck home to me in a fresh way. They are the kind that a true friend gives as a warning and an encouragement to persist in living well. He deserves to be quoted at length:

---

[6]Edith Eva Eger, *The Gift: 14 Lessons to Save Your Life* (New York: Scribner, 2020), 5, 7.
[7]Eger, *Gift*, 11.
[8]Abraham Joshua Heschel, *The Prophets* (Peabody, MA: Hendrickson, 2017), 147.

Evil propagates itself by a chain reaction. . . . If one man injures another, there are three ways in which evil can win a victory and only one way in which it can be defeated. If the injured person retaliates, or nurses a grievance, or takes it out on a third person, the evil is perpetuated and is therefore victorious.

Evil is defeated only if the injured person absorbs the evil and refuses to allow it to go any farther. . . . Without doing anything to perpetuate evil, (what Christ did was that) he submitted to all that sin could do to him until death carried him beyond its power. But he did more than this: "he died for our sins." He drew off on to himself the evil effects of other men's sins; he faced the powers of evil and drew their fire. . . . By drawing off on to himself the hostility with which men regard one another, and by allowing it to put him on the Cross, he has slain the hostility . . . (which) involved the abolition of the law, and so constituted a victory over the angelic guardians of legal rebellion.[9]

Furthermore, Jesus not only absorbed the evil, but he empowered us to overcome evil. By first absorbing the evil, he bore the penalty for the charges the accuser legally held against us in the heavenly courtroom. A judicial transaction took place between the Trinity, humanity, and the accuser. When Jesus took on himself the punishments and sentence of death that we rightly deserve, the price to deliver us from evil was paid by God himself. By Jesus willingly laying down his life to remove our charge of *guilty*, we became innocent in the eyes of the court.

All who receive the price that Jesus paid for their violations are thereby restored to their original position as an image-bearer with the full rights and authority of heaven. Because of God's mercy on full display at the cross, we get to leave the prison of guilt and judgment. We are released from the control of the warden of the jail and all his guards. Satan, demons, and the horde of evil's henchmen and thieves no longer have the legal right to hold us captive, afflict us, accuse us, or torment us. We are legally free. In response to God's mercy and love, there are steps we need to take to live into our new freedom.

The first step is to receive Jesus' payment for the penalty of our transgressions. When we receive the transfer from us to Jesus of the weight of our bitterness, anger, and all the wrongs we have done, our debts are forgiven, and our chains are removed. We receive our walking papers.

---

[9]G. B. Caird, *Principalities and Powers: A Study in Pauline Theology*. The Chancellor's Lectures for 1954 at Queen's University, Kingston, Ontario (Eugene, OR: Wipf & Stock, 1956), 98-99.

The second step is to leave prison and return to our Father's house as freed men and women. God rejoices when we return. He clothes us, puts a signet ring of authority on our finger, a crown of beauty on our head, and we eat at his table. Some people never take this second step. Some people stay in their prison. Somewhat like animals that have lived in captivity their whole lives, when the cage doors open, some are reluctant to leave their familiar cell. We must learn how to live free, for at first this new life might not feel natural.

The third step is to embrace our new purpose. We need to learn how to step into our position and authority as sons and daughters of the Most High King. As part of God's royal family, God gives us the privilege and the power to rule with him according to his ways, as he intended in creation. That's the reason the Bible calls us *a new creation* and Jesus *the Second Adam.* We are charged once again to serve and protect the people and the spaces that are within the responsibility God gives us. As in the beginning, we are to reign with Christ over the earth, and stop evil, corruption, and abuse of every kind. This is the way we restore peace and goodness where God sends us. We can increase our understanding of what our purpose looks like by observing Jesus' life on the earth. He feared nothing and no one. He healed, helped, and delivered all who came to him. He took authority over animals and nature. He was never intimidated by the religious or political powers but boldly spoke truth to them and refused to submit to oppressive authority.

In order to find the abundant life Jesus came to give us, we can't live like beaten or degraded prisoners in the ways that held us captive. Nor are we to sit passively beside our old cage, staring at heaven, waiting for people to throw us food or waiting for *God* to do what he tells *us* to do. As we step into new life that God has given us, we find purpose and joy even in the midst of opposition and challenges. After Jesus' resurrection from death, he gave us the power to carry out God's will. Jesus was given all authority (*exousia*) in heaven and on earth (Mt 28:18). Everyone that receives him and believes in him is given the right (*exousia,* authority) to be God's children (Jn 1:12). Jesus gave us the power (*dynamis*) through the Holy Spirit to bear witness to what Christ has done and to do the work of God to bring his kingdom into our circumstances (Acts 1:8; Jn 20:21; Lk 10:9).

Our mission on earth, should we accept it, is to be a blessing to every nation and person, healing lives, and stopping evil. Like Jesus, we are to take up the authority he has given us and go. The Great Commission is not only about words. Although words are important and powerful, actions must flow from our words.

When we are obeying God's commands, all the authority of his kingdom backs us up and empowers our words and actions. We must not tolerate wrong or cower before evil. We must not be silent in the face of violence, abuse, and injustice. By the power entrusted to us in the name of Jesus, we must act as God's agents to do his will.

In humility we know that we can see only part of God's very big picture. There are situations and mysteries that go unsolved or unresolved. However, this I know—God's will is our good. God's mercy is greater than our sin. God's power to overturn evil by doing his good is greater than our suffering. Though many wills assert themselves, in time, God's will for good will prevail. Brokenness will be healed, either in this life or the next. This present darkness will be overcome with the bright glory of love. For those who mourn, one day suffering, pain, and evil will be swept away and seen no more. But meanwhile, the Spirit of God still hovers over the face of the deep, calling forth light in the darkness and inviting us as God's image-bearers to join with him to turn chaos into order, fill the emptiness with purpose, and create flourishing spaces out of the barren void.

> Love must be sincere. Hate what is evil; cling to what is good. Be devoted to one another in love. Honor one another above yourselves. Never be lacking in zeal, but keep your spiritual fervor, serving the Lord.
>
> Be joyful in hope, patient in affliction, faithful in prayer. Share with the Lord's people who are in need. Practice hospitality.
>
> Bless those who persecute you; bless and do not curse. Rejoice with those who rejoice; mourn with those who mourn. Live in harmony with one another. Do not be proud, but be willing to associate with people of low position. Do not be conceited.
>
> Do not repay anyone evil for evil. Be careful to do what is right in the eyes of everyone. If it is possible, as far as it depends on you, live at peace with everyone.

Do not take revenge, my dear friends, but leave room for God's wrath, for it is written: "It is mine to avenge; I will repay," says the Lord.

On the contrary:

"If your enemy is hungry, feed him;

if he is thirsty, give him something to drink. . . ."

Do not be overcome by evil, but overcome evil with good. (Rom 12:9-21)

BIBLIOGRAPHY

Acolatse, Esther E. *Powers, Principalities, and the Spirit: Biblical Realism in Africa and the West*. Grand Rapids, MI: Eerdmans, 2018.

Albrecht, Karl. "Science Class Isn't Working." *Psychology Today*, September 29, 2017. www.psychologytoday.com/us/blog/brainsnacks/201709/science-class-isnt-working.

Annus, Amar, and Alan Lenzi. *Ludlul Bēl Nēmeqi: The Standard Babylonian Poem of the Righteous Sufferer*. Helsinki: Neo-Assyrian Text Corpus Project, 2010.

Arnold, Clinton E. *Powers of Darkness: Principalities & Powers in Paul's Letters*. Downers Grove, IL: IVP Academic, 1992.

Averbeck, Richard E. "Ancient Near Eastern Mythography as It Relates to Historiography in the Hebrew Bible: Genesis 3 and the Cosmic Battle." In *The Future of Biblical Archaeology: Reassessing Methodologies and Assumptions*, edited by A. R. Millard and James Karl Hoffmeier, 328-56. Grand Rapids, MI: Eerdmans, 2004.

———. "Having a Baby the New-Fashioned Way: An Old Testament Perspective." Trinity Evangelical Divinity School, Deerfield, IL, April 21, 2009.

———. "Wisdom from the Old Testament." In *Why the Church Needs Bioethics: A Guide to Wise Engagement with Life's Challenges*, edited by John F. Kilner, 25-42. Grand Rapids, MI: Zondervan, 2011.

Bailey, Daniel P. "Jesus as the Mercy Seat: The Semantics and Theology of Paul's Use of Hilasterion in Romans 3:25." PhD diss., University of Cambridge, 1999.

Baker-Fletcher, Karen. *Dancing with God: The Trinity from a Womanist Perspective*. St. Louis: Chalice, 2006.

Barad, Karen. *Meeting the Universe Halfway: Quantum Physics and the Entanglement of Matter and Meaning*. 2nd ed. Durham, NC: Duke University Press, 2007.

Barr, James. "Was Everything That God Created Really Good? A Question in the First Verse of the Bible." In *God in the Fray: A Tribute to Walter Brueggemann*, edited by Tod Linafelt and Timothy K. Beal, 55-65. Minneapolis: Fortress, 1998.

Bartholomew, Craig G., and Michael W. Goheen. *The Drama of Scripture: Finding Our Place in the Biblical Story*. 2nd ed. Grand Rapids, MI: Baker Academic, 2014.

Beale, G. K. *The Temple and the Church's Mission: A Biblical Theology of the Dwelling Place of God*. Downers Grove, IL: IVP Academic, 2004.

Beale, Gregory K. "Eden, the Temple, and the Church's Mission in the New Creation." *Journal of the Evangelical Theological Society* 48 (2005): 5-31.

Black, M. C., K. C. Basile, M. J. Breiding, S. G. Smith, M. L. Walters, M. T. Merrick, J. Chen, and M. Stevens. "The National Intimate Partner and Sexual Violence Survey: 2010 Summary Report." National Coalition Against Domestic Violence, n.d. www.speakcdn .com/assets/2497/male_victims_of_intimate_partner_violence.pdf.

Blankert, Tim, and Melvyn R. W. Hamstra. "Imagining Success: Multiple Achievement Goals and the Effectiveness of Imagery." *Basic and Applied Social Psychology* 39, no. 1 (2017): 60-67.

Block, Daniel I. *Covenant: The Framework of God's Grand Plan of Redemption.* Grand Rapids, MI: Baker Academic, 2021.

———. *The Gods of the Nations: A Study in Ancient Near Eastern National Theology.* 2nd ed. Eugene, OR: Wipf & Stock, 2013.

———. *How I Love Your Torah, O Lord! Studies in the Book of Deuteronomy.* Eugene, OR: Cascade Books, 2011.

———. "What Do These Stones Mean? The Riddle of Deuteronomy 27." *Journal of the Evangelical Theological Society* 56, no. 1 (2013): 17-41.

Boda, Mark J. *A Severe Mercy: Sin and Its Remedy in the Old Testament.* Winona Lake, IN: Eisenbrauns, 2009.

Boda, Mark J., and Jamie Novotony, eds. *From the Foundations to the Crennellations: Essays on Temple Building in the Ancient Near East and Hebrew Bible.* Alter Orient Und Altes Testament 366. Münster: Ugarit-Verlag, 2010.

Bogost, Ian. "What Is 'Evil' to Google? Speculations on the Company's Contribution to Moral Philosophy." *The Atlantic*, October 15, 2013. www.theatlantic.com/technology /archive/2013/10/what-is-evil-to-google/280573/.

Boyd, Gregory A. *God at War: The Bible and Spiritual Conflict.* Downers Grove, IL: IVP Academic, 1997.

Brownstone, Sydney. "What Does Google's 'Don't Be Evil' Actually Mean After Snowden." *Fast Company*, August 28, 2014. www.fastcompany.com/3034969/what-does-googles -dont-be-evil-actually-mean-after-snowden.

Bruckner, James K. *Implied Law in the Abraham Narrative: A Literary and Theological Analysis.* Englewood Cliffs, NJ: Sheffield Academic, 2002.

Brueggemann, Walter. *Genesis.* Interpretation: A Bible Commentary for Teaching and Preaching. Atlanta: Westminster John Knox, 1986.

Buber, Martin. *Good and Evil.* Upper Saddle River, NJ: Pearson, 1980.

Byrne, Rhonda. *The Secret.* New York: Atria, 2006.

Caird, G. B. *Principalities and Powers: A Study in Pauline Theology,* The Chancellor's Lectures for 1954 at Queen's University, Kingston Ontario. Eugene, OR: Wipf & Stock, 2003.

Cassuto, U. *A Commentary on the Book of Genesis (Part I): From Adam to Noah.* Jerusalem: Varda Books, 2012.

CBS News. "Poll: Nearly 8 in 10 Americans Believe in Angels." CBS News, December 23, 2011. www.cbsnews.com/news/poll-nearly-8-in-10-americans-believe-in -angels/.

Childs, Brevard S. *Myth and Reality in the Old Testament*. 2nd ed. London: SCM Press, 1962.

———. *Old Testament Theology in a Canonical Context*. Philadelphia: Fortress, 1990.

Clark, Randy. "A Study of the Effects of Christian Prayer on Pain or Mobility Restrictions from Surgeries Involving Implanted Materials." DMin diss., United Theological Seminary, 2013.

Coates, George W. "The God of Death: Power and Obedience in the Primeval History." *Interpretation* 29, no. 3 (1975): 227-39.

Coelho, Paulo. *The Alchemist, A Fable About Following Your Dream*. Anniversary ed. San Francisco: HarperOne, 2014.

Coke, Ethan. "Judges." Essay written for OT 308 Historical Books and the Prophets. Northern Seminary, Lisle, IL, January 29, 2022.

Collins, C. John. *Genesis 1–4: A Linguistic, Literary, and Theological Commentary*. Phillipsburg, NJ: P&R, 2006.

Collins, John J. "Prince." In *Dictionary of Deities and Demons in the Bible*, edited by Karel van der Toorn, Bob Becking, and Pieter W. van der Horst. Grand Rapids, MI: Eerdmans, 1999.

Copan, Paul. *Is God a Moral Monster? Making Sense of the Old Testament God*. Grand Rapids, MI: Baker Books, 2011.

Corbett, Steve, Brian Fikkert, John Perkins, and David Platt. *When Helping Hurts: How to Alleviate Poverty Without Hurting the Poor . . . and Yourself*. Chicago: Moody, 2014.

Corradi, Max. "Understanding the Law of Cause and Effect: Karma in Buddhism." *Sivana East*, n.d. https://blog.sivanaspirit.com/bd-sp-law-cause-effect-karma/.

Coxon, Peter W. "Nephilim." In *Dictionary of Deities and Demons in the Bible*, edited by Karel van der Toorn, Bob Becking, and Pieter W. van der Horst. Grand Rapids, MI: Eerdmans, 1999.

Crenshaw, James L. "Introduction: The Shift from Theodicy to Anthropodicy." In *Theodicy in the Old Testament*, 1-16. IRT 4. Philadelphia: Fortress, 1973.

Davidson, Richard M. "The Divine Covenant Lawsuit Motif in Canonical Perspective." *Journal of the Adventist Theological Society* 21, no. 1–2 (2010): 45-84.

Davies, Brian. *The Reality of God and the Problem of Evil*. New York: Continuum, 2006.

Day, John. "God and Leviathan in Isaiah 27:1." *Bibliotheca Sacra* 155 (1998): 423-36.

Day, Peggy L. *An Adversary in Heaven: Satan in the Hebrew Bible*. Atlanta: Brill, 1988.

Dispenza, Joe. *Becoming Supernatural: How Common People Are Doing the Uncommon*. 2nd ed. Carlsbad, CA: Hay House, 2019.

Dostoevsky, Fyodor. *The Brothers Karamazov: A Novel in Four Parts with Epilogue*. Translated by Richard Pevear and Larissa Volokhonsky. New York: Picador, 2021.

Douglas, Sally. "A Decoding of Evil Angels: The Other Aetiology of Evil in the Biblical Text and Its Potential Implications in Our Church and World." *Colloquium* 45, no. 1 (2013).

Eger, Edith Eva. *The Gift: 14 Lessons to Save Your Life*. New York: Scribner, 2020.

Ehrman, Bart D. *God's Problem: How the Bible Fails to Answer Our Most Important Question—Why We Suffer*. New York: HarperOne, 2009.

Eichrodt, Walther. "Faith in Providence and Theodicy in the Old Testament." In *Theodicy in the Old Testament*, 17-41. IRT 4. Philadelphia: Fortress, 1973.

Emanuel, David M. "Satan." In *Lexham Theological Wordbook*, edited by Douglas Mangum. Lexham Bible Reference Series. Bellingham, WA: Lexham, 2014.

Faro, Ingrid. *Evil in Genesis: A Contextual Analysis of Hebrew Lexemes for Evil in the Book of Genesis*. Studies in Scripture & Biblical Theology. Bellingham, WA: Lexham, 2021.

———. "God's Comfort for Human Brokenness." In *Divine Suffering*, edited by Andrew J. Schmutzer, 222-50. Eugene, OR: Pickwick, 2023.

———. "The Question of Evil and Animal Death Before the Fall." *Trinity Journal* 36, (2015): 1-21.

Fleming, Daniel E. "Religion." In *Dictionary of the Old Testament: Pentateuch*, edited by T. Desmond Alexander and David W. Baker, 670-84. Downers Grove, IL: InterVarsity Press, 2002.

Fokkelman, J. P. *Narrative Art in Genesis: Specimens of Stylistic and Structural Analysis*. 2nd ed. Eugene, OR: Wipf & Stock, 2004.

Foster, Cody J. "Did America Commit War Crimes in Vietnam." *New York Times*, December 1, 2017. www.nytimes.com/2017/12/01/opinion/did-america-commit-war -crimes-in-vietnam.html.

Frederick, John. "Mercy and Compassion." In *Lexham Theological Wordbook*, edited by Douglas Mangum and Derek R. Brown. Lexham Bible Reference Series. Bellingham, WA: Lexham, 2014.

Freeman, Tzvi. Editing the Past. *Daily Dose of Wisdom* (blog). Accessed February 16, 2023. www.chabad.org/library/article_cdo/aid/985005/jewish/Editing-the-Past.htm.

Fretheim, Terence E. *Creation Untamed: The Bible, God, and Natural Disasters*. Illustrated ed. Grand Rapids, MI: Baker Academic, 2010.

———. "Exodus, Book Of." In *Dictionary of the Old Testament: Pentateuch*, edited by T. Desmond Alexander and David W. Baker, 248-58. Downers Grove, IL: InterVarsity Press, 2003.

———. "Is Genesis 3 a Fall Story?" *Word and World* 14 (1994): 144-53.

Garr, W. Randall. "'Image' and 'Likeness' in the Inscription from Tell Fakharieh." *Israel Exploration Journal* 50, no. 3 (2000): 227-34.

———. *In His Own Image and Likeness: Humanity, Divinity, and Monotheism*. Boston: Brill, 2003.

Gleaves, G. Scott. "Evil." In *Lexham Theological Wordbook*, edited by Douglas Mangum and Derek R. Brown. Lexham Bible Reference Series. Bellingham, WA: Lexham, 2014.

Goldingay, John. *Daniel*. Word Biblical Commentary 30. Rev. ed. Grand Rapids, MI: Zondervan Academic, 2019.

———. *Old Testament Theology*. Vol. 2, *Israel's Faith*. Downers Grove, IL: IVP Academic, 2016.

Goldstein, Joseph. "Cause and Effect: Reflecting on the Law of Karma." *The Buddhist Review Tricycle*, 2008. https://tricycle.org/magazine/cause-and-effect/.

Görman, Ulf. *A Good God? A Logical and Semantical Analysis of the Problem of Evil*. Studia Philosophiae Religionis 5. Stockholm: H. Ohlsson, 1977.

Gregg, Brian Han. *What Does the Bible Say About Suffering?* Downers Grove, IL: IVP Academic, 2016.

Guillaume, Philippe. "Animadversiones: Metamorphosis of a Ferocious Pharaoh." *Biblica* 85, no. 2 (2004): 232-35.

Hamilton, Victor P. *The Book of Genesis: Chapters 1-17*. New International Commentary on the Old Testament. 3rd ed. Grand Rapids, MI: Eerdmans, 1990.

Hamilton, Victor P., and David Noel Freedman. "Satan." In *Anchor Bible Dictionary*. New York: Doubleday, 1996.

Hartley, John E. *The Book of Job*. 2nd ed. Grand Rapids, MI: Eerdmans, 1988.

Heiser, Michael S. *Angels: What the Bible Really Says About God's Heavenly Host*. Bellingham, WA: Lexham, 2018.

———. *Demons: What the Bible Really Says About the Powers of Darkness*. Bellingham, WA: Lexham, 2020.

———. "Deuteronomy 32:8 and the Sons of God." *Bibliotheca Sacra* 158, no. 629 (January-March 2001): 52-74.

———. "Divine Council." In *The Lexham Bible Dictionary*, edited by John D. Barry et al. Bellingham, WA: Lexham, 2016.

———. "The Divine Council in the Pentateuch: A Conference Paper." San Antonio, TX, 2017.

———. "New Testament Terms for Unseen Divine Beings." In *Faithlife Study Bible*. Bellingham, WA: Lexham, 2016.

———. *The Unseen Realm: Recovering the Supernatural Worldview of the Bible*. Bellingham, WA: Lexham, 2015.

Henten, Jan Willem van. "Angel (II)." In *Dictionary of Deities and Demons in the Bible*, edited by Karel van der Toorn, Bob Becking, and Pieter W. van der Horst. Grand Rapids, MI: Eerdmans, 1999.

Heschel, Abraham J. *The Prophets*. New York: Harper Perennial Modern Classics, 2001.

Hill, Andrew E., and John H. Walton. *A Survey of the Old Testament.* 3rd ed. Grand Rapids, MI: Zondervan Academic, 2009.

History.com editors. "My Lai Massacre." *History.com,* April 17, 2020. www.history.com /topics/vietnam-war/my-lai-massacre-1#:~:text=The%20My%20Lai%20massacre %20was,Lai%20on%20March%2016%2C%201968.

Hwang, Jerry. *Hosea: A Discourse Analysis of the Hebrew Bible.* Edited by Daniel I. Block. Grand Rapids, MI: Zondervan Academic, 2021.

Jacobs, Mignon R. "The Conceptual Dynamics of Good and Evil in the Joseph Story: An Exegetical and Hermeneutical Inquiry." *Journal for the Study of the Old Testament* 27 (2003): 309-38.

Jeans, James. *The Mysterious Universe.* Edited by Vesselin Petkov. Montreal, QC: Minkowski Institute Press, 2020.

Jeffrey, David. "Prejudice and Pride: Classical Education and the Modern Scholar." *Christianity and Literature* 27, no. 2 (1978): 53-66.

Jørstad, Mari. "The Ground That Opened Its Mouth: The Ground's Response to Human Violence in Genesis 4." *Journal of Biblical Literature* 135 (2016): 705-15.

Kalimi, Isaac. *Metathesis in the Hebrew Bible: Wordplay as a Literary and Exegetical Device.* Peabody, MA: Hendrickson Academic, 2018.

Katz, Judith, Noam Saadon-Grossman, and Shahar Arzy. "The Life Review Experience: Qualitative and Quantitative Characteristics." *Consciousness and Cognition,* no. 48 (February 2017): 76-86.

Keener, Craig S. *Miracles: The Credibility of the New Testament Accounts.* Grand Rapids, MI: Baker Academic, 2011.

———. *Miracles Today: The Supernatural Work of God in the Modern World.* Grand Rapids, MI: Baker Academic, 2021.

Knierim, Rolf P. *The Task of Old Testament Theology: Method and Cases.* Grand Rapids, MI: Eerdmans, 1995.

Knuth, Stacy, and Douglas Mangum. "Cherubim." In *The Lexham Bible Dictionary.* Bellingham, WA: Lexham, 2016.

Koch, Klaus. "Is There a Doctrine of Retribution in the Old Testament?" In *Theodicy in the Old Testament,* edited by James L. Crenshaw. Issues in Religion and Theology. Philadelphia: Fortress, 1983.

Korpel, Marjo Christina Annette. *Rift in the Clouds: Ugaritic and Hebrew Descriptions of the Divine.* Münster: Ugarit-Verlag, 1990.

Kwiatkowski, Marisa. "The Exorcisms of Latoya Ammons." *IndyStar,* January 5, 2014. Updated January 27, 2022. www.indystar.com/story/news/2014/01/25/the-disposession -of-latoya-ammons/4892553/.

Laato, Antti, and Johannes C. de Moore. "Introduction." In *Theodicy in the World of the Bible,* edited by Antti Laato and Johannes C. de Moore, vii-liv. Leiden: Brill, 2003.

Lamb, William. "Parliamentary Debates: Official Report: Session of the Parliament of the United Kingdom of Great Britain and Ireland." Presented at the British Member of Parliament Report, London, 1817.

Lanfer, Peter T. "Allusion to and Expansion of the Tree of Life and Garden of Eden in Biblical and Pseudepigraphal Literature." In *Early Christian Literature and Intertextuality*, vol. 1, *Thematic Studies*, edited by Craig A. Evans and H. Daniel Zacharias, 96-108. Library of New Testament Studies 391. New York: T&T Clark, 2009.

Langberg, Diane. *Suffering and the Heart of God: How Trauma Destroys and Christ Restores*. Greensboro, NC: New Growth, 2015.

"Law of Cause and Effect—Foundation of Buddhism." In *Tibetan Buddhist Encyclopedia*, February 26, 2016. http://tibetanbuddhistencyclopedia.com/en/index.php/Law_of _Cause_and_Effect_—_Foundation_of_Buddhism.

Leibniz, Gottfreid Wilhem. *Theodicy: Essays on the Goodness of God*. LaSalle, IL: Open Court, 1985.

Levenson, Jon D. *Creation and the Persistence of Evil*. Princeton, NJ: Princeton University Press, 1994.

Lewis, C. S. *Mere Christianity*. San Francisco: HarperOne, 2015.

———. *The Great Divorce*. San Francisco: HarperOne, 2015.

———. "The Inner Ring." C. S. Lewis Society of California, 1944. www.lewissociety.org /innerring/.

Livingston, G. Herbert. *The Pentateuch and Its Cultural Environment*. Grand Rapids, MI: Baker, 1987.

Longman, Tremper III. *Daniel*. NIV Application Commentary. 4th ed. Grand Rapids, MI: Zondervan, 1999.

Longman, Tremper, III, Daniel G. Reid, and Willem A. VanGemeren. *God Is a Warrior*. Grand Rapids, MI: Zondervan Academic, 1995.

Lupton, Robert D. *Toxic Charity: How Churches and Charities Hurt Those They Help, and How to Reverse It*. San Francisco: HarperOne, 2012.

Maciolek, Cathryne, and Mandy Lehto. "Visualize It: The Technique Used to Win the Game, Get Rich, and Fight Illness." *Psychology Today*, November 8, 2011. www.psycho logytoday.com/us/blog/the-psychology-dress/201111/visualize-it.

Mandela, Nelson. *Long Walk to Freedom: The Autobiography of Nelson Mandela*. London: Abacus, 2004.

Maor, Eli. *E: The Story of a Number*. Princeton, NJ: Princeton University Press, 1994.

Mariottini, Claude F. *Divine Violence and the Character of God*. Eugene, OR: Wipf & Stock, 2022.

Mark, Joshua J. "Ludlul-Bel-Nimeqi." In *World History Encyclopedia*, January 20, 2023 www.worldhistory.org/article/226/ludlul-bel-nemeqi/.

Martens, Elmer A. "Sin, Guilt." In *Dictionary of the Old Testament: Pentateuch*, edited by Desmond Alexander and David Baker. Downers Grove, IL: InterVarsity Press, 2003.

Maté, Gabor. *When the Body Says No: The Cost of Hidden Stress*. London: Vermilion, 2019.

Mathews, Kenneth. *Genesis 11:27–50:26: An Exegetical and Theological Exposition of Holy Scripture*. Nashville: Holman Reference, 2005.

McDowell, Catherine L. *The Image of God in the Garden of Eden: The Creation of Humankind in Genesis 2:5–3:24 in Light of the Mīs Pî, Pīt Pî, and Wpt-r Rituals of Mesopotamia and Ancient Egypt*. Siphrut: Literature and Theology of the Hebrew Scriptures 15. Winona Lake, IN: Eisenbrauns, 2015.

McGuire-Moushon, J. A. "Divine Beings." In *Lexham Theological Wordbook*, edited by Douglas Mangum. Lexham Bible Reference Series. Bellingham, WA: Lexham, 2014.

Meier, S. A. "Angel (I)." In *Dictionary of Deities and Demons in the Bible*, edited by Karel van der Toorn, Bob Becking, and Pieter W. van der Horst. Grand Rapids, MI: Eerdmans, 1999.

Merrill, Eugene H. "Image of God." In *Dictionary of the Old Testament: Pentateuch*, edited by T. Desmond Alexander and David W. Baker, 441-45. Downers Grove, IL: Inter-Varsity Press, 2002.

Mettinger, T. N. D. "Cherubim." In *Dictionary of Deities and Demons in the Bible*, edited by Karel van der Toorn, Bob Becking, and Pieter W. van der Horst. Grand Rapids, MI: Eerdmans, 1999.

Mill, John Stuart. "Inaugural Address." Speech, St. Andrews University, Scotland, 1867.

Millard, A. R., and P. Bordriiul. "A Statue from Syria with Assyrian and Aramaic Inscriptions." *Biblical Archaeologist* (Summer 1982): 135-41.

Moberly, R. W. L. "Did the Serpent Get It Right." *Journal of Theological Studies* 39, no. 1 (1988): 1-27.

———. *The Old Testament of the Old Testament: Patriarchal Narratives and Mosaic Yahwism*. Eugene, OR: Wipf & Stock, 2001.

———. *The Theology of the Book of Genesis*. Old Testament Theology. New York: Cambridge University Press, 2009.

Moltmann, Jürgen. *God in Creation: A New Theology of Creation and the Spirit of God*. Minneapolis: Fortress, 1993.

Moltmann, Jürgen, and Miroslav Volf. *The Crucified God: 40th Anniversary Edition*. Minneapolis: Fortress, 2015.

Montopoli, John. "Public Speaking Anxiety and Fear of Brain Freezes." National Social Anxiety Center, February 20, 2017. www.nationalsocialanxietycenter.com/2017/02/20/public-speaking-and-fear-of-brain-freezes/.

Moo, Douglas J. "Nature in the New Creation: New Testament Eschatology and the Environment." *Journal of the Evangelical Theological Society* 49 (2006): 449-88.

Mullen, E. T. Jr. "Divine Assembly." In *Anchor Bible Dictionary*, vol. 2. New Haven, CT: Yale University Press, 1992.

Mullenberg, James. *The Way of Israel: Biblical Faith and Ethics*. New York: Harper, 1961.

Murphy, Roland E. *The Tree of Life: An Exploration of Biblical Wisdom Literature*. 3rd ed. Grand Rapids, MI: Eerdmans, 2002.

——. "Wisdom and Creation." *Journal of Biblical Literature* 104, no. 1 (1985): 3-11.

Murray, Michael. *Nature Red in Tooth and Claw: Theism and the Problem of Animal Suffering*. Oxford: Oxford University Press, 2011.

Neiman, Susan. *Evil in Modern Thought: An Alternative History of Philosophy*. Princeton Classics. Princeton, NJ: Princeton University Press, 2015.

Newsom, Carol A. *New Interpreter's Bible: 1&2 Maccabees, Job, Psalms*. Nashville: Abingdon, 1996.

Nourkova, Veronika V. "Compressed Life Review: Extreme Manifestation of Autobiographical Memory in Eye-Tracker." *Behavioral Sciences* 10, no. 3 (2020): 1-14. https://doi.org/10.3390/bs10030060.

Padilla, Lace M., Sarah H. Creem-Regehr, Mary Hegarty, and Jeanine K. Stefanucci. "Decision Making with Visualizations: A Cognitive Framework Across Disciplines." *Cognitive Research Journal* 29 (2018). https://doi.org/10.1186/s41235-018-0120-9.

Palmer, Michael. *Atheism for Beginners: A Course Book for Schools and Colleges*. Cambridge: Lutterworth, 2013.

Pannenberg, Wolfhart. *Systematic Theology*. Vol. 3. Translated by Geoffrey W. Bromiley. Grand Rapids, MI: Eerdmans, 2009.

Parkin, David, ed. *The Anthropology of Evil*. Oxford: Wiley-Blackwell, 1991.

Patterson, Todd L. "The Righteous and Survival of the Seed: The Role of Plot in the Exegesis and Theology of Genesis." PhD diss., Trinity Evangelical Divinity School, 2012.

——. *The Plot-Structure of Genesis: "Will the Righteous Survive?" in the Muthos-logical Movement from Complication to Dénouement*. Biblical Interpretation Series 160. Leiden: Brill, 2018.

Peckham, John. "Rules of Engagement: God's Permission of Evil in Light of Selected Cases of Scripture." *Bulletin for Biblical Research* 30, no. 2 (2020): 243-60.

——. *Theodicy of Love: Cosmic Conflict and the Problem of Evil*. Grand Rapids, MI: Baker Academic, 2018.

Perel, Esther. "Rethinking Infidelity . . . a Talk for Anyone Who Has Ever Loved." TED Talk, 2015. www.youtube.com/watch?v=P2AUat93a8Q.

Peterson, Brian Neil. "Nephilim." In *The Lexham Bible Dictionary*, edited by John D. Barry et al. Bellingham, WA: Lexham, 2016.

Plantinga, Cornelius. *Not the Way It's Supposed to Be: A Breviary of Sin*. Grand Rapids, MI: Eerdmans, 1999.

Richter, Sandra L. *Stewards of Eden: What Scripture Says About the Environment and Why It Matters*. Downers Grove, IL: IVP Academic, 2020.

——. *The Epic of Eden: A Christian Entry into the Old Testament*. Downers Grove, IL: IVP Academic, 2008.

Riley, G. J. "Demon." In *Dictionary of Deities and Demons in the Bible*, edited by Karel van der Toorn, Bob Becking, and Pieter W. van der Horst. Grand Rapids, MI: Eerdmans, 1999.

Rosenberg, Ross. *The Human Magnet Syndrome: Why We Love People Who Hurt Us*. Eau Claire, WI: Premier, 2013.

Ross, Allen. *Creation and Blessing: A Guide to the Study and Exposition of Genesis*. Grand Rapids, MI: Baker, 2009.

Ross, Hugh. *Hidden Treasures in the Book of Job: How the Oldest Book in the Bible Answers Today's Scientific Questions*. Grand Rapids, MI: Baker Books, 2014.

Routledge, Robin. *Old Testament Theology: A Thematic Approach*. Downers Grove, IL: IVP Academic, 2012.

Sacks, Jonathan. *Koren Shalem Siddur, Ashkenaz*. Jerusalem: Koren Publishers Jerusalem, 2017.

Scott, Manny. "A Complicated Truth About School Shooters." MannyScott.com, May 2022. www.youtube.com/watch?v=3MIwGbylYsk.

Seal, David. "Satan." In *The Lexham Bible Dictionary*, edited by John D. Barry et al. Bellingham, WA: Lexham, 2016.

Stafford, Betty. "The Growing Evidence for 'Demonic Possession': What Should Psychiatry's Response Be?" *Journal of Religion and Health* 44, no. 1 (2005): 13-20.

Stewart, Alexander Coe. "Heaven Has No Sorrow That Earth Cannot Feel: The Ethics of Empathy and Ecological Suffering in the Old Testament." *Canadian Theological Review* 4, no. 2 (2015): 19-34.

Stocker, Abigail, and John D. Barry. "Seraphim." In *The Lexham Bible Dictionary*, edited by John D. Barry et al. Bellingham, WA: Lexham, 2016.

Stokes, Ryan E. "Satan, Yhwh's Executioner." *Journal of Biblical Literature* 133, no. 2 (2014): 251-70.

Straus, M. A., and R. J. Gelles. *Physical Violence in American Families: Risk Factors and Adaptations to Violence in 8,145 Families*. Piscataway, NJ: Transaction, 1990.

Stump, Eleonore. *Wandering in Darkness: Narrative and the Problem of Suffering*. Oxford: Oxford University Press, 2012.

Stump, Jim. "Naming Natural Evils: Is the Coronavirus Evil?" *Sapientia Henry Center Trinity University*, November 6, 2020. https://henrycenter.tiu.edu/2020/11/naming -natural-evils/.

Swartz, Michael D. *The Signifying Creator: Nontextual Sources of Meaning in Ancient Judaism*. New York: NYU Press, 2014.

Sweeney, Marvin A. *TANAK: A Theological and Critical Introduction to the Jewish Bible*. Minneapolis: Fortress, 2011.

Tanner, Beth LaNeel. "Book Three of the Psalter: Psalms 73–89." In *The Book of Psalms*, edited by Nancy L. deClaisse-Walford, Rolf A. Jacobson, and Beth LaNeel Tanner, 581-684. New International Commentary on the Old Testament. Grand Rapids, MI: Eerdmans, 2014.

Tate, Marvin. *Psalms 51–100*. Word Biblical Commentary 20. Grand Rapids, MI: Zondervan Academic, 2015.

Tejwani, Vickram, Duc Ha, and Carlos Isada. "Public Speaking Anxiety in Graduate Medical Education—A Matter of Interpersonal and Communication Skills?" *Journal of Graduate Medical Education* 8, no. 1 (2016): 111.

"The Purpose of Creation: 'Today the World Was Born.'" *Sichos in English*, Timeless Patterns in Time, n.d. www.chabad.org/holidays/jewishnewyear/template_cdo/aid/4456 /jewish/The-Purpose-of-Creation.htrr.

Thompson, Curt. *Anatomy of the Soul: Surprising Connections Between Neuroscience and Spiritual Practices That Can Transform Your Life and Relationships*. 3rd ed. Carol Stream, IL: Tyndale Refresh, 2010.

Tigay, Jeffrey H. *The JPS Torah Commentary: Deuteronomy*. Philadelphia: Jewish Publication Society, 2003.

Tsumura, David Toshio. "The Creation Motif in Psalm 74:12-14? A Reappraisal of the Theory of the Dragon Myth." *Journal of Biblical Literature* 134, no. 3 (2015): 547-55.

Turse, Nick. "The Vietnam War Crimes You Never Heard Of." *George Washington University, History News Network* (blog), 2017. https://historynewsnetwork.org/article/1802.

Van der Kolk, Bessel A. *The Body Keeps the Score: Brain, Mind and Body in the Healing of Trauma*. New York: Penguin Books, 2015.

Van der Toorn, Karel. "God (1)." In *Dictionary of Deities and Demons in the Bible*, edited by Karel van der Toorn, Bob Becking, and Pieter W. van der Horst. Leiden, Netherlands: Brill, 1999.

Van der Toorn, Karel, Bob Becking, and Pieter W. van der Horst, eds. *Dictionary of Deities and Demons in the Bible, Second Edition*. Revised 2nd edition. Grand Rapids, MI: Eerdmans, 1999.

Vanhoozer, Kevin J. *Faith Speaking Understanding: Performing the Drama of Doctrine*. Louisville: Westminster John Knox, 2014.

Verma, Adarsh. "Google Drops 'Don't Be Evil' Motto from Its Code of Conduct." *Fossbyte*, February 26, 2021. https://fossbytes.com/google-drops-dont-be-evil-motto-code -of-conduct/.

Walton, John H. "Creation in Genesis 1:1–2:3 and the Ancient Near East: Order Out of Disorder After Chaoskampf." *Calvin Theological Journal* 43 (2008): 48-63.

———. "Demons in Mesopotamia and Israel: Exploring the Category of Non-Divine but Supernatural Enemies." In *Windows to the Ancient World of the Hebrew Bible: Essays in Honor of Samuel Greengus*, edited by Bill T. Arnold, Nancy L. Erickson, and John H. Walton. Winona Lake, IN: Eisenbrauns, 2014.

———. "Genesis." In *Zondervan Illustrated Bible Backgrounds Commentary Volume 1: Genesis, Exodus, Leviticus, Numbers, Deuteronomy*, 3-179. Grand Rapids, MI: Zondervan, 2009.

Walton, John H., and N. T. Wright. *The Lost World of Adam and Eve: Genesis 2–3 and the Human Origins Debate*. Downers Grove, IL: IVP Academic, 2015.

Weiland, Bianca. "The Science Behind Visualization." *Activacuity*, January 24, 2016. www.activacuity.com/2016/01/the-science-behind-visualization/.

Wenham, Gordon J. "Sanctuary Symbolism in the Garden of Eden Story." In *"I Studied Inscriptions Before the Flood": Ancient Near Eastern, Literary, and Linguistic Approaches to Genesis 1–11*, edited by Richard S. Hess and Tsumura, 399-404. Winona Lake, IN: Eisenbrauns, 1994.

Wenham, Gordon John. *Genesis 1–15*, Word Biblical Commentary 1. Grand Rapids, MI: Zondervan Academic, 2014.

Westermann, Claus. *Genesis 1–22*. Translated by John J. Scullion. Continental Commentary. Minneapolis: Augsburg, 1984.

———. *The Promises to the Fathers: Studies on the Patriarchal Narratives*. Philadelphia: Fortress, 1980.

White, Ellen. *Yahweh's Council: Its Structure and Membership*. Tübingen: Coronet Books, 2014.

White, Hugh C. "Direct and Third Person Discourse in the Narrative of the 'Fall.'" *Semeia* 18 (1980): 107-11.

Wiesel, Elie. *A Jew Today*. New York: Vintage, 1979.

Willard, Dallas. *The Divine Conspiracy: Rediscovering Our Hidden Life in God*. San Francisco: Harper, 1998.

Wilson, Lindsay. *Job*. Grand Rapids, MI: Eerdmans, 2015.

Wray, T. J., and Gregory Mobley. *The Birth of Satan: Tracing the Devil's Biblical Roots*. New York: St. Martin's, 2005.

Wright, Archie T. *The Origin of Evil Spirits: The Reception of Genesis 6:1-4 in Early Jewish Literature*. Rev. ed. Minneapolis: Fortress, 2015.

Wright, Christopher J. H. *Old Testament Ethics for the People of God*. Downers Grove, IL: IVP Academic, 2004.

———. *The Mission of God: Unlocking the Bible's Grand Narrative*. Downers Grove, IL: IVP Academic, 2006.

Wright, N. T. *Evil and the Justice of God*. Downers Grove, IL: InterVarsity Press, 2014.

Yahuda, A. S. *Language of the Pentateuch in Its Relation to Egyptian Part 1*. London: Kessinger, 2003.

Zapada, Kimberly. "How to Manifest Anything You Want or Desire: Yes, That Even Includes Love . . . and Money." *Oprah Daily*, December 20, 2020. www.oprahdaily.com/life/a30244004/how-to-manifest-anything/.

Zevit, Ziony. *What Really Happened in the Garden of Eden?* New Haven, CT: Yale University Press, 2013.

Zucker, Moshe, ed. *Saadya's Commentary on Genesis*. New York: Jewish Theological Seminary of America, 1984.

GENERAL INDEX

SCRIPTURE INDEX